J O H N

Readings: A New Biblical Commentary

JOHN

Mark W G Stibbe

JSOT PRESS

To Alie

28538353

Copyright © 1993 Sheffield Academic Press

Published by JSOT Press
JSOT Press is an imprint of
Sheffield Academic Press Ltd
343 Fulwood Road
Sheffield S10 3BP
England

Typeset by Sheffield Academic Press
and
Printed on acid-free paper in Great Britain
by Bookcraft (Bath) Limited
Bath

British Library Cataloguing in Publication Data

Stibbe, Mark W.G.
    John.—(Readings: A New Biblical
    Commentary, ISSN 0952-7656)
    I. Title II. Series
    226.5

ISBN 1-85075-414-4
ISBN 1-85075-433-0   pa

Contents

6   John

Preface

When I completed my PhD thesis on John 18–19 in 1989, my external examiner asked me whether he thought the method of narrative criticism could be applied to the whole Gospel. It had worked well with the passion narrative in John 18–19. But could it work as well with other parts of the gospel, for example the farewell discourses in John 13–17?

When the PhD was published in 1992 under the title *John as Storyteller*, this question was raised again. One of the reviewers expressed the hope that I would apply the method to the rest of John's Gospel.

Between these two events, Dr David Orton invited me to do the *Readings* commentary on John. In the light of what my external examiner had said I felt that I could not refuse. Nor did I want to, especially since there is, as yet, no narrative-critical commentary on the Fourth Gospel. Consequently, in this book I have tried to work through the whole of the Gospel using elements of the narrative-critical method which I describe in *John as Storyteller*.

In undertaking this task I have sought to explore in more detail the views which I put forward in my article, 'The Elusive Christ: A New Reading of the Fourth Gospel' (see Stibbe 1991 in the bibliography). The reader might like to consult that before reading this commentary. I have also used *The Greek New Testament* (ed. Kurt Aland *et al.*; 3rd edn) and the NIV translation of John's Gospel. References to Plato's *Phaedo* are from thePenguin Classics edition (trans. Hugh Tredennick; Middlesex, 1954).

There are a number of people to whom I am grateful for support during the writing of this commentary. I wish first of all to thank the Sheffield Academic Press for the invitation to write, and for their help in publishing it. I would especially like to thank Richard Davie.

I would like also to thank my colleagues on the staff at St Thomas's Church, Crookes in Sheffield. Much of this book would not have been written without their encouragement and comments. I am grateful to Robert, Paddy, Derek, John and David for their friendship. They have been most responsive companions on this journey.

My thanks also go to the undergraduate students and staff in the Department of Biblical Studies at Sheffield University. During my courses on John's Gospel over the last three years I have learnt much from them as I have listened to their stimulating and often provocative feedback.

Thanks most of all must go to my wife Alie, who has had to endure my bouts of reclusive writing, and to our children Philip, Hannah and Johnathan, who have always cheered me up when I felt unworthy of the task before me.

This book is dedicated to Alie.

Introduction

People who write new commentaries on the Fourth Gospel cannot avoid looking over their shoulders at the great commentaries of the past. The Fourth Gospel, of all the texts in the New Testament, has been best served by commentators. The most recent notable contributions have come from the pens of R.E. Brown, R. Schnackenburg, C.K. Barrett, B. Lindars and E. Haenchen (see the bibliography). Many others have also written less celebrated but nonetheless valuable commentaries in the last three decades; we can number among these J. Marsh, R. Tasker, G. Beasley-Murray, D. Carson, G. Sloyan and K. Grayston. As I embarked on this *Readings* commentary for the Sheffield Academic Press, I was tempted to ask: 'What is there new to say about John's Gospel using the commentary genre?'

In this brief introduction I want to propose that this book marks something of a paradigm shift in the writing of commentaries on the Fourth Gospel. Until the beginning of the 1980s, the study of the Fourth Gospel was dominated by historical criticism, the history of religions approach, source criticism, and redaction criticism. Broadly speaking, historical critics discussed the value of John's data concerning the historical Jesus; history of religions scholars looked at the influence of first century philosophical and religious movements on the fourth evangelist; source critics attempted to uncover the original sources used in the composition of the Gospel; and redaction critics worked tentatively towards a reconstruction of the Johannine community from evidence within the Gospel and the Johannine Epistles. In the main, these methodologies were not concerned with the aesthetic qualities of the final form of the text as we now have it.

In 1983 R. Alan Culpepper published his book *Anatomy of the Fourth Gospel*, subtitled *A Study in Literary Design*. The emphasis of this book was not what lies behind or outside of the Fourth Gospel, but rather what lies in front of our eyes as we look exclusively at the Fourth Gospel as a literary unity. In itself this was not an entirely new departure. In *The Gospel of John as Literature: An Anthology of Twentieth Century Perspectives*, I shall be demonstrating how scholars in both Germany and Great Britain were committed to the literary, dramatic and poetic qualities of John's Gospel in both the nineteenth and early twentieth century. What was new about Culpepper's book was his emphasis upon the narrative qualities of the Fourth Gospel (e.g.

narrator, point of view, time, plot and characterization) and upon the communication between the narrator of the Gospel and the reader. Having criticized former scholars for treating the Gospel like an 'archeological tell', he provided the tools for appreciating it as an 'artistic tale'.

Recent research on the Fourth Gospel has, in a sense, been footnotes to Culpepper. Although there are still some influential scholars who employ methods such as source and redaction criticism, the vast majority of Johannine scholars now work with methodologies designed to awaken the reader to the aesthetic, narrative dynamics which elicit certain reader responses. In North America, South Africa, Holland, France and Great Britain, there has been a torrent of articles and books using methods such as structuralism, narrative criticism, reader response criticism, feminist literary criticism, speech act theory, deconstruction, semiotics, and rhetorical criticism. Indeed, so great has been the output since the publication of Culpepper's book that it is hard even for the specialist to keep up with it all.

In the shift from mainly historical to mainly literary approaches to John's Gospel, the one thing which has been noticeable by its absence is a commentary using the narrative and reader response approaches pioneered by Culpepper. There have been moves towards such a contribution such as P. Ellis's composition-critical commentary in 1983 which broke some new ground. R. Kysar's very short, popular book entitled *John's Story of Jesus* in 1984 also paved the way towards a predominantly text-immanent commentary. However, no one has written a commentary designed to elucidate the context, structure, plot, settings, form, plot-type, characterization, narrator, point of view, time, irony, symbolism, themes, literary devices and reader response of each passage of the Fourth Gospel. Neither has anyone, as yet, produced a commentary in which scholars, students, ministers and interested laypeople can be helped towards a literary appreciation of each section of the Gospel.

In this work I want to fill this gap by providing a narrative-critical reading of each passage of John's story. This commentary will not be exhaustive because the commentators in this series have all been asked to work within a limit of 100,000 words. However, I have attempted to expose some of the salient features of each passage using the method of narrative criticism. In the remainder of this introduction I shall briefly outline the narrative-critical approach to Johannine texts.

Context
The first step will be to look at the context of the text under discussion. I have found that there are essentially two levels of contextualization which the reader must appreciate. The first is the immediate context of a

passage. For example, the immediate context of Jn 18.1-27 is the passion narrative. John 18.1-27 forms the first sub-section of the passion narrative in chs. 18–19. Any discussion of its immediate context must therefore answer two questions. First, 'how does what immediately precedes John 18 prepare for it?' Secondly, 'how does Jn 18.1-27 prepare for what immediately follows?'

The second level of contextualization involves the Gospel as a whole. At this level I am concerned with the overall context of a passage. Thus, in the case of a text like John 20, I shall be showing how some of the themes in John 1 are reintroduced in John 20 in order to suggest a kind of ring composition in which the end of the Gospel resonates with its beginning. Examination of the overall context of a passage is vital for our understanding of both the structure and the plot of the Gospel. In structural terms, such a discussion succeeds in keeping the part related to the whole. In terms of plot, it succeeds in giving us an idea of how the passage under scrutiny contributes to the development of the Gospel story in its entirety.

Structure

From context I almost always turn to structure. We shall see that in most cases the author has arranged each narrative or discourse with consummate artistry. Often each text has a very noticeable 'literary design', to use Culpepper's phrase. Even in the case of the long discourses we shall frequently uncover some of the author's favourite structural devices: chiasmus (inverted parallelism), inclusio (ring composition), number patterns (divisions into three and seven in particular) and parallelism (conscious similarities between related sections).

However, the reader should not infer from this that the Gospel as a whole is structured with the same artful design as many of the individual episodes. One thing I have discovered in the writing of this commentary is the plausibility, on literary and structural grounds, of the evolutionary hypothesis of composition. Proponents of the evolutionary hypothesis argue that John's Gospel was composed over about sixty years, and that a redactor added material into the Gospel during the final stages, thereby disturbing what is predominantly the fourth evangelist's handiwork. What the evangelist created was almost certainly an artfully constructed narrative. Something of this architectural dexterity is still visible in many of the episodes. However, when the editor of the Gospel added and relocated material, some of this literary design was partially disrupted.

For example, the number of units in the first section of the Book of Signs looks, in the final form of the text, like this:

John 2.1–4.54: From Cana to Cana

a	2.1-11	Cana, first miracle
b	2.12	Transitional passage
c	2.13-25	Jesus at the Temple
d	3.1-15	Jesus and Nicodemus
e	3.16-21	Narrator's summary
f	3.22	Transitional passage
g	3.23-30	Jesus and John the Baptist
h	3.31-36	Narrator's summary
i	4.1-3	Transitional passage
j	4.4-42	Jesus and the Samaritan woman
k	4.43-45	Transitional passage
l	4.46-54	Cana, second miracle

This section seems both to encourage and also refute an examination of its overall structure. On the one hand, a sense of overall design is suggested through the use of inclusio. The section begins at Cana and ends at Cana. Both stories are called 'signs' and both seem to be composed of a request–rebuke–response structure. On the other hand, the relationships between the parts in this section prove much more obscure and the original design does seem to have been disrupted.

There is a sense in which a later editor has deconstructed the text of the evangelist. First of all, the editor has almost certainly moved the Cleansing of the Temple (2.13-25) from the conclusion to the Book of Signs (ch. 12) to Jn 2.13. Secondly, material has been added which shows all the hallmarks of later theological reflection: the theology of salvation in 3.16-21, and the development of the Baptist's Christology in 3.31-36. If we take these passages out we are left with a finely structured section which abounds in chiasmus, inclusio and parallelism:

a^1	2.1-11	The first Cana sign
b^1	2.12	Transitional passage
c^1	3.1-15	Jesus and Nicodemus
d^1	3.22	Transitional passage
e	3.23-30	Jesus and John the Baptist
d^2	4.1-3	Transitional passage
c^2	4.4-42	Jesus and the Samaritan woman
b^2	4.43-45	Transitional passage
a^2	4.46-54	The second Cana sign

What this highlights is the difficulty faced by anyone who attempts to propose a tidy structure for the Fourth Gospel in its entirety. Whoever the redactor was, he or she had a proto-deconstructionist mind-set, content to disrupt the *logic* of the evangelist's story through the adding and moving of material.

Form

I have consistently found it important to move from an analysis of structure to an analysis of the form of a passage. By 'form' here I do not mean the design of a text in the final stage of its tradition history. I have used the word 'structure' for this purpose. By 'form' I mean the genre of the whole Gospel and of its constituent parts. The genre of the Gospel as a whole I understand to be *bios*, ancient biographical writing (Segovia 1991a: 32-33). The genre of the individual sections of the Gospel varies. The author makes use of a prologue, of different forms of miracle story (I have detected four on literary grounds), the *paroimia* (symbolic word-picture, Jn 10.1-21, 15.1-11), the betrothal type-scene (Jn 4.4-42), the homily (Jn 6.25-59), the *Isaianic* trial scene (for example, Jn 8.12-59), the farewell genre, the passion narrative and the resurrection appearance story. Attention to form in this sense is vital in narrative criticism. It is particularly important in the farewell discourses (Jn 13–17), where the author cleverly employs and subverts the formal characteristics of the farewell genre.

Plot-Type

Alongside discussion of the forms used by the author, I will sometimes examine what is called the *mythos* or 'plot-type' of a text. This term is used by Northrop Frye in his archetypal approach to story patterns. In his highly influential book, *Anatomy of Criticism* (1971), Frye's proposal is that all storytellers will redescribe events using one of four fundamental plot-types or *mythoi*. These are tragedy (the *mythos* of autumn), satire (the *mythos* of winter), comedy (the *mythos* of spring) and romance (the *mythos* of summer). John's Gospel is no exception. To take one example: John begins the first major section of his Gospel (Jn 2.1–4.54) with a story rooted in the comic *mythos*. The wedding at Cana, with its misunderstanding, the implication of drunkenness, the Dionysian motif of wine, and the ignorance of the chief steward, has elements of comedy. However, if it is comic, it is in a sense in the wrong place. Weddings occur at the conclusion—the 'eucatastrophe' or 'happy ending'—of comic stories, not at their beginnings. Why then does the writer of the Gospel *begin* the story of Jesus with a 'happy ending'? What does this tell us about the relationship between narrative form and realized eschatology?

My belief is that the author uses the four *mythoi* of story in a creative way throughout the Gospel. The Gospel as a whole has a U-shaped plot. The descent and ascent of Jesus is in its own way U-shaped. Jesus comes down to the world below and then goes up into the world above. This is an essentially comic plot-shape. However, there are also elements of the other three *mythoi* in John's story. There is romance in John 2–4 where Jesus is the bridegroom, John the Baptist the best man, and where the question seems to be, 'Where and who is the bride?' In John 5–10, the *mythos* turns from the summer of romance to the winter (10.22) of satire. Here the invective of Jesus against the Jews marks a change in mood and in genre. In John 11–12 we return to the *mythoi* of comedy and romance, before moving into the autumn of tragedy in John 13–19. In the final chapters of the Gospel, the *mythos* of spring emerges powerfully once again. Comedy is inseparable from resurrection, and that is precisely what we find in John 20–21. Here the Gospel ends, the U-shaped plot completed, with all four *mythoi* having been creatively used and combined.

Plot

One of the next steps in the commentary will be an analysis of the plot of a passage. We shall see that the events in some sections of the Gospel are very carefully arranged with a beginning, a middle and an end. In the plot of Jn 11.1-44 for example, there is a clever use of progression involving settings. At the beginning of the story Jesus is outside Judea, where he hears of Lazarus' illness. At the middle of the story Jesus is outside the village of Bethany, where Lazarus is now buried. At the end of the story Jesus is outside the tomb, from which Lazarus is about to emerge. Here the storyteller uses plot in order to home in on the tomb of Lazarus. In such cases the use of plot, settings, point of view and progression are all used with effect to create a sense of movement and suspense.

Time

My discussion of plot also includes an analysis of the time-shapes in John's narrative. The creation of a plot involves the organization of events into a temporal sequence. In my examination of John's use of time I shall employ Culpepper's terminology, which itself derives from Gérard Genette's work *Narrative Discourse* (1980). I have found Culpepper's distinction between narrative time (the time it takes to read a narrative) and story time (the time sequence within the narrative world itself) very useful (1983: 70-73). It is of particular value in the case of the Book of the Passion (Jn 13–21). Here, in chs. 13–19, seven chapters of narrative cover a period of 24 hours, while in the Book of Signs (Jn 1–12), twelve chapters cover a period of two to three years. A distinction between narrative time (the time it takes to read a story) and story time (the time scale of events within a story) allows us to see the extent to which the author has slowed the pace of the plot at the start of John 13.

Also of value is Culpepper's use of terms like 'analepsis' (flashback) and 'prolepsis' (flash-forward) (1983: 56-70). These are also taken from Genette's theory of narrative. I shall be following Culpepper's use of these terms. In the farewell discourses we shall see the importance of 'internal prolepses' and 'external prolepses'. Internal prolepses are anticipations of events later on in the course of the Gospel. External prolepses are anticipations of events after the end of John's story, in the life of the post-resurrection Christian community which the writer was addressing. The need to distinguish between these two kinds of flash-forward will emerge in the commentary on John 13–17.

However, I have also supplemented Culpepper's terminology with David Higdon's four time-shapes, which he defines as process, retro-spective, barrier and polytemporal time-shapes (Higdon 1977). All four of these are used in John's Gospel. Process time-shapes are often used by the narrator as temporal indicators. In particular, the narrator is fond of giving the impression of the passing of days and of exact hours when events occur. Retrospective time-shapes are used when the narra-tor addresses readers directly in order to remind them of something earlier in the Gospel. Barrier time-shapes are notations of the prescribed time limit within which the hero's task has to be completed (the 'hour' of Jesus). Polytemporal time-shapes are used when the narrator wants to suggest the fusion of different temporal horizons, such as the eternal within the temporal, or the 'present' of the original readers in the past of Jesus' ministry.

Author, Narrator, Reader

So far I have been speaking in this introduction of an author, a narrator and various readers of John's Gospel. In the commentary I shall often use the phrase 'the reader' in a general sense. Sometimes, however, it will be important to distinguish between author and narrator on the one hand, and three specific kinds of reader on the other.

The author of the Gospel is the first-century writer who redescribed the various historical sources in the form of a continuous narrative. The narrator is the character whom the author has created in order to tell the story. This character sometimes withdraws from view, content to let characters speak. This form of narration is called 'showing'. Equally often the narrator's voice describes events. This form of narration is called 'telling'. It is important not to confuse this narrator with the author of the Gospel. The author of John's Gospel has actually con-structed a narrator with a specific point of view and a specific purpose. This point of view is the omniscient perspective of one who sees the events of the story in the light of the resurrection of Jesus and, indeed, in the light of eternity. The purpose is a rhetorical one. It is to persuade the reader to believe that Jesus of Nazareth was and is the Son of God (Jn 20.31).

But then who are the readers? There are first of all the original readers of the Gospel. By this I mean the historical readers whom the author

was addressing in (I propose) the late first century. These original readers were members of the Johannine community. Though some of them
may well have been Greeks and Samaritans, I believe they were predominantly Jewish Christians who had become alienated from Judaism
as a result of the *birkat ha minim*, the curse against the Christian
heretics formulated around 85 CE. Sometimes I shall speak of these
readers in the course of the commentary. They are the contemporaries
of the author.

The second type of readers are what I call first-time readers. First-
time readers are simply newcomers to John's story, people who are
reading the Gospel for the first time. Any narrative approach to John's
Gospel needs to take into account what it is like to read the story
wihout ever having seen it before. However, there are limitations to
any discussion of first-time readings. When I have mentioned them in the
commentary I have been very aware that such naive readings are the
construction of my own imagination, not the record of actual readings.

The third type of readers are paradigmatic readers. Any initial reading
of the Gospel is inevitably an inadequate one. It is only as first-time
readers progress to a constant re-reading that they start to become
aware of the deep subtleties of John's storytelling. What appeared at a
first reading to be transparent turns out on subsequent readings to be
opaque. Paradigmatic readers are therefore people who proceed from a
carnal to a spiritual reading (Kermode 1979: ch. 1), from a superficial to
an in-depth appreciation of John's narrative art. Here John's secrets are
revealed through the complex use of symbolism, narrative echo effects,
irony and intertextuality. Paradigmatic readers, it should be added, are
ones who do not resist the narrator. They are ones who agree to read
the story from above not from below (in other words, with faith and
understanding).

Characterization

One of the fundamental requirements of the New Testament narrative
critic is an examination of the way in which authors redescribe the historical characters in their sources. Culpepper uses terminology drawn
from the criticism of the modern novel in his assessment of Johannine
characterization. However, I have argued elsewhere that the fourth
evangelist does not draw characters in a novelistic way but in a manner
reminiscent of Hebrew storytellers (Stibbe 1992: 24-25). In this respect,
Robert Alter's *The Art of Biblical Narrative* (1981) proves useful. Alter
stresses the 'artful reticence' in Hebrew characterization. That is to say,
he highlights the way in which character traits are suggested only indirectly. Unlike the modern novel, where the narrator often provides
extensive internal commentary on the consciousness of characters, the

Fourth Gospel suggests motives, attitudes and temperaments in an implicit way (mainly through speech and action).

This is particularly true of Jesus. In my article entitled 'The Elusive Christ' (Stibbe 1991), I have proposed that the essential character-trait of the Johannine Jesus is his elusiveness. He is quintessentially the elusive Christ, the Johannine Pimpernel. The Jews, in particular, find him most evasive. Yet Jesus cannot be grasped by them either physically (when they try to arrest him) or theologically (when they try to understand him). He is the light shining in the darkness, a light which the darkness can neither apprehend nor comprehend (Jn 1.5). Yet this quality of elusiveness is not usually indicated by direct, explicit commentary on the part of the narrator. As in Hebrew storytelling it is suggested first of all through Jesus' words. His language is rich in misunderstood metaphors, enigmatic word-pictures and discontinuous dialogue. It is also suggested through his actions. Jesus is sought by people but rarely found. He moves from one place to another in a consistently evasive manner. John's characterization of Jesus seems to focus on this dimension of elusiveness. Truly Jesus is *ho sklēros logos* (Jn 6.60), the Difficult Word.

One of the main purposes of this commentary is to develop the thesis of my article 'The Elusive Christ' by highlighting those facets of John's characterization which contribute towards this portrait. We shall find, as we proceed through the story, that the critical challenge given to every character in the Gospel is that of penetrating the filter of apparent offensiveness caused by Jesus' elusive language and presence. In practically every episode we shall find a character confronted by the question, 'Who is this man?' or 'Where does he come from?' The quality of elusiveness is, as we shall see, an important key to understanding John's portrait of Jesus.

Literary Devices
In telling this distinctive story of Jesus, the author uses a great number of literary devices which I shall introduce and explain in the commentary. The most frequent are: focus, dualism, contrast, juxtaposition, narrative echo effects, asides, proverbs, *double entendre*, dual stage-setting, closure, forensic imagery, judicial rhetoric, dynamic and stative verbs, reality effects, parody, *amēn-amēn* sayings, the historic present, and narrative settings (especially ones which play on the idea of 'inside' and 'outside').

Irony
Most important of all is the constant use of irony. The narrator of John's Gospel is supremely an ironist. An ironist commonly sets up two levels of meaning: one which is misunderstood by the characters within the

story, the other which is understood by the paradigmatic reader outside the story. In any discussion of John's narrative art, attention must constantly be given to the presence of irony. This almost always has to do with the issue of *anagnorisis*, or recognition. John's narrator is interested in tragic irony, always keen to exploit the *agnoia* or 'ignorance' of those who come face to face with Jesus. Often such people claim to know who or what Jesus really is, while the paradigmatic reader knows only too clearly (because of the hints given by the narrator) that this is not so.

Truth Value

These, then, are some of the literary strategies which I shall be seeking to elucidate in this narrative commentary. By way of conclusion, I want —in true Johannine style—to return to some of the thoughts with which I began this introduction. There I showed how the advent of narrative criticism has brought a new, text-immanent perspective into Fourth Gospel research, one which is now not so concerned with historical matters. Does this mean, then, that my narrative-critical commentary is based on the view that John's story is worthless in the ongoing quest for the historical Jesus and that its truth value as a narrative historiography is no longer credible?

It is often thought that a commitment to narrative criticism is synonymous with the view that the Gospels are all fictions. This view is not without basis, since much of the work of people like Culpepper is grounded in the judgment that John is novelistic narrative—that John's story is, in short, a fictional novel. However, I want openly to state that this is not a view to which I subscribe. I have argued in *John as Storyteller* that the tradition in the Fourth Gospel comes from an eyewitness source, that it has been treated conservatively, and that John's Gospel is therefore of value for our attempt to rediscover the historical Jesus (Stibbe 1992: ch. 4). In this respect I propose that the truth-value of John's Gospel is related to the historical value of its description of Jesus.

However, I want also to say that the kind of history which we have in John's Gospel is unusual insofar as it is charismatic history; that is, it is historical tradition interpreted creatively and christologically with the aid of the *paraklētos*, the Spirit of truth. I have the strongest suspicion that the author of the Fourth Gospel was the prominent member of a school of people in the Johannine church who were especially gifted in the ministry of prophecy. These people spent much time, I propose, reflecting on the historical reminiscences of the beloved disciple. In that long-term process of reflection, they may often have been led inspirationally into a profound appreciation of the eternal significance implicit and inherent within the contingent realities of their oral and written traditions. I propose, therefore, that the truth value of John's Gospel is also related to the poetic value of its redescription of Jesus.

In terms of narrative history, the Gospel of John is both a Gospel of reference and a Gospel of mimesis. Aristotle wrote of poetry that it was more valuable than history because history is concerned with the contingent while poetry is concerned with the universal. Aristotle proposed that it is *mimesis*, the universalization of actions, which accounts for the greater value of the poetic over the historical. What is remarkable about John's story is its fusion of poetry and history, of the universal and the particular. John's story of Jesus is not just an historical account of the life of Jesus (which would be priceless in itself). It is also and above all a narrative in which the author, inspired by the Spirit of truth, evokes the transcendent significance of Jesus from the traditions concerning his earthly words and works. It is a work of poetic history.

It is partly for this reason that John's Gospel will always come across to many readers, both now and in the future, as the regenerative and liberating Word of God. Jesus said, 'You will know the truth, and the truth will set you free' (Jn 8.32). It is my hope that this commentary will help readers to experience not only something of the beauty of the written word but more importantly something of the power of the living Word, Jesus the Messiah.

Commentary

John 1.1-18

Introduction

Most stories begin with a sense of 'once upon a time', with a sense of a beginning somewhere in the past. John's story of Jesus begins with a sense of 'once before time'. The opening verses of John's Gospel, composed in the form of a dramatic prologue, take us back to the very beginning of all things, indeed to the very creation of time through the agency of the Word.

This magnificent overture has three functions: interactional, intertextual and intratextual (Malbon 1991: 177). The interactional function concerns the communication between the narrator and the reader. The narrator's voice and point of view is established in the Prologue. From now on the relationship will be one of an omniscient narrator communicating with a privileged reader.

The intertextual function has to do with the relationship of Jn 1.1-18 with other literary texts. Right at the beginning of the Gospel, the narrator lets the reader know what other texts are important for the interpretation of the story. The intertextual relationship between John's story of Jesus and the Old Testament stories of Moses is established in the Prologue and, as we shall see, will prove to be of particular significance for our understanding of John 5–10.

The intratextual function of the Prologue is to introduce the reader to certain narrative qualities which will be ubiquitous in the Gospel. Amongst the most important elements introduced here are the protagonist, the plot and the themes. I shall look briefly at these three functions in the commentary that follows.

Interactional Function of the Prologue. One of the most important functions of the Prologue is the creation of a relationship between the narrator of the story and the reader (whether the original, first-time or paradigmatic reader).

The narrator is introduced to the reader in Jn 1.1-18. This narrator turns out to have several noteworthy characteristics. First of all, he or she is a figure who views Jesus-the-Word from an omniscient perspective. The reader is given the impression from the start that the story is being told by one who views events from a transcendent and eternal vantage point. This narrator is seemingly present before the creation of the world (v. 2), during creation (v. 3), before the appearance of the pre-existent Word (vv. 6-9) and during the lifetime of the incarnate Word (vv. 10-13). The narrator tells the story 'from above'. Little wonder that the author has been portrayed since the earliest time as an eagle among the four evangelists.

Secondly, the narrator seems to speak on behalf of a group or a community of people. This is not purely a third-person narration. He or she employs more of a We–Thou than an I–Thou form of address. This can be seen by the use of third person plural pronouns in vv. 14-18. The Word made his dwelling among 'us' (v. 14). 'We' have seen his glory (v. 14). From the fulness of his grace 'we' have received one blessing after another (v. 16). Clearly the voice of the narrator is the voice of a community spokesperson.

Intertextual Function of the Prologue. The next vital purpose of the Prologue is to provide the reader with some hints concerning the literary traditions which have influenced John's storytelling.

The protagonist of the Prologue is Jesus of Nazareth, called 'Jesus Christ' in v. 17, but referred to until then as the Logos or Word. The most probable intertextual background for John's use of this title lies in the Jewish mythology of personified Wisdom. Much of what is said about the Word in John's Prologue is said of personified Wisdom. Wisdom existed before the creation of the world (Prov. 8.22-23), and was with God (Sir. 1.1). Wisdom was active in the creation of the world (Wis. 9.9), and is said to be better than life (Prov. 8.35) and like light (Eccl. 2.13). Wisdom came into the world and was rejected (1 En. 42.2). However, she set up her tent among men (Sir. 24.8) and dispensed glory and grace (Sir. 24.16). In portraying Jesus as the creative and life-giving Word, the narrator creates an intertextual relationship between the protagonist and the figure of Wisdom.

The narrator also sets up an intertextual relationship between the story of Jesus and the story of Moses. Comparisons between Jesus and Moses, and between Jesus' death and the Exodus, recur throughout John. This network of Moses symbolism is initiated in the Prologue. The verb translated 'dwelt among us' in v. 14 literally means 'pitched tent' and should remind the paradigmatic reader of the theme of tenting in Exod. 25.8-9. In v. 14 the narrator writes, 'We have seen his glory', which has parallels with the divine presence associated with Mount Sinai where Moses saw the $k^eb\bar{o}d$ $Yahweh$, 'the glory of the Lord' (Exod. 24.15-16). The phrase 'full of grace and truth' in v. 14 reflects the Hebrew pairing, $hesed$ and $'emet$ which we find in Exod. 34.6. The point about this relationship between Jesus-the-Word and Moses is made in v. 17: 'the Law was given through Moses; grace and truth came through Jesus Christ'. In other words, even though elements of God's grace and truth came to Israel through the gift of the Law, the fullness of these things has come to humankind through Jesus Christ.

The narrator not only establishes an intertextual relationship between this story and the stories of Wisdom and of Moses, the same thing is also done with the opening of the book of Genesis. There is hardly a work of literature with more of a sense of a beginning than John's Gospel. Both the phrase 'in the beginning' and the title 'the Word' are significant in creating this impression. Both create resonances with the story of Genesis 1. 'In the beginning', of course, echoes the first words of Gen. 1.1. The description of Jesus as the Word echoes 'And God said' in the same narrative. The Johannine Prologue abounds in such intertextual resonances.

Intratextual Function of the Prologue. The third and final function of the Prologue is to give the reader some vital background information concerning the protagonist and plot of the Gospel, and to introduce many of the major themes and some of the chief literary characteristics which it contains.

The narrative beginning of John's Gospel first of all introduces the protagonist of the Gospel. Here Jesus is depicted as the Word of God. What is said about the Word in the opening two verses focuses on three dimensions: existence, divinity and relationship. The use of the verb 'was' embraces all three nuances. The first 'was' ('In the beginning was the Word') implies existence. Before the world began, asserts the narrator, Jesus-the-Word existed. The second 'was' ('The Word was with God') implies relationship. Before the world began, Jesus-the-Word was with God, or in God's presence. The third 'was' ('The Word was God') predicates divinity of Jesus. Before the world began, claims the narrator, the being of Jesus-the-Word could not be separated from that of God.

The following relationships which Jesus-the-Word shares are the object of the narrator's focus.

a. The relationship between Jesus-the-Word and God (vv. 1-2). There is both difference and identity in this relationship. Jesus-the-Word is both separate from God and the same as God ('the Word was with God, and the Word was God'). As such, there is a uniqueness about him; he is the One and Only (v. 14), the One and Only from the bosom of God the Father (v. 18), the one who reflects the undiminished *kābōd* (glory) of God (v. 14).

b. The relationship between Jesus-the-Word and Creation (vv. 3-5). Jesus-the-Word is depicted here as the Creator of all things. He is the all-powerful, life-giving principle in the universe (vv. 4-5). He does not stand aloof from Creation like some Gnostic phantom or the Unmoved

Mover. Far from it, Jesus-the-Word has become flesh and pitched camp in the hostile world which humanity inhabits (v. 14).

c. The relationship between Jesus-the-Word and John the Baptist (vv. 6-9). Jesus-the-Word is the one to whom the Baptist points. Both are, in different senses, 'from God'. Jesus is the true light who descends *from* God; John is the witness to that light sent *by* God. The Baptist himself testifies to his subordinate position to Jesus in the only words in direct speech in vv. 1-18: 'He who comes after me has surpassed me because he was before me' (v. 15).

d. The relationship between Jesus-the-Word and his enemies. Many of his own people do not recognize Jesus (vv. 10-11). The perversity of this rejection is suggested by the fact that its locus is ironically the world which the Word has created.

e. The relationship between Jesus-the-Word and the community of faith. Another group separate from the enemies are highlighted: those who accept Jesus (v. 12), believe in his name (v. 12), become children of God (vv. 12-13), behold his glory (v. 14), and receive continual blessings (v. 16).

The Prologue of the Gospel therefore introduces us to the hero. In particular, we are introduced to the elusiveness of Jesus, which is his major character trait in John's Gospel. Jesus is depicted throughout the story as the one who evades people both at the level of presence and at the level of language. Certainly from ch. 5 onwards, people seek Jesus but he hides from them. People speak to Jesus, but he often makes his meaning obscure.

This central feature of John's characterization of Jesus is announced in four ways in the Prologue. First of all, there is an elusiveness about the narrator's introduction of Jesus in 1.1-18. The commentaries do not make the obvious point that Jesus' name is actually delayed until v. 17; until then Jesus is referred to with the rather enigmatic personification, 'the Word'. For the first-time reader of the Gospel, the possessor of this title may prove elusive until he is unveiled in v. 17. Compare this with the overt naming of the Baptist in v. 6 ('His name was John'), and the importance attached to believing in the 'name' of Jesus in v. 12, and the point becomes radiantly clear: John wants to portray Jesus right from the very beginning of his Gospel as the deity who is elusive.

The second quality in the Prologue which highlights this feature is the statement of the narrator in v. 5: 'The light shines in the darkness, but the darkness has not understood it'. Here the 'light' is a symbol standing for Jesus. What the narrator is revealing is the fact that Jesus cannot be either apprehended or comprehended. He cannot be either 'overcome' or 'understood' (*katelaben* contains both nuances). He is the hidden Messiah, the elusive God.

The third aspect which promotes this character-trait is the narrator's judgment in v. 10, 'He was in the world, and though the world was made through him, the world did not recognize him'. The important thing to notice here is the narrator's claim that the world did not know or recognize who Jesus really was. This anticipates the presentation of Jesus throughout the story as the Concealed Revealer, the one whose identity remains elusive even within the world which he has made.

The final aspect of the Prologue which underlines this elusiveness is more indirect. In v. 18 the narrator concludes with the words, 'No-one has ever seen God, but God the One and Only, who is at the Father's side, has made him known'. The invisibility and transcendent elusiveness of God is emphasized here and at two other points in the Gospel (5.37 and 6.46). The background for this lies in Exodus, this time in 33.20 where we are told that no one can see God and live. What we have at the end of the Prologue is therefore the implication that the elusiveness of Jesus reflects the elusiveness of God.

If the first intratextual function of the Prologue is to introduce the protagonist, the second is to introduce the plot. Many scholars have noticed that vv. 10-13 encapsulate the plot of the whole Gospel. Verses 10-11 point to the lack of recognition of Jesus and to his rejection by his own race in chs. 1–12 (part one of the Gospel story). Verses 12-13 point to the adoption and acceptance of the disciples as the children of God in chs. 13–21 (part two of the story). Something of the whole plot of John's story is therefore indicated at this early stage.

The third intratextual function of the Prologue is to establish some of the leading themes of the Gospel. By 'themes' here is meant those recurrent ideas in John's narrative which give unity, coherence and depth to the story. The following themes emerge in vv. 1-18:

a. Jesus' Origins (vv. 1-2). The opening words of the Gospel depict Jesus' origins in heaven with God before the world was made. The critical question to answer in John's story will prove to be, 'Where does Jesus really come from?' Those who see Jesus as one who has come from God in a literal sense (as someone who has descended from heaven) have made the breakthrough from misunderstanding to true knowledge. Most of the characters of John's story do not reach this goal of genuine faith. They are left with Pilate's unenlightened mystification in 19.9: 'Where do you come from?'

b. Life (v. 4). The narrator states that in Jesus-the-Word was life, *zōē*. The word 'life' occurs 36 times in John's story, in contrast to the 16 occasions in the Synoptics. In John's Gospel, *zōē* does not mean natural life. The word *psuchē* is used for life in that sense (see 13.37, 15.13). *zōē* in the Fourth Gospel means 'the life of the age to come'. This is super-natural not natural life.

c. **Light and Darkness (vv. 4-9).** In the Prologue, Jesus-the-Word is described as 'the light of the world'. Over and against this light, stands a hostile entity which John describes as 'darkness'. The point made in the Prologue and throughout John's Gospel is that the darkness never grasps the light, it never masters the light intellectually (in terms of un-derstanding) or physically (in terms of physical destruction). Of the 73 NT occurrences of *phōs* (light), 23 occur in John's Gospel; and of the 17 NT occurrences of *skotia* (darkness) 8 are in John's story.

d. **Sending (v. 6).** The occurrences of *apostellō* and *pemp ō* are numerous in the Fourth Gospel. The two verbs are used interchange-ably. Jesus is described as being sent by the Father using both these verbs (*apostellō* in 3.17, 34; 5.36, 38; 6.29, 57; 7.29; 8.42; 10.36; 11.42; 17.3, 8, 18, 21, 23, 25; and *pempō* in 4.34; 5.23, 30, 37; 6.38-39, 44; 7.16, 18, 28, 33; 8.16, 18, 26, 29; 9.4; 12.44-45, 49; 13.20; 14.24; 15.21; 16.5). Here in the Prologue John the Baptist is described as one sent from God (*apestalmenos para theou*). This anticipates the descriptions of Jesus as sent from God.

e. **Witness (vv. 7-8).** In vv. 7-8, John the Baptist is portrayed as a witness. The terminology of testimony and witness permeates the Gospel story. We shall see many occasions when words such as 'witness' and 'judgment' are used with a careful ambiguity. They often suggest that the Gospel is a law-suit in which Jesus the Judge is ironically on trial for his messiahship. When the context indicates that Jesus is on trial, words like *marturia* will be seen as forensic and not just missiological terms.

f. **The World (v. 9, 10).** *kosmos* is introduced here. The word is used 78 times in John. The reader should note the use of personification in v. 10. The world is depicted as having personal characteristics. It can choose to reject or recognize its creator, the Word. The fact that the world does not acknowledge Jesus shows that John has no time for what literary theorists call 'the pathetic fallacy'—the fallacious view that nature sympathizes with the poet and/or the hero. The world in John's story is actively hostile to the protagonist. That is why, unlike Mk 15.33, John's story has no dark clouds at Golgotha.

g. **Knowledge (v. 10).** When the narrator says that the world did not 'recognize' Jesus-the-Word, he or she uses the verb *gin ōskō* (to know). Knowledge is a key theme in the Gospel. *ginōskō* is used 56 times and *oida* (another word meaning 'to know') 85 times.

h. Believing (v. 7, 12). In the Prologue, belief in Jesus' name is stressed as crucial for regeneration. The name referred to may well be the *egō eimi* (*I am*) which Jesus uses (the divine name). Of the 98 occurrences of *pisteuō* in John, 36 are followed by *eis* (believing 'in' or 'into'). On two occasions it is used of belief in the Father, 31 times of belief in Jesus and four times of belief in the name of Jesus (as here). The sense of this phrase is as follows: salvation and regeneration (being born of God) are dependent on active commitment, dynamic trust and personal faith. The subject of this kind of believing is the disciple and the object is Jesus, the I Am.

i. Rebirth (v. 13). In v. 13 the narrator speaks of those who are *ek theou egennēthēsan*, 'born of God'. In ch. 3, Jesus will tell Nicodemus that he must be *gennēthē anōthen* and *gennēthē ex hudatos kai pneumatos* ('born from above/again' and 'born of water and the spirit'). At this early stage of the story, the narrator is therefore portraying all that is necessary for salvation: dynamic, personal faith and supernatural rebirth.

j. Seeing (v. 14, 18). In v. 14 the narrator speaks of having seen the glory of God in the life of Jesus-the-Word. The verb here is *theaomai* (6 times in the Fourth Gospel). John also uses *blepō* (17 times), *the ōreō* (24 times), *eidon* (36 times) and *horaō* (31 times). Seeing who Jesus really is becomes an important theme, one which will be used with particular irony in John 9, the story of the man born blind.

k. Glory (v. 14). *doxa* is introduced here. It occurs 18 times in John. The word sometimes refers to the honour that human beings can attain (5.41). It also means the praise that people can give to God (7.18). Finally, there is the *doxa* (Hebrew *shekinah*) majesty of God (here in 1.14).

l. Truth (v. 14). Truth is a leading concept in the Fourth Gospel. *alēthēs* (truth, truthful) occurs 14 times (twice in the Synoptics), *alēthinos* (true, genuine) 9 times (once in the Synoptics), and *alētheia* (truth) 25 times (seven times in the Synoptics). *alētheia* in John seems to denote 'heavenly or divine reality'.

If the third intratextual function of the Prologue is to introduce the reader to the leading themes of the Gospel, the fourth is to indicate some of the rhetorical strategies which we shall see throughout the story. The first of these is the *step-stair progression* in 1.1-18 (Stanton 1989: 116). This is the process in which lines begin by repeating the end of the previous line:

In the beginning was the *Word*
And the *Word* was with *God*
And what *God* was, the *Word* was.
The *Word* was in the beginning with *God*.

All things were made through *him*,
And without *him* was not anything *made*.
What was *made* in him was *life*
And the *life* was the *light* of men.
And the *light* shines in the *darkness*
And the *darkness* did not master it.

The reader will find that the narrator uses a step-stair style throughout the Gospel. As the commentary on ch. 1 will show, themes mentioned in one narrative are picked up in the subsequent narrative. At that point, one or two new themes are mentioned which are then raised in the following narrative. So the process goes on.

Another characteristic of the Gospel's rhetoric is the use of the device known as *inclusio*. This is the technique whereby a passage ends where it began, a form of ring composition in which the closure of a text picks up the language of its opening sentences. In the Prologue, this is visible in the way the narrator returns at the end of the passage (v. 18) to the subject with which it began (vv. 1-2), namely the relationship between Jesus-the-Word and God the Father.

Another rhetorical feature introduced in the Prologue is the use of *dualism*. In 1.1-18, the opposition of light and darkness is mentioned in v. 5: 'The light shines in the darkness, but the darkness has not understood it'. Here the antithesis connotes hostility. Another contrast is between the Baptist and Jesus. In v. 8 the narrator stresses that John-the-Witness and Jesus-the-Word are not to be confused. John is the best man, not the groom (3.29), the lamp but not the light (5.35). Here the antithesis is to do with hierarchy not hostility. Other contrasts in the Prologue are between those who reject Jesus (vv. 10-11) and those who accept him (vv. 12-13), between flesh and glory (v. 14), and between Jesus and Moses (v. 17). The technique of presenting things in stark, binary oppositions is a recurrent characteristic of the Gospel's literary style.

The device of *symbolism* is also introduced. A symbol is a concrete image pointing to an abstract reality. In the Prologue, one of the commonest archetypal symbols of literature is employed: the symbol of light. Here light is a symbol of revelation. However concealed and elusive Jesus is in John's story, he is always the revealer of truth, the one who discloses the heavenly realities of the world above. Light is a visible image pointing to the concept and reality of revelation. Over and against this light is darkness, another primordial and archetypal symbol.

In John's story, darkness stands for the forces in opposition to Jesus: the devil, the Jewish authorities, the world, Judas, the Romans who help arrest Jesus and so on. Darkness is the symbol which points to the quality of perverse hostility to Jesus. The whole Gospel is permeated by this symbolic opposition of light and darkness.

Another rhetorical technique which is introduced in the Prologue is *irony*. Irony is an oppositional structure. It contrasts two levels of understanding: the way in which characters within the narrative world understand Jesus, with the way in which the reader, standing with the narrator above the narrative world, understands Jesus. As Aristotle saw very clearly, recognition or *anagnorisis* is something which can be exploited with ironical and dramatic effect. In John's story, the main irony is introduced in v. 10: 'He was in the world, and though the world was made through him, the world did not *recognize* him'. As the plot develops, the narrator will bring on stage a whole range of characters: the disciples, Nathaniel, the Jews, Nicodemus, John the Baptist, the Samaritan woman, the official's son, the crippled man at Bethesda, the crowds, the man born blind, Caiaphas, Annas, Pilate and so on. To each of these characters, the narrator issues the same challenge: the challenge to recognize what the paradigmatic reader can see, the real origin and identity of Jesus of Nazareth.

Another device introduced here is *chiasmus*. Chiasmus is essentially inverted parallelism. If a passage has five sections, then section 5 will be expected to parallel section 1, section 4 to parallel section 2, and section 3 to function as the centrepiece. Peter Ellis's composition-critical commentary on John's Gospel (1984) is particularly alert to the use of chiasmus. Some literary specialists have recently argued for the presence of a chiastic structure in Jn 1.1-18. The following symmetrical structure has been proposed (Staley 1986: 249):

A^1	1.1-5
B^1	1.6-8
C^1	1.9-11
D	1.12-13
C^1	1.14
B^1	1.15
A^1	1.16-18

A final device worthy of mention is *multivalence*, or multiple layers of meaning. One of the features which makes this prologue so memorable is the fact that it seems to operate at two levels. At the first level, the Prologue celebrates the genesis of the world. At the second level, the Prologue seems to celebrate the genesis of the Gospel. At this secondary, concealed level, we may be encouraged to see in the incarnation of the Word a kind of allegory of the composition of the Gospel itself. This prologue, after all, depicts Jesus as the Logos, the Word. This title suggests 'speech', something which we find so much of throughout the Fourth Gospel. Could it be that the journey of the Word into human flesh is, in part, an allegory of the incarnation of oral tradition in textualized narrative? Could it be that the Prologue of the Fourth Gospel not only celebrates the incarnation of the Word but also the evolution from orality into textuality in the composition history of John's story?

As we shall find throughout the Fourth Gospel, the sense of transparency in John's storytelling will often be a false impression. In reality John's narrative is memorable precisely because, as has often been said, it is like a pool in which children can paddle and elephants can swim. It is polyphonic or multivalent narrative.

John 1.19-28

Context

The Prologue prepares for this narrative with some subtlety. In 1.6-9 the narrator states three things about the Baptist: first, that he himself is not the light; second, that he came to witness to the light; and third, that through his witness all people might believe. In Jn 1.19-42, we have three narratives which fulfil these three expectations in succession. First, in 1.19-28, the Baptist stresses that he is not the light ('I am not the Christ, Elijah or the Prophet'). Second, in 1.29-34, he bears witness to the light ('Look, the lamb of God!'). Third, in 1.35-42, we see people coming to faith in Jesus as a result of his testimony (two disciples—one of them Andrew—and Simon Peter).

Structure

John 1.19-28 has been artfully constructed as follows:

A^1	19-20	The Baptist's testimony: 'I am not the Christ.'
B^1	21-22	Question: 'Who are you? Elijah or the Prophet?'
C	23	Isaiah 40.3, The Baptist as the voice in the desert
B^2	24-25	Question: 'Why baptize if you're not Elijah or the Prophet?'
A^2	26-28	The Baptist's testimony to 'the one who comes after me'

This is an example of inverted parallelism, or chiasmus. In the arrangement of these verses, vv. 26-28 echo the subject of vv. 19-20 (the Baptist's testimony), vv. 24-25 echo the subject of vv. 21-22 (the questioning of the Baptist in relation to Elijah and the Prophet), and v. 23 stands as the centrepiece. This shows that the paradigmatic reader is to focus on the Isaianic prophecy concerning the Baptist's heraldic function.

Two further points must be made about structure: first of all, the use of inclusio or ring composition. In this narrative we see a wide-ranging inclusio. In vv. 20-21, John twice denies that he is the Christ with a resounding *ouk eimi*, 'I am not!' This forms an inclusio with the twofold *ouk eimi* of Peter in Jn 18.15-27 in response to his interrogators in Annas's courtyard. Peter's two 'I am nots' in reference to Jesus will therefore recall those of the Baptist. Whereas the Baptist is a faithful witness, Peter will prove inadequate. Secondly, the reader should notice that the interrogators in this story ask the Baptist three times about his identity. We shall see throughout this commentary that John often uses threefold patterns in his storytelling.

Narrator and Point of View

The narrator's function in this narrative is largely informational. We are given details about the Jews in Jerusalem and the interrogators in v. 19, about the openness of the Baptist's testimony in v. 20, about who is speaking in vv. 21-22, about the source of the Baptist's quotation in v. 23, about the identity of the questioners in vv. 24-25, and about the set-ting for these interrogations in v. 28. Since most of the passage is in direct speech, the role of the narrator largely merges into the background.

Characters and Characterization

There are five characters in 1.19-28. Three of these take on the role of accusers: the priests, Levites and Pharisees. The Jews appear as the instigators of the interrogations in v. 19; however, no real note of hostility is detectable in the phrase *hoi Ioudaioi*.

The Baptist takes centre stage. His characterization is subtle. In the introduction I showed how the Johannine characterization of Jesus has redescribed the hero in terms of an elusive Christ. Throughout the Gospel we shall see Jesus using the device known as 'discontinuous dialogue' in maintaining this aura of evasiveness. Here we see the Baptist using precisely this tactic under interrogation. His answers to begin with are non-answers (two 'I am nots'). When he finally does answer the questions of the priests and Levites, it is with an OT quotation which must have seemed enigmatic to say the least. Perhaps this is why the Pharisees change the subject from the identity of the Baptist to his function: 'Why then do you baptize?' John's answer is again elusive. 'I baptize with water', he says, 'But among you stands one...who comes after me'.

The characterization of the Baptist should be seen as an anticipation of the elusiveness of Jesus and as an indication of the unanimity between the Baptist and the Messiah. The question, 'who are you?' will not only be asked of the Baptist (as it is here), it will also be the key question addressed to Jesus in the Gospel.

Themes

These comments on elusiveness reveal that, at this juncture, the theme of the elusive Christ is not far from the story. Indeed, even though Jesus is not visibly on stage, his elusive presence is felt in the Baptist's rather obscure remark that 'among you stands one you do not know' (notice the theme of knowledge). The reference here is clearly to the mysterious and elusive presence of Jesus himself.

The theme of sending is present in this narrative. *apostellō* is used in v. 19 and v. 24, and *pempō* in v. 22.

The theme of witness is raised in the first sentence. The narrator says that this was the *marturia* of the Baptist. Here the legal as well as the missiological connotation comes to the fore. What follows is an implied trial scene in which the Baptist plays the part of the witness, and in which the priests, Levites and Pharisees play the part of the accusers. The idea of confession is important. The Baptist boldly and humbly confesses with the words 'I am not!' Later in John's story, we shall see a number of occasions when Jesus underlines his divinity using the revelatory 'I am'.

Literary Devices

Irony is present in 1.19-28. The statement, 'among you stands one you do not know', plays on the foundational irony in the Gospel which has to do with the failure of recognition. Indeed, it picks up the comment in the Prologue that 'though the world was made through him, the world did not recognize him' (1.10).

There is another irony in the threefold use of the verb 'send'. The reader now knows from the Prologue that John the Baptist is really the one who is sent, sent from God. Here something is made of the fact that the interrogators are sent from the Jews in Jerusalem. This sets up an ironic contrast in 1.19-28 between the Baptist, sent from God, and the priests, Levites and Pharisees, sent from the Jews. Later on in the commentary we shall see how the narrator uses such ironies in order to parody the Jewish antagonists of Jesus.

Setting

The reader should finally note the clear indication of setting in 1.28: 'This all happened at Bethany on the other side of the Jordan'. This reference to Bethany is important in terms of the structure of the Gospel. The Book of Signs (Jn 1–12) begins with an introductory chapter located in Bethany beyond the Jordan (1.28) and concludes with action in and around the Bethany near Jerusalem (11.1, 18; 12.1). Even though these are not the same place, the use of the same place name at both the beginning and the end of the Book of Signs can be seen as another example of the device of inclusio.

John 1.29-34

Context
In vv. 29-34, Jesus appears overtly for the first time on the stage of the story. The Baptist points to Jesus and gives three testimonies about the latter's identity. He emphasizes the superiority, authority and priority of Jesus over himself and his ministry. Of particular importance is the baptism of Jesus. This is not described directly in the Fourth Gospel but is referred to as a past event very briefly in v. 33. The main reason for this is because the elusiveness of God in John's story requires that there should be no open heaven except at 12.28 (even there the voice from heaven proves elusive to the majority).

Characterization
Jesus appears now for the first time in person. The name *Iēsous* at last, after 29 verses, signals the physical presence of the protagonist. Up until now, Jesus has been the centre of the reader's attention even if he has not yet been the centre of the narrator's action. Even in 1.19-28, where Jesus appears to be absent, he is at the centre of things in the Baptist's allusions to 'the Lord' (v. 23), 'one you do not know' (v. 26), and 'one who comes after me' (v. 27).

Jesus is the character who emerges *in medias res*. In terms of narrative focus, he emerges always in the middle, the centre of things. In terms of plot, he emerges in the middle of his life-story (there are no birth or childhood narratives in the Fourth Gospel). Jesus' centrality can be seen from the fact that the name *Iēsous* appears 239 times in the Gospel. The only time when it disappears from focus is in chs. 14–17. Since Jesus is speaking for the most part in these chapters, this is hardly surprising. Truly, Jesus is the focus of the Gospel.

The only other character besides the Baptist who is mentioned in 1.29-34 is the Spirit (v. 32 and 33). The introduction of the Spirit in 1.32 is crucial. Here the Spirit descends like a dove from the sky and rests on Jesus. The Spirit and Jesus are united in this act of supernatural *katabasis* (descent). From the baptism onwards, the distance between the Spirit and Jesus is mediated. Jesus is the Spirit-inspired Messiah.

Themes

A number of key themes reappear here (seeing, witness, world, recognition, sending). Some new themes also emerge: first of all, the theme of the Lamb of God (*amnos tou theou*) in v. 29. There are two intertextual backgrounds for this phrase: the Suffering Servant in Isaiah 53 and the Passover Lamb of Exodus 12. Deutero-Isaiah is an important literary quarry for the author in the composition of themes for this story (Lincoln 1993). Key themes in Deutero-Isaiah are prominent also in the Gospel: Isaiah 40–55 has trial scenes, 'I am' sayings, the themes of glory, revelation, God-as-shepherd, knowledge, descent from Abraham, flowing water, sight and blindness, darkness and light, witness, belief, salvation, the temple, truth, lifting up, pasture, and so on. John's story has quotations from Deutero-Isaiah at two vital moments: in 1.23 ('I am the voice of one calling in the desert', Isa. 40.3) and in 12.38 ('Lord, who has believed our message?', Isa. 53.1). It is likely that the Lamb of God title derives in part from the Suffering Servant who is led like a lamb to the slaughter in Isa. 53.7.

However, there is evidence in John's story of a rich Passover symbolism. The whole of the Gospel could be described as a *Passover plot* in that it moves through the three Passover festivals in 2.13, 6.4 and 13.1. The point of travelling up to Jerusalem at Passover time in Second Temple Judaism was to take a lamb to the priests in the Temple to be slaughtered and prepared for the Passover meal. In the final Passover in Jn 13–19, the passion of Jesus coincides with this slaughter of the lambs, and the description of the death of Jesus is given some subtle paschal overtones as we shall see in the commentary on 19.16b-42. The suggestion is that Jesus is the true Passover Lamb, the Lamb of God who takes away the sin of the world. Thus the Lamb of God theme in 1.29 is a careful and creative fusion of two literary traditions from Deutero-Isaiah and Exodus 12.

Another new theme is that of revelation. In v. 31 the Baptist says that his destiny has been to facilitate the revelation of Jesus (*phanerōthē*) to Israel. The verb *phanero ō* is found nine times in John's story and connotes an emergence from concealment and obscurity. This word is again linked to the central plot motif of the elusiveness of Jesus Christ. Jesus is concealed from human understanding until he sovereignly chooses to reveal himself.

A final, important new theme in this narrative is the theme of resting/abiding/staying. John speaks of the Spirit resting on Jesus (*emeinen* in v. 32, and *menon* in v. 33). The verb *menō* (rest) occurs 40 times in the Fourth Gospel (only 12 times in the Synoptics). Usually the verb is used to describe the Son's relationship with the Father and the Son's relationship with the disciple. Here the relationship is between the Spirit and the Son.

Narrative Christology

This section of John's story is a perfect example of narrative Christology, of christological confession couched in story form. A great christological credo is suggested in a very few words. From the mouth of the Baptist, we learn that Jesus is the Lamb of God, the one who existed before John, the one to be revealed to Israel, the recipient of God's Spirit, the one who baptizes with the Holy Spirit, the Son of God—all this in six verses.

The narrator states in Jn 20.30-31 that the primary purpose for narrating the Gospel is to evoke faith in Jesus as the Christ, the Son of God. Everything in the Gospel is therefore designed to evoke a specific christological faith in the reader. The Baptist's climactic confession of Jesus as Son of God in 1.34 is the first of eight occasions where *ho huios tou theou* is used to describe Jesus (1.34, 49; 5.25; 10.36; 11.4, 27; 19.7; 20.31). This is the most important christological title in the Fourth Gospel. In using *ho huios tou theou*, the narrator does not want us to think merely of a messianic title, impressive though that would be on its own. We are to see in this description an affirmation of the divinity of Jesus of Nazareth. The reader who penetrates that level of meaning, and believes what he or she understands, is the one who has experienced the liberating power of God's truth (Jn 8.32).

John 1.35-42

Context

After 35 verses, we are at last introduced properly to the protagonist of John's story. In the Prologue Jesus was eulogized as the Word of God. In 1.19-28 he was mentioned as someone standing mysteriously and elusively among the Pharisees. In 1.29-34 he was merely seen coming towards John. Now, in 1.35-42, Jesus turns round and utters his first words to the two disciples. At last the elusive Christ makes himself accessible and speaks to those who are searching for him.

The present story not only resonates with the beginning of the Gospel. There are also distinct prolepses (flash-forwards or anticipations) of the Gospel's conclusion. Jesus' words, 'What are you seeking?' (v. 38) also occur at 18.4, 7 and 20.15. Yet again we see John linking the beginning and the conclusion of his Gospel with the device of inclusio.

Characterization

Andrew, John, Simon and Jesus are the four characters mentioned in the story. Simon is introduced as Andrew's brother, but other than the fact that he is given the name Peter, his role is not developed. Little is made of his call and commission. Likewise, little is made of the Baptist. He is given the role of witness, again confessing Jesus as *amnos tou theou* (Lamb of God). However, he disappears after v. 36 as the narrator's focus shifts to Jesus. In this short narrative we see the narrator beginning to use minor characters as foils for Jesus' words and works.

Jesus himself is defined throughout ch. 1 in relation to the titles which others use of him. Already we have seen the Baptist confess Jesus as Lamb of God, pre-existent one, the one baptized in the Holy Spirit and Son of God. Now we see the two ex-disciples of the Baptist call Jesus 'Rabbi' (v. 38) and 'Messiah' (v. 41). The narrator frequently portrays the disciples addressing Jesus as 'Rabbi' (Master) in the first part of the Gospel (chs. 1–12), while he most frequently has them calling Jesus 'Kurios' (Lord) in the second part. As for 'Messiah', this only occurs in the form *messias* here and at 4.25, but occurs frequently as *christos* at 1.20, 25, 41; 3.28; 4.25, 29; 7.26, 27, 31, 41 (x2), 42; 9.22; 10.24; 11.27; 12.34; 20.31, and twice with *Iēsous* at 1.17 and 17.3. John 1.41 is the first overt reference to Jesus as the Christ outside the Prologue. John 1.35-42 is another example of narrative Christology—of christological belief expressed through the medium of story.

This is also the first of three references to the disciple called Andrew. Here his role is that of witness and evangelist. He helps his brother Simon to faith in Jesus the Messiah. When we see him again in 6.8-9 he again is seen bringing someone to Jesus, this time a young boy with five loaves and two small fish before the feeding of the five thousand. In 12.22 we see Andrew and Philip helping to bring some Greeks to the attention of Jesus. Andrew's character is defined in relation to his role: he is an evangelist *par excellence*.

Themes

Although there are some now familiar Johannine themes—seeing, v. 36, 38, 39(x2); also staying/remaining, v. 38, v. 39 (x2)—a number of new key concepts emerge in this narrative. First of all, the word *mathētēs* (disciple) appears in v. 35 and v. 37. The theme of discipleship is important in John's story.[1]

Connected with the idea of discipleship is the idea of following. John

---

1   *Mathētēs* occurs at 1.35, 37; 2.2, 11, 12, 17, 22; 3.22, 25; 4.1, 2, 8, 27; 6.3, 8, 12, 16, 22 (x2), 24, 60, 61, 66; 7.3; 8.31; 9.2, 27, 28 (x2); 11.7, 8, 12, 54; 12.4, 16; 13.5, 22, 23, 35; 15.8, 16, 17, 29; 18.1 (x2), 2, 15 (x2), 16, 17, 19, 25; 19.26, 27, 38; 20.2-4, 8, 10, 18-20, 25, 26, 30; 21.1, 2, 4, 7, 8, 12, 14, 20, 23, 24.

introduces this idea in 1.37 (*ēkolouthēsan*), 1.38 (*akolouthountas*) and v. 40 (*akolouthēsantōn*). 'Following' in the sense of discipleship is mentioned at 8.12; 10.4, 27; 12.26; 13.36; 21.19, 22. The fact that the verb is used in this sense four times in seven verses (37, 38, 40, 43) indicates that the narrator is initiating a major theme at this stage.

Two other themes which emerge are seeking and finding. The verb for seeking (*zēteō*) is used 34 times in John (14 in Matthew, 10 in Mark, 25 in Luke, 117 in the NT). The majority of uses in John concern seeking Jesus: 1.38; 6.24, 26; 7.11, 34, 36; 8.21; 11.56; 13.33; 18.4, 7, 8; 20.15. In the present context, Jesus asks the two disciples, *ti zēteite*, 'What are you seeking?' Since these are the first words of Jesus in the Gospel, they are of great significance. The Gospel story is, as I showed in the introduction, an exciting exploration of the idea of Jesus as the elusive Christ. The quest for Jesus is perhaps one of the most important aspects of the Gospel's plot—one responsible for the suspense and drama of John's story. Here, the words 'What are you seeking?' initiate the theme and are loaded with profound, religious significance.

The other keyword is 'finding' (*heuriskō*). In v. 41 Andrew finds Simon (*heuriskei*) and in v. 41 he says to his brother, 'We have found the Messiah!' (*heurēkamen*). *heuriskō* is used 19 times in John's story: 1.41 (x2), 43, 45; 2.14; 5.14; 6.25; 7.34-36 (x3); 9.35; 10.9; 11.17; 12.14; 18.38; 19.4, 6; 21.6. Seeking and finding are connected to Jesus' elusiveness. Only at 1.41, 1.45 and 6.25 is Jesus said to have been found by anyone.

Another important theme is that of coming to Jesus. Here Jesus invites the disciples to 'Come and see'. There is a deeper meaning implied in these simple words: 'Come into relationship with me and receive true sight'. 'Coming to Jesus' is used to describe active faith in John's story (see 3.21; 4.29-30; 5.40; 6.35, 37, 45; 7.37).

Narrator

The role of the narrator is more clearly evident in this story than in the other two scenes after the Prologue. A particularly important aspect of the storytelling appears here: the tendency to provide explanatory parentheses. There are three in this passage alone:

38	'which means Teacher'
41	'that is, the Christ'
42	'which, when translated, is Peter'

There are many of these asides in the Gospel (see 2.9, 22; 4.2, 9, 25; 6.6, 59, 64, 71; 7.5, 39; 8.27; 9.7; 10.6; 11.2, 18, 51; 12.6, 16; 13.11; 18.10, 14, 40; 19.13, 14, 17, 31, 35-36, 42; 20.9, 16, 30-31; 21.7, 14, 19, 23, 24-25). On at least four occasions (9.7; 19.13, 17; 20.16) these asides contain Greek translations of Hebrew or Aramaic terms. This is the function of the three parentheses in 1.38, 1.41 and 1.42. Evidently there were Greeks in the author's original readership.

John 1.43-51

Context

The plot of the Nathaniel narrative imitates the plot of the narrative preceding it. This suggests that the two stories are to be linked together. They share the same formal characteristics ('the call story'):

1.35-42	1.43-51
Andrew and Peter from Bethsaida	Philip from Bethsaida
Two disciples find and follow Jesus (one of them named as Andrew)	Jesus finds Philip and invites him to follow him
Jesus says, 'Come and see' to the two disciples	Philip says, 'Come and see' to Nathaniel
Andrew says to Peter, 'We have found the Messiah'	Philip says to Nathaniel, 'We have found the one Moses wrote about'
Jesus calls Simon 'Peter', the Rock	Jesus describes Nathaniel as 'a true Israelite'

Characterization

Three characters are mentioned: Jesus, Philip and Nathaniel. A new facet of Jesus' character appears: his supernatural *gn ōsis* (knowledge) about people. For the main part, however, he is again defined by the titles used of him. He is the one written about by Moses and the prophets. He is the master of the disciples who attach themselves to him (Rabbi). He is the Son of God and king of Israel. He is, by his own assertion, 'the Son of Man'. This last title is important in John's story:

	Description	Activity
1.51	The one on whom the angels ascend and descend	Mediation between earth and heaven
3.13	The one who has gone in and out of heaven	Mediation between earth and heaven
3.14	The one who must be lifted up	Passion
5.27	The one who has authority to judge	Judgment
6.27	The one who gives the food of eternal life and on whom God's favour rests	Life-giver
6.53	The one whose flesh and blood bring life	Life-giver

	Description	Activity
6.62	The one who ascends to where he was before	Mediation between earth and heaven
8.28	The one who will be lifted up	Passion
9.35	The one who is both the object of faith and worship	Life-giver
12.23	The one who is to be glorified through the cross	Passion
12.34 (×2)	The one who must be lifted up	Passion
13.31	The one who is to be glorified through the cross	Passion

In using the title 'Son of Man' (*ho huios tou anthrōpou*), Jesus describes himself as the eschatological Heavenly Man who mediates the polarity of earth and heaven through the cross. When Pilate exclaims, 'Behold the man!' (19.5), this theme reaches its climax.

Philip is characterized in this passage as the model disciple. The word *mathētēs* (disciple) connotes the idea of imitation. Indeed, the rabbinic master–pupil relationship in first-century Palestinian Judaism could be summed up in this idea. The Rabbi taught by information and demonstration, and his disciples imitated him. Here Philip imitates Jesus. Just as Jesus finds Philip, so Philip finds Nathaniel. Just as Jesus wins the attention of enquirers with the enticing 'Come and see', so Philip attracts Nathaniel with the same words, 'Come and see'.

Nathaniel's appearance is significant. He is the first of a number of named individuals who are distinctive to John's story. Nathaniel, Nicodemus and Lazarus are characters who receive detailed attention on the occasions when they appear. Here Nathaniel is portrayed as a man of mixed qualities. He is capable of regional prejudice ('Can anything good come from Nazareth?') but he is also a man of transparent integrity ('one in whom there is nothing false'). He is a representative character ('a true Israelite'), yet also an individual ('How do you know *me*?'). He is unlike Jacob in character (there was plenty of guile in Jacob) and yet like Jacob in charisma (like Jacob, Nathaniel will see a vision of angels ascending and descending). This wealth of paradoxes is suggested in very few words. As ever, John's characterization displays artful reticence.

Themes

There are new themes in this story. The themes of seeing/coming to Jesus and finding/following/belief have appeared before. New themes include: ascent and descent, the supernatural knowledge of Jesus and the 'even greater things' (1.51, 5.20, 14.12). The theme of ascending and descending is used at a number of levels in the Gospel. Here it is angelic beings who ascend and descend upon the Son of Man. In the majority of instances it will be Jesus who is presented as descending from heaven and ascending to heaven. We shall see later that the narrator also uses these words for Jesus' itinerary. Often Jesus is portrayed as going down or going up to a geographical area. The use of the same verbs in these instances function as a constant reminder of the celestial *katabasis* (descent) and *anabasis* (ascent) of Jesus.

Literary Devices

Yet again we see an *inclusio* with the end of John's story. The narrative begins with the words of Jesus to Philip, *akolouthei moi* (Follow me, 1.43). In the conclusion of the Gospel, these words will appear on the lips of Jesus, this time to Peter in 21.19.

Time-shapes are again in evidence. The phrase *tē epaurion* gives the impression of process time. After the timelessness of the Prologue, the references to the passing of days in 1.29, 35 and 43 help to earth John's story.

There are three references to 'the next day' in ch. 1. The preference for number patterns is evident here. The author's marked tendency to structure material in tripartite patterns is visible in the three confessions of Jesus in 1.43-51, one by Philip and two by Nathaniel.

We have in 1.43-51 the first example of the *double Amen formula*. Jesus says, 'I tell you the truth' (*am ēn, amēn* in v. 51) to Nathaniel. Other examples of this are at 3.3, 5, 11; 5.19, 24-25; 6.26, 32, 47, 53; 8.34, 51, 58; 10.1, 7; 12.24; 13.16, 20-21, 38; 14.12; 16.20, 23; 21.18.

The narrator uses the device of *focus* skilfully. The Gospel states that the mission of Jesus is to the world (1.10, 3.16). There is a universal scope to Jesus' work which results in an equally cosmic, narrative focus. What the Nathaniel narrative shows for the first time is the narrator's ability to move from a cosmic to a highly specific perspective. Nathaniel is an individual who is the object of a precise and particular literary study. However, his personal story is also taken up into the world story depicted by the narrator (3.16). Personal history and universal history are carefully fused.

Another literary device which contributes to the sense of meaningful history is the narrator's use of the *historic present* tense. In 1.45, Philip *finds* Nathaniel (present tense) and *says* (present), 'We have found the Messiah'. This brings the past into the reader's present and implies a purposeful continuity of mission. Furthermore, the constant appearance of *legō* (to say/speak) in the present tense helps to reduce the effects of the transition from orality to textuality in the Gospel's composition. By having characters speaking in the present tense, the Gospel recreates the living aspect of speech characteristic of oral storytelling.

Another noteworthy device is the narrator's language of *movement and stasis*. We shall see later in the commentary that the movements of characters, and also where they stand in relation to other characters, will have symbolic significance. In 1.43-51, Nathaniel is seen approaching Jesus (*erchomenon pros auton*). In 1.36, John sees Jesus walking by (*peripatounti*). In 1.38, Jesus sees the disciples following him (*akolouthountas*). In 1.29 John sees Jesus approaching him (*erchomenon pros auton*, exactly the same as Nathaniel's movement towards Jesus in 1.47). These verbs of movement have symbolic overtones of 'coming into faith and discipleship'.

But stative verbs are important too. John is standing at a certain point (*heistēkei*) when Jesus passes by in 1.35. Later on in the Gospel, where various characters are positioned will be of vital importance in the narrator's implicit commentary on events. Where Judas and Peter are standing in Jn 18.1-27 will prove to be significant in determining their loyalty to Jesus.

A final device worthy of mention is the use of *proverbs*. Nathaniel's 'Can anything good come from Nazareth?' sounds very much like a local proverb. Other examples of Johannine proverbs are: 2.10; 3.8; 4.35, 37, 44; 12.24, 25a; 13.16; 15.13, 20.

John 2.1-11

Context
There is a marked change of setting at the start of ch. 2 (from Bethany to Cana); this indicates the start of a new narrative section. The introduction of the miracles of Jesus, described as *sēmeia* (signs) also indicates a new beginning. The word *sēmeion* (sign, 2.11) and the related word *ergon* (work) occur at a number of points from here on. Jesus' miracles are important because they are revelatory; they disclose the real identity of Jesus.

The reader should note that 2.1-11 is part of a block of narrative material beginning at 2.1 and extending to 4.54. This depicts a Cana-to-Cana itinerary. The stories within this section focus on faith-responses to Jesus. Having introduced the theme of belief and faith in 2.11, the narrator now explores some varied reactions to the early stages of Jesus' ministry of signs and wonders (4.48):

	Subject	*Faith-Response*
2.1-11	The wine miracle at Cana. First sign	The disciples believe (v. 11) in Jesus because of the Cana sign.
2.12-22	The Cleansing of the Temple	The Jews demand a sign (v. 18) and misunderstand Jesus (vv. 19-21).

2.23-25	Many people see signs from Jesus in Jerusalem	Many believe in Jesus because of the signs. Jesus does not entrust himself to them because he knows their true motives.
3.1-21	Jesus' conversation with Nicodemus	Nicodemus knows Jesus is 'from God' because of his signs, but he also misunderstands Jesus.
3.22-36	John the Baptist's witness to Jesus	John reveals true faith in Jesus as well as true understanding.
4.1-42	Jesus' conversation with the Samaritan woman	The woman believes in Jesus and leads her whole village to faith.
4.43-54	The healing miracle at Cana. Second sign	The official and his whole household believe on the basis of the sign.

Broadly speaking, the overall theme of John 2–4 concentrates on responses to Jesus' charismatic ministry. Another overarching idea is the theme of Jesus' radical break with Judaism and his inauguration of a new order of things. In the Cana episode in 2.1-11, Jesus replaces the old rituals of purification. The phrase, 'they have no more wine' (2.3) symbolizes the inadequacy of Judaism; Judaism now has no more to offer humanity by way of salvation. The fact that there are only six jars (2.6) further signals the failure and incompleteness of the old order. The saving of the good wine until now shows that Jesus is the fulfilment of Judaism (2.10). This thought continues in 2.13-22; here Jesus replaces the Temple in Judaism with the temple of his body, the new place for humanity's encounter with God. In 3.1-21, Jesus explains his new teaching on the kingdom of God, that humanity enjoys the privileges of this kingdom through regeneration. In 3.22-30, we see the Baptist emphasizing that the Christ is bringing in a new order. In 4.1-42, the narrator portrays Samaritans coming to faith in the Messiah, and Jesus speaking of a new form of worship—not in the holy places of Jerusalem and Samaria but 'in spirit and in truth'. In the final story of the Cana-to-Cana cycle, Jesus brings the life of the age to come into history in his restoration of the official's son. A major theme of John 2–4 is, therefore, the dawn of a new age in Jesus Christ.

Structure
John 2.1-11 provides us with another example of a chiasmus:

A^1	1-2	Introduction	Cana, a wedding, disciples present
B^1	3-5	Dialogue	Jesus and his mother, about wine
C	6-8	Dialogue	Jesus and the servants
B^2	9-10	Dialogue	The master and Jesus, about wine
A^2	11	Conclusion	Cana, first sign, disciples believe

The introduction and conclusion have verbal parallels in the words *Kana* and *hoi math ētai*. The two dialogues in vv. 3-5 and vv. 9-10 are both linked by the common theme of wine. In vv. 3-5, the mother of Jesus says, 'They have no more wine' (v. 3). In vv. 9-10, the master of ceremonies enquires where the wine has come from. This leaves vv. 6-8 as the centrepiece. The narrator wants the reader to focus on the stone water jars, the water, and their symbolic value (see 'Symbolism' below).

Characterization

There are six characters: the mother of Jesus, Jesus, his disciples, the servants at the wedding banquet, the master of ceremonies, and the bridegroom. What is noticeable is the lack of narrative focus on the couple actually being married and their close family and attendants. Maybe this is because the narrator does not want to mention bridegrooms, brides and bridegroom's friends in a story where these figures are to have different, symbolic and messianic connotations (3.27-30). The most likely reason is that the narrator wishes to highlight the sign performed by Jesus, and that all other material is incidental.

The mother of Jesus is portrayed as the one who approaches her son with the observation that the wine has run out. This is one of two occasions in John's story when she performs a function in the narrative. On both occasions (here and in 19.25-27), she is not called Mary by the narrator, and she is addressed by Jesus as *gunai*, 'woman'. Jesus' reference to his 'hour' here (the hour of his return to the Father, embracing his death), links the Cana episode to the crucifixion where the mother of Jesus is also present. In both stories, the mother is a minor character with personality (see below) and symbolic value. Jesus' use of *gunai* may be intended as an allusion to Gen. 3.15, in which case she is to be seen as the New Eve in the New Creation of Jesus' ministry.

The disciples of Jesus are not prominent except in the narrator's introduction and conclusion. All that we learn about them is that they put their faith in Jesus on the basis of this miracle (2.11). The narrator has only mentioned five specific disciples in the story so far. In ch. 1, he alludes to Andrew, an unnamed disciple, Simon Peter, Philip and Nathaniel. However, we can assume that a larger group than this is implied in the words, *hoi mathētai*. What is interesting to note at this stage is the narrator's preference for 'the disciples' over and against 'the Twelve'. The latter occurs only at 6.67, 70 and 20.24.

The characterization of Jesus is complex and developed. What is the meaning of his reaction to his mother in v. 4? These words do not sound like the response of a loving son. Indeed, it sounds like a rebuke: 'Woman, why are you involving me in this?' The next comment, 'My hour has not yet come', hardly sounds like an obvious reason for Jesus' attitude. In fact, it sounds like an example of discontinuous dialogue—of

Jesus' tendency to transcend normal levels of discourse with enigmatic statements.

The paradigmatic reader, however, knows that the hour of Jesus refers to his return to the Father through the cross. Furthermore, this reader also knows that, in John's story, the cross is to be the place where Jesus' real identity is to be disclosed. In 8.28, Jesus says, 'When the Son of Man is lifted up, then you will know that I am' (*egō eimi*— the divine name). The paradigmatic reader, knowing already that the cross is the place of revelation, is able to interpret Jesus' words to his mother in 2.4 as follows: 'Woman, why are you involving me in this business? Don't you know that now is not the hour for my true identity to be revealed to the world? The moment of revelation will be on the cross. If you urge me to perform this sign now, everyone here will recognize me for who I really am. Therefore do not press me.'

However, the mother of Jesus—interestingly—does not easily take 'no' for an answer. Maybe she is, in a practical and caring way, concerned that the wedding banquet should not end in disaster. Her reaction to Jesus' rebuke is consequently not some submissive withdrawal into the wings but rather a complete refusal to be swayed by her son's resistance. Her reaction is to turn to the servants of the banquet and say, 'Do whatever he tells you'. This now leaves Jesus with no choice but to do something! He is involved now whether he likes it or not.

Even so, Jesus will not be compromised. Out of respect for his mother he does become involved, but he does so furtively. The miracle which follows is no dramatic and overt display. It is depicted as the secret work of a hidden Messiah, of the elusive Christ. That is why the fifth character, the master of ceremonies (*architriklinos*) turns to the bridegroom (the sixth character) to ask him why the vintage wine is being served now. If the miracle had been performed as a public spectacle in full view of everyone, then the *architriklinos* would never have had to ask this question. But the sign has been performed unobtrusively. Jesus merely asks the servants to fill the six jars with water, and then to draw some out and take it to the master of ceremonies. There is no invocation of the Spirit, no loud cry to the Father, just a covert transformation which only the servants, the mother of Jesus and the disciples know about. Thus, Mary's implicit request is answered and Jesus' true identity remains undisclosed.

Symbolism

The story begins with the phrase, 'On the third day' (*kai tē hēmera tē tritē*). On the surface this merely looks like a statement of process time. We have had references to the passing of days in the previous three narratives (*tē epaurion*). 'On the third day' appears to be another such temporal indicator. However, 'on the third day' has powerful connotations in both earliest and present-day Christianity. Since the first generation church, 'on the third day' has prefaced statements of the resurrection in credal formulae. Thus, in 1 Cor. 15.4 we read that Jesus Christ was raised on the third day (*tē hēmera tē tritē*). The opening words of the Cana narrative therefore have strong symbolic resonances. They show that the sign is an eschatological event. The implicit commentary seems to be as follows: the wine miracle marks the dawn of a new age.

The idea of a new age dawning through the Cana miracle is not only suggested by the symbolism of the third day. It is also suggested by the *gamos*, the wedding motif. In a Gospel which emphasizes realized eschatology, the wedding at Cana functions as a symbol of the eschatological marriage of the bridegroom Jesus (Jn 3.29) with his church (Isa. 54.4-8). The feast at Cana symbolizes the messianic banquet attending that event (Isa. 25.6).

There may also be a realized eschatology implicit in the chronology here. The narrator dates this miracle on the seventh day of the story—counting days from the ministry of the Baptist in ch. 1.

1st day	1.19-28	The Baptist's testimony about himself
2nd day	1.29-34	The Baptist's testimony about Jesus
3rd day	1.35-39	Andrew and another follow Jesus
4th day	1.40-42	Simon Peter becomes a disciple
5th day	1.43-50	Philip and Nathaniel
6th day	(none)	The journey to Galilee (see 1.43 and 2.1)
7th day	2.1-11	The wedding at Cana

This implies that the seven days of chs. 1 and 2 are an echo of the seven days of Creation, and that what we have in the coming of Jesus the Messiah is a New Creation (Brown 1966: I, 106).

Form

The Cana wedding sign is a miracle story. It has formal similarities with the Cana story in 4.46-54. In both there is a request–rebuke–response sequence. In 2.1-11, the mother of Jesus makes a request to her son. She is rebuked. But then Jesus responds with a miracle. In 4.46-54 we see a similar sequence. The official makes a request to Jesus. Jesus rebukes the crowd. But then Jesus responds with a miracle of healing. The fact that both miracles share an identical setting (Cana) as well as an identical form suggests that they come from the same collection of miracles. This collection is almost certainly a signs source because the action of Jesus in both 2.1-11 and 4.46-54 is described as a *sēmeion*. However, it is likely that these are the only two narratives derived from John's celebrated signs source. On no other occasion do we have a story set in Cana, described as a 'sign' and emplotted according to a request–rebuke–response sequence. The widely argued view that the whole of John 1–12 and some of John 21 is based on a Signs Gospel cannot be sustained by the evidence.

Plot-Type

The reader needs to be alert to the literary-critical as well as the form-critical genre of 2.1-11. The first Cana miracle has some comic elements. There is humour in the ignorance of the *architriklinos* which contrasts with the superior knowledge of his *diakonoi* (servants) in v. 9. There is a comic touch in the implied reference to the customary drunkenness of wedding guests in 2.10. The very context of the wedding suggests comedy. Comic stories often conclude with the appearance of a new society, and this new society is marked by a party or festive ritual, of which weddings are the most common. From a literary point of view, the wedding setting in Jn 2.1-11 therefore helps to create a mood of romantic comedy. Indeed, what we have in 2.1-11 is something unique in literary terms: it is the occurrence of the 'happy ending' right at the start of the story ('a happy beginning!'). From a theological point of view, it helps to create the sense of the last things appearing at the beginning! In other words, the comic *mythos* in 2.1-11 is related to John's realized eschatology.

Literary Devices

Literary devices are used throughout Jn 2.1-11. The use of the *historic present tense* (see the commentary on 1.43-51) is again visible here. The narrator four times has *legō* in the present (vv. 3, 5, 7, 10). This lifts the spoken word out of the past and makes it a present speech-event for the reader. By using this device, the narrator recreates that sense of living address which was lost when oral storytelling became written narrative.

Note also the use of *time-shapes* in the first Cana miracle. I have examined 'on the third day', a process time-shape with strong symbolic overtones. In Jesus' reference to the 'hour' in 2.4, we have the first example of a barrier time-shape. The hour refers to the appointed time of Jesus' return to the Father. By that appointed time, Jesus must be able to say of his saving work that 'it is finished'. The concept of the hour functions as a barrier in that it sets up a prescribed time limit in which the protagonist must have fulfilled his quest. Mentioning the hour as early as 2.4 is important because it establishes the goal in the mind of the reader, and helps to create a sense of anticipation and suspense.

John 2.12

This is the first of four passages in the first section of the Book of Signs which exist mainly to orient the reader within Jesus' itinerary. Far from being pointless additions to the story, they in fact contribute in a number of important ways to the plot. The four bridge passages are:

1.   2.12   Jesus travels with his family to Capernaum
2.   3.22   Jesus travels into the Judaean countryside
3.   4.1-3   Jesus travels from Judea to Galilee
4.   4.43-45   Jesus revisits Galilee after visiting Samaria

These texts first of all help us to establish the exact itinerary of Jesus. The journey in 2.1–4.54 takes Jesus from Cana (the starting point in 2.1) to Capernaum (mentioned in the bridge passage here at 2.12) to Jerusalem (2.13–3.21) into the Judean countryside (3.22), then *en route* back to Galilee (4.1-3), into Samaria to a village called Sychar (4.5) before finally arriving back in Galilee (4.43-45) and returning to the place where he started his itinerary (Cana, 4.46). Jesus' first itinerary is therefore a circular one.

The first literary function of these bridge passages is to create a sense of movement. This function relates to space. The second function relates to time. One of the striking aspects of the storytelling in John is the way in which two contrasting concepts of history are combined. On the one hand, he presents us with history as structured, directional, purposive. On the other hand, he also portrays history as fragmentary (2.12 is an 'itinerary fragment'). The meaningful view of history is suggested by the way in which the sequence of seven days in 1.19–2.11 is made to symbolize the first week of a new Genesis. The episodic view of history is suggested by statements such as 2.12: 'After this he went down to Capernaum with his mother and brothers and his disciples. There they stayed for a few days.' Here the days serve no symbolic function. The *pollas hēmeras* in Capernaum are part of the temporal flux of Jesus' ministry.

From a deconstructionist perspective, the insignificance of the passing of days in 2.12 could be said to undermine the view of time which the narrator has established up to this point. The prologue of the Gospel has hinted at a world of inherent structure and rationality in its description of Jesus as the Logos. The Gospel begins with a magnificent gesture of logocentricism. This is then further indicated by the story time in 1.19–2.11, which is set forth as a symbolic sequence of seven days. Now, in 2.12, however, the narrator provides us with a form of history-writing which is more chronicle than narrative. He gives us the briefest description of a visit of Jesus to Capernaum which lasted an unspecified number of days. In statements like this, the emplotted nature of history seems to be forsaken for a moment. In its place, the contradictory idea of history as the very opposite of narrative is suggested.

However, one must be cautious about pursuing this interpretation too far. Even in John 2.12 there is a sense of meaning which is not immediately visible. This deeper level of emplotment is suggested through the narrator's use of the verb *katabainō* in 2.12: 'Jesus went down (*katebē*) to Capernaum'. This verb will be used throughout the Fourth Gospel, sometimes of Jesus coming down from heaven, sometimes of Jesus going down to a geographical location (see 4.47, 49, 51). The latter references are used as reminders of the main plot of John's story, which has to do with the descent and ascent of Jesus (see also 2.13, where the narrator uses *anabainō* for Jesus' journey *up to* Jerusalem). Even in the apparent deconstruction of narrative history in 2.12 there is still therefore an indication of emplotment and narrativity.

John 2.13-25

Context
This is the first of three allusions to the Passover in the Gospel. The other two are at 6.4 ('The Jewish Passover feast was near') and at 13.1 ('It was just before the Passover feast'). These three Passovers are important in the creation of a sense of plot (beginning, middle and end). The first Passover occurs at the beginning of the Book of Signs (2.13). The second occurs in the middle (6.4). The third occurs at the end (12.1). The present story has an important role in the construction of a Passover plot in the first twelve chapters.

The sign at Cana and the sign in the Temple are linked. Both explore the theme of the replacement of the old order of worship with a new order centred on Jesus and his work. Jesus replaces the water of Jewish purification with the new wine of the kingdom in 2.1-11. Here in vv. 13-22 he replaces the Temple in Jerusalem with the new temple of his body. From now on, people will no longer meet in the Temple to gain access to God; they will indwell the temple of his risen presence.

Structure
Like the Cana miracle, 2.13-25 shows evidence of compositional artistry. Again we see the devices of inclusio and chiasmus:

A^1	13	Jesus in Jerusalem at the Passover
B^1	14-17	The disciples' post-resurrection remembrance
C	18-21	The new temple of Jesus' body
B^2	22	The disciples' post-resurrection remembrance
A^2	23-25	Jesus in Jerusalem at the Passover

Characterization

Jesus' characterization reveals a number of qualities. First of all, his pilgrimage to Jerusalem shows that he is a pious Jew who observes the feasts even if he seeks to fulfil and transcend them. Secondly, his outrage at the discovery of the merchants in the outer courts of the Temple reveals his devotion to his Father's house—a devotion which we are told will 'consume' him (v. 17, a prolepsis of the passion). Thirdly, the language of Jesus from v. 19 onwards reveals a new characteristic. Here he takes a concrete object from his immediate, local context and infuses it with symbolic, spiritual meaning. The object in this instance is the Temple building which Jesus uses as a metaphor for his own body. This is a strategy which we shall see again in the coming chapters. In 3.8 Jesus takes *pneuma*, the desert wind, and uses it as a metaphor for the Spirit in his conversation with Nicodemus. In ch. 4, Jesus will take the running water at Jacob's well and use it as a symbol of the water of the Spirit, this time in dialogue with the Samaritan woman.

The other characters are the merchants selling animals, the money lenders and the disciples. The first two groups are merely mentioned in passing. The disciples, however, are said to have understood Jesus' words and actions later, in the light of the resurrection and their subsequent interpretation of the Scriptures. They are therefore backstage witnesses of the action. Their presence in the Temple precincts is presupposed but not highlighted.

This just leaves 'the Jews'. This group has already been mentioned in 1.19 when the Jews in Jerusalem send priests and Levites to investigate John the Baptist. Here the same group in Jerusalem start to appear in their characteristic, negative light. However, caution needs to be exercised in interpreting the narrator's stance towards this group. In this passage alone, we can see a certain variety in connotation when *hoi Ioudaioi* is used. In 2.13 the narrator speaks of the Passover of the Jews (*tōn Ioudaiōn* which just denotes Judaism). Here the 'Jews' is used in a neutral way. However, in 2.18 and 20, *hoi Ioudaioi* is beginning to be defined by the context. The antagonism of this group in 2.18 suggests a hostile use of the 'Jews'. From now on, there are over 70 references to the Jews in the story. Some of these will suggest Judaism or the nation of the Jews in general, as in 2.13. In other instances, the same phrase will connote a group hostile to Jesus and characterized by intense unbelief (as in 2.18, 20). The context will determine whether the neutral or the hostile sense is implied.

Narrator and Point of View

The presence of the narrator becomes obvious again here. This is principally because the amount of direct speech decreases and the amount of narratorial asides increases. In the ten verses of the story, only four have any direct speech in them. The rest is the commentary of the narrator, who introduces the context in v. 13, describes the action in vv. 14-15, reports Jesus' words in v. 16, provides a later interpretation of all this in v. 17, describes the dialogue between Jesus and the Jews in vv. 18-20, gives an interpretative aside in v. 21, and provides us with a post-resurrection perspective in v. 22. Here we have the full spectrum of involvement from objective, third-person description to the penetrative elicitation of secret meanings.

In 2.13-25, the narrator describes events from an enlightened, post-resurrection point of view. The remembrance motif brings this out strongly. Jesus will promise his disciples in 14.26 that the *paraklētos*, the Holy Spirit, will teach them everything and will also remind them of what he has said. This is a reference to the very different understanding which the disciples will have after the coming of the Spirit. In 12.16, the narrator shows that this new hermeneutic is enjoyed after the resurrection: 'At first his disciples did not understand all this. Only after Jesus was glorified did they realize that these things had been written about him and that they had done these things to him' (notice the close parallel with 2.22).

What we have in 2.13-25 is a narrator who describes events retrospectively. He or she is the spokesperson of a group whose interpretation of the past is very different from the understanding of events at the time. During the ministry of Jesus, the disciples sometimes misunderstand the true import of Jesus' words and acts. After the resurrection, however, they remember what Jesus said and did, they interpret it in the light of OT Scripture, and they understand/believe. Something of this process is preserved in the Temple cleansing story. The event is remembered, it is filtered through the Scripture of Ps. 69.9, and then understood as an event signifying the establishing of a new house of God in the person of Jesus—risen, glorified, but present to his own in the *paraklētos*. Thus the narrator and point of view in this story are prominent.

Themes and Reader Response

Certain keywords resurface here: 'finding' (v. 13), 'sign' (v. 18), 'disciples' (v. 22) and 'believing' (v. 22). A new theme is raised in the concept of remembrance (*emnēsthēsan*, vv. 17, 22). The crucial theme, however, is the theme of the Temple. In v. 14, Jesus goes into the Temple area (*hieron*, the outer courts). He drives the merchants out of this area (*hieron*, v. 15). In v. 16, in his angry denunciation, Jesus refers to the Temple as the *oikos tou patros*. Here the word *oikos* (house) replaces *hieron* (outer Temple area) as the keyword. In v. 17, the word *oikos* appears again in the quotation from Ps. 69.9 ('zeal for your house'). In v. 19, the word *naos* (the inner area of the Temple) replaces *oikos* when Jesus says 'destroy this Temple' (*naos*). The word is taken up by the Jews in v. 20 and by the narrator in v. 21. In v. 21 the narrator identifies the *naos* referred to by Jesus as his body (*sōma*). What we therefore have in this narrative is a cluster of keywords which connote the Temple. They evolve as follows:

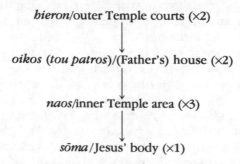

hieron/outer Temple courts (×2)

oikos (*tou patros*)/(Father's) house (×2)

naos/inner Temple area (×3)

sōma/Jesus' body (×1)

It is important to spot the binary opposition between outer and inner (suggested by the words *hieron* and *naos*) in order to notice the gradual progression in the story. What we have at the start of the narrative is movement around the outer areas of the Temple (vv. 14-15). What we have by the end of the story is a homing in on the inner areas of the Temple (vv. 19-21). This movement from the outer to the inner is reflective of the movement in understanding. As paradigmatic readers, we move in the story from an external, superficial inter-pretation of the Temple as a building in Jerusalem, to the heart of what the Temple really means, the body of Jesus. Unlike the Jews, who remain purely at the outer area (the literal interpretation), we the readers proceed to the innermost sanctuary of the narrator's intention. Like a symbolic high priest, the narrator guides the paradigmatic reader through the veil of misunderstanding into the most holy place of revelation. Here we are told that the real Temple, the new Temple, is the body of Jesus—wherever Jesus Christ, by his Spirit, is known.

Literary Devices

The device of 'punning' is related to this insider/outsider hermeneutic. In 2.16 and 2.20, we see a number of 'puns' based on the word *oikos*. In 2.16, Jesus says, 'How dare you turn my Father's house' (*oikos tou patros*) into a market (*oikon emporiou*)'. In 2.20, the Jews speak of how long the Temple took to build (*oikodomēthē*). They question how it could possibly be raised. Here they use the word *egereis*, which can be used of buildings but which is also used of Jesus' resurrection. These puns reveal that the narrator is concerned to maximize the effects of playing on Temple-related words, especially *oikos*. Those 'in the know' can enjoy the puns. Those who are outsiders (the Jews) cannot.

Another literary device worthy of mention is the narrator's ability to use a passage as both *conclusion and introduction*. John 2.23-25 provides a conclusion to ch. 2 but also prepares us for the Nicodemus narrative in ch. 3. Several words are used in 2.23-25 that offer an interpretative background for the dialogue between Jesus and Nicodemus which follows. The narrator says that Jesus knew everything about a person (*anthrōpou*) and also what was in a person (*anthrōpō*). The first words of ch. 3 are: *hēn de anthrōpos*, 'There was a man' (referring to Nicodemus). The *anthrōpos* of 3.1 picks up the *anthrōpos* (×2) of 2.25, suggesting that Nicodemus is one of the *polloi*, the 'many', in Jerusalem who believe. Also, the narrator says that many people saw the signs which Jesus did. Nicodemus, in 3.2, will claim that he knows that Jesus is sent from God because no one can do the signs which Jesus does (*ta sēmeia poiein*) unless he is from God. This recalls the narrator's words in 2.23 (*ta sēmeia ha epoiei*). Again, the suggestion is that Nicodemus is one of the *polloi*. Finally, the reference to Jesus' knowledge in 2.24 (*ginōskein*) will be picked up both by Nicodemus's *oidamen* (3.2) and by Jesus' *oidamen* in 3.11.

The significance of this device should not be underestimated. The narrator will often use passages as both conclusion and introduction. This again relates to the narrator's understanding of history. The inability to suggest an ultimate closure to a narrative and indeed to the Gospel story as a whole (see the commentary on Jn 21) indicates a unique perspective on Jesus-history. Stories in John are often 'open-ended'. This is because the narrator's point of view is saturated in 'realized eschatology', the belief that the end of all things has entered the middle of history in the person of Jesus. If the end is already here, then how can any story involving Jesus truly end?

John 3.1-21

Structure
Certain structural features should be noted in Jn 3.1-21. In the arrangement of 3.1-15, the author once again has revealed a predilection for tripartite structures. These verses are arranged artistically around three questions and three answers (Brown 1966: I, 136). Nicodemus asks:

2	Paraphrased: 'Where do you come from?' (the key question)
4	'How can a man be born again when he is old?'
9	'How can this be?'

Jesus' answers become progressively longer:

3	'You must be born again'
5-8	'You must be born of water and the Spirit'
10-15	'You are Israel's teacher, yet you do not understand'

The entire piece is based on a contrast between Jesus and Nicodemus. Nicodemus is depicted as 'a man' (*anthrōpos*) in v. 1, while Jesus, at the very end of the dialogue, describes himself twice as 'the Son of Man' (*ho huios tou anthrōpou*). Here 'a man' comes face to face with *the* Heavenly Man. The archetype of Jewish wisdom and pedagogy encounters the personification of heaven's Truth.

John 3.1-21 also contains several examples of inclusio (Brown 1966: I, 137). The following is a list of the parallels between vv. 1-2 and vv. 19-21:

1	'a man' // v. 19 'men'
2	'coming to Jesus' // v. 21 'coming into the light'
2	'by night' // v. 19 'darkness'
2	'doing' // v. 20 'doing'
2	'God is with him' // v. 21 'wrought in God'

Characterization

Nicodemus is portrayed as a man of the Pharisees, one of the rulers of the Jews. The Pharisees are mentioned 19 times in John's story and are synonymous with the Jewish authorities. This impression is reinforced in v. 1 by the proximity of the words *Pharisaiōn* and *Ioudaiōn*. These Pharisees have already been mentioned twice in the Gospel, at 1.19 and 1.24. Nicodemus' use of the plural, 'we know' in v. 2 suggests that he is a representative of a group, possibly the *polloi* in Jerusalem who believe in Jesus on the basis of the miracles (2.23-25). His meeting with Jesus takes place at night, which indicates that he wanted the meeting to occur in secret. Nicodemus may be being depicted in a partly negative light. However, the fact that he comes to Jesus at all means that the he is not a lost soul. The idiom 'to come to Jesus' has already been used as a synonym for 'coming to faith', so some sort of genuine seeking is implied.

Nicodemus' partial faith is borne out by two descriptions of Jesus which he verbalizes. He confesses that Jesus is both 'from God' and that God is 'with him'. He even addresses Jesus as 'Rabbi'. However, Nicodemus is also an inveterate literalist. His understanding of 'from God' does not connote heavenly origin. Nor does his definition of 'God with Jesus' connote ontological oneness. For Nicodemus, Jesus is 'from God' in the same way that the Baptist is 'from God': that is, he is a prophet who walks in the Spirit of God. His literalism here is a sign that he is 'from below', not 'from above'. That is why he cannot interpret rebirth 'from above/again (*anōthen*, vv. 3, 7)' and 'of the Spirit'. Even though he is the most prominent teacher in Israel (note the definite article in v. 10, '*the* teacher of Israel'), he does not understand Jesus' earthly teaching at the true level. Nicodemus is the embodiment of misunderstanding.

Jesus in this narrative is portrayed as the revealer of heaven's secrets. He speaks of the necessity of initiation into the rule of God through regeneration in water and the Spirit. He discloses truths about the elusiveness of the Spirit by comparing the Spirit with the desert wind. He indirectly communicates the fact that he has unrestricted access to and from heaven, and that he is the Son of Man, the one whose lifting up will give eternal life to all those who behold him in faith. In speaking of these things, however, Jesus proves to be the elusive Christ, a concealing revealer. He speaks in puns, *double entendres* and metaphors which require more than a modicum of wit to interpret. He also uses discontinuous dialogue by transcending the level of discourse used by his questioner.

Thus in Jn 3.1-21 the narrator depicts the first of a number of dramatic encounters between Religion (represented here by Nicodemus of the Pharisees) and Revelation (Jesus). In all cases, such encounters will present the reader with a sense of *krisis* or judgment. The verdict will be that religion and its institutions are insufficient for salvation. Only believing in the Revealer will bring a person to life in God.

Themes

A large cluster of Johannine themes enrich the Nicodemus dialogue.

a. Coming to Jesus. The theme of 'coming to Jesus' reappears in the movement of Nicodemus described by the narrator in v. 2 (*ēlthen pros auton*).

b. Darkness. The symbolic opposition of light and darkness resurfaces in the *nuktos* of v. 2. Darkness is also mentioned in v. 19 as a symbol of evil, the arena of human sinfulness.

c. Knowledge. Nicodemus says, 'we know' (v. 2). Jesus says, 'we know' (v. 11). Jesus points to Nicodemus's lack of knowledge by saying that Nicodemus does not know (*ouk oidas*) the movements of God's Spirit (v. 8). Who is really the possessor of knowledge is the main subject of the dialogue. Nicodemus' ignorance and Jesus' divine *gnōsis* grow more obvious as the story unfolds.

d. Jesus' Origins. In the story before us, Nicodemus confesses that Jesus is 'from God' (v. 2), yet he misunderstands the full import of what he is saying.

e. Signs. The theme of Jesus' signs reappears in v. 2. Nicodemus bases his judgment of Jesus on the latter's performance of signs and wonders.

f. Rebirth. In 1.13 the narrator spoke of those who accept Jesus as the born-of-God (*ek theou egennēthēsan*). Here Jesus tells Nicodemus that he must be born again/from above (*gennēthē anōthen*, 3.3, 7). The idea of birth is picked up again in vv. 7-8.

g. Sight. Jesus speaks of 'seeing' God's rule (v. 3) and of testifying to what he has seen (v. 11). The question which the reader is asking throughout this story is, 'Will Nicodemus *see*?'

h. Water. Regeneration is through water and the Spirit (v. 5). Water is a symbol of baptism here. This will be picked up in 3.23 where the narrator speaks of the plentiful supplies of water for the Baptist's ministry.

i. The Spirit. *Pneuma* appears again at v. 5 (*pneumatos*), v. 6 (*pneumatos* and *pneuma*), v. 8 (*pneuma/pneumatos*). What is interesting about Jesus' portrayal of the Spirit in v. 8 is that the Spirit's elusiveness is stressed. No one knows where the Spirit comes from or where the Spirit goes to. This indicates the identity between Jesus and the Spirit. Both are elusive.

j. Witness. In v. 11 Jesus speaks twice of testimony (*marturoumen/marturian*). This legal terminology creates the courtroom atmosphere pervasive throughout John.

k. Descent and Ascent. In 1.51 Jesus had spoken of the descent and ascent of the angels upon the Son of Man. Here the Son of Man title occurs for the second and third time (vv. 13 and 14). The idea of descent and ascent resurfaces with it (*anabebēken/katabas*, v. 13). In 3.13 it is the Son of Man himself (Jesus) who ascends and descends from heaven. He is the one who mediates the binary opposition of above and below, heaven and earth.

l. Lifting up. The verb *hupsoō* occurs twice (v. 14). Jesus compares his coming death on the cross with the lifting up of the serpent in the wilderness by Moses.

m. Life. The theme of life appears in vv. 15, 16 and 21. Here Jesus speaks of the believer receiving life eternal (*zōēn aiōnion*, v. 15). The combination, 'life eternal', occurs 17 times in the Gospel. This is the first time Jesus speaks about his mission of giving spiritual life.

n. Faith. The verb *pisteuō* is used in vv. 15, 16, 18 (×3). See v. 15: 'that everyone who believes in him may have life eternal'.

Literary Devices

The presence of *puns* in this dialogue is memorable. Jesus' use of *pneuma* in v. 8 is a fine example. Like the Hebrew *ruach*, *pneuma* denotes both 'wind' and 'spirit'. As such, Jesus can play on the word with dexterity while talking to Nicodemus. Furthermore, at the end of the dialogue Jesus plays on the verb *hupsoō*. While 'lifting up' connotes glorification at the spiritual level, at the physical level it has overtones of being hauled up or elevated onto the cross. Jesus has both meanings in mind because the cross in John's story is seen as the place where Jesus is glorified (12.28).

Linked with this is the use of *double entendre*. The well-known double meaning in v. 3 and v. 7 clearly troubles Nicodemus. When Jesus speaks of being born again, the word often translated 'again' can also be rendered 'from above' (*anōthen*). Jesus has both meanings in mind, but Nicodemus reveals his limited understanding by interpreting from below (as 'again'). The use of puns and *double entendre* in the narrative reinforces the ironic divide between above and below which is a characteristic feature of the Nicodemus episode.

The most colourful device is that of *parody*. Parody is essentially the art of satirical imitation. In this dialogue, Jesus notes Nicodemus' use of language in the latter's opening words and then uses them later as a critique of Nicodemus' interpretative inadequacies. Thus, Nicodemus approaches Jesus and applauds him as a teacher (*didaskolos*). He uses that word in his confident assertion, 'we know you are a *didaskolos* from God' (v. 2). In vv. 10-11 Jesus parodies Nicodemus' unjustfied confidence with an entirely justified assertion of his own. He does this by using Nicodemus' language. Jesus says, 'You are the teacher (*didaskolos*) of Israel and yet you do not know (*ginōskeis*) these things. I tell you the truth, *we* speak of what *we know* (*oidamen*)'. Here Jesus' use of 'teacher' and 'we know' are used to parody Nicodemus' lack of knowledge.

Narrator and Point of View

The narrator's voice replaces that of Jesus in v. 16. In v. 16, the point of view is retrospective: the one speaking talks in the past of a God who 'loved' and who 'gave'. Since the previous verses (14-15) have been about the 'lifting up' of the Son of Man on the cross, the supreme, divine act of love referred to in 3.16 must be the death of Jesus. At this point in John 3, the narrator therefore takes us out of the story and up to a level where we can view matters from the viewpoint of eternity. Looking back at Jesus-history after the resurrection, the narrator takes us into the bosom of the Father in order to reveal the divine initiative and purpose in the giving of the *monogenēs*, God's one and only Son.

The fundamental revelation which the narrator gives the reader in vv.16-21 concerns the nature of God and the nature of humanity. Indeed, the narrator's words highlight the fundamental aspects of the God–humanity dualism:

> 16-18   The nature of God—love for the world
> 19-21   The nature of humanity—love of the world

In vv. 16-18, the narrator reveals heavenly secrets about God's nature. Having taken us deeper into the identity and mission of the Spirit and the Son in 3.1-15, the narrator now takes us deep into the mystery of God the Father. There is therefore a progression in John's storytelling from revelation about the Spirit (3.5-8), to revelation about the Son (3.13-15), to revelation about the Father (3.16-21). The narrator guides us into the very heart of the Triune God.

The fundamental revelation about God is contained within Jn 3.16. The narrator discloses that 'God so loved the world that he gave his one and only Son, that whoever believes in him shall not perish but have eternal life'. Much is said about the character of God by way of implicit commentary in these words. There are intertextual echoes with the story of Abraham and Isaac in Gen. 22.1-19 in Jn 3.16. A parallelism is suggested between Abraham and Isaac and God the Father and his Son. God's love is like Abraham's in that God too is prepared to give up his son. In this act of love towards the world, God the Father gives up (*edōken*) his one and only son. In using *monogenēs* here to describe Jesus the Son (v. 16, also v. 18), Jesus and Isaac are associated with one another. Three times Isaac is called Abraham's son, his only son (Gen. 22.2, 12, 16). In the prologue of John's story, and here in 3.16-21, Jesus is portrayed as God's Son, his only Son (*monogenēs*).

The narrator's characterization of God in Jn 3.16-21 focuses on the revelation of divine love. The verb used for God's love is *agapaō*, self-giving love expressed in action (*agapaō* is used 36 times in John, 26 times in the Synoptics). The object of this love is the world (*kosmos*, v. 16, 17 [×2], 19) which we already know is hostile to its Creator (1.10-11). The desire of God is that no one should perish (*apollumi*, 10 times in John), but that all who believe (*pisteuō* again, and in v. 18 three times) should have eternal life. God wants all people to be saved (*sōthe*, v. 17) not condemned (*krinē*).

If vv. 16-18 present a brief portrait of God, vv. 19-21 present a frank, realistic and decisive portrait of humanity. The verdict (*krisis*) in v. 19 is that people preferred darkness (*skotos*) to light (*phōs*). Here there is irony in the fact that people loved darkness more than light. The word for 'loved' is the same as in v. 16 for God's love (*agapaō*). People love darkness because their evil deeds can remain hidden rather than be exposed. However, humanity is faced with a choice: to do evil (*ho phaula prassōn*) or to do the truth (*ho de poiōn ten alētheian*).   Those who do evil are of the darkness, but those who do the truth are of the light.

John 3.22-30

Context
After the dialogue with Nicodemus (3.1-15), and the narrator's commentary (3.16-21), the narrator provides a brief itinerary fragment (3.22). Now, at 3.23, the same pattern of dialogue–narrator's commentary–itinerary fragment is repeated. We start with the Baptist dialogue (3.23-30), proceed through the narrator's commentary (3.31-36) before concluding with another itinerary fragment which echoes 3.22 (4.1-3).

Characterization
Though a number of characters appear in this story (Jesus, his disciples, a certain Jew, the disciples of the Baptist, the Baptist himself), the focal character is the Baptist. This is one of a very few times in John's story where Jesus is physically absent. However, it is noticeable that Jesus is still the subject of the questioning that is taking place. Jesus may not be present in person, but he is still the centre of our attention.

The Baptist is portrayed as the faithful and humble witness. His faithfulness is suggested by the use of the word 'stand' in v. 29. He is the friend who stands with (*hestōkōs*) the bridegroom (Jesus). As I have already noted in the commentary on 1.35 (which also speaks of the Baptist's standing in relation to Jesus), stative verbs have connotations of allegiance in John's story.

The Baptist's humility is indicated by his climactic pronouncement, 'He must become greater; I must become less' (v. 30). There is no sense in these words that the Baptist is aggrieved that everyone is now going to Jesus rather than to him. Most people would be threatened by such a turn of events. John gladly accepts it and announces that this is precisely the way things should be. He states that a person can only receive as much in terms of prominence as heaven will allow (v. 27).

John's status as witness is indicated by a number of details. First of all the occurrence of the verb *martureō* in the narrative (vv. 26 and 28). The Baptist's open witness to Jesus is again emphasized. Secondly, in another example of the narrator's use of asides, the reader is informed in v. 24 that 'This was before John was put in prison'. The reference to imprisonment acts as a hint of the Baptist's martyrdom.

Narrative Echo Effects

This narrative gives us the opportunity to highlight a literary device frequently used in John. John's story revels in echo effects. One part of the story resonates with other parts through the repetition of various key words. There are two passages prior to and two after 3.23-30 with which the story is connected. Later on, we will hear Jesus speaking twice in 15.11 and 16.24 of his desire to make the joy of the disciples complete. The Baptist's expression of the same desire in 3.29 is a proleptic echo of that theme. Also, the reference to everyone flocking to Jesus in 3.26 prepares us for the same complaint made by the Pharisees in 12.19: 'Look, how the whole world has gone after him'.

The most important echoes are with narratives which precede 3.23-30 (analepses, flashbacks). There are a number of analepses with 1.19-34 (the first two stories focusing on the Baptist) in 3.23-30. In 3.28, John says, 'I am not (*ouk eimi*) the Messiah'. This parallels his announcement in 1.19, 'I am not (*ouk eimi*) the Christ'. In 3.28, John claims that he has been sent ahead of Jesus the Messiah. This echoes 1.23 where John describes himself as the one preparing the way of the Lord. In 3.30 John says that he must become lesser while Jesus must become greater. This echoes 1.30 where John points to Jesus as the superior one who will 'come after me'. Clearly the narrator wants to link the first and last appearances of the Baptist through the use of analeptic echo effects.

The most interesting echoes, however, are with the Cana miracle in Jn 2.1-11. There are four echoes with 2.1-11: 1. In 3.23 the narrator tells us that there was plenty of water. This recalls the plentiful supply of water in 2.6 which Jesus transforms into wine. 2. In 3.25 a certain Jew approaches the Baptist's disciples about the matter of ceremonial washing (*katharismou*). In the wedding feast at Cana, the narrator points to six jars used for ceremonial washing (*katharismon*). 3. In 3.29, the theme of marriage surfaces in the Baptist's description of Jesus as the bridegroom (*numphion*, twice). The narrator has used the word 'bridegroom' already, in 2.9 (*numphion*). 4. Finally, in 3.30 the Baptist says that he must decrease. The word here is *elattousthai* (from *ellatoō*) and denotes inferiority. A similar, related word is used for the inferior wine in 2.10 (*elassō*).

Implicit Commentary

What is the purpose of the narrative echo effects between the wedding at Cana and the curtain call for the Baptist? It seems as though the wedding motif in chs. 2–4 is extremely important to the narrator. In 2.1-11, the symbolic import of the Cana miracle is that the eschatological wedding, along with the messianic banquet, has now begun. In John's realized eschatology, the wedding promised at the end of time between

Yahweh and his people has arrived ahead of time—in the here-and-now of Jesus' ministry.

However, the Cana wedding story almost completely ignores the figures of the bridegroom and bride, as I noted in the commentary. This is because the narrator wants to introduce these figures later. Here in 3.23-30 we discover that the Baptist is the bridegroom's friend, and that Jesus is the bridegroom. Thus, the eschatological marriage between Yahweh and his people takes place in Jesus-history. Jesus is the messianic bridegroom to whom John the Baptist, the eschatological best man, points. Who, then, is the bride? Asking this question leads the paradigmatic reader to look out for a female character who will fulfil this symbolic role. By the end of John 4, we will have met her.

John 3.31–36

Narrator's Commentary

Just as 3.1-15 is followed by the narrator's commentary, so 3.23-30 is followed by a summary. In these verses the narrator evokes some of the themes which we found in 3.1-15:

Subject	3.1-15	3.31-36
From above	*anōthen* (v. 3, 7)	*anōthen* (3.31)
Heavenly origins	*ek tou ouranou* (3.13)	*ek tou ouranou* (3.31)
Earth/Heaven	*epigeia/epourania* (3.12)	*ek tēs gēs/ek tou ouranou* (3.31)
Witnessing to what has been seen	*ho heōrakamen marturoumen* (3.11)	*ho heōraken...marturei* (3.32)
Failure to receive the testimony	*ten marturian hēmōn ou lambanete* (3.11)	*tēn marturian autou oudeis lambanei* (3.32)
The Spirit	*pneuma* (3.8)	*pneuma* (3.34)
Faith and Life	*pisteuō/zōē* (3.15, 16)	*pisteuō/zōē* (3.36)

Again the evidence of ring composition or inclusio suggests that the author is no careless compiler of Jesus tradition.

John 4.1-3

In 4.1-3, we have an itinerary fragment. This, as I have already noted, recalls and qualifies the itinerary fragment in 3.22. As such, a sense of closure is evoked before the change in setting in 4.4, where we move to Samaria. This next section is intimately related to the marital symbolism of John 3.1–4.3 (Jesus = bridegroom, the Baptist = best man). Indeed, in symbolic terms, Jn 4.4-42 could be entitled, 'Here comes the bride'!

John 4.4-42

Context
The story of the Samaritan woman and the story of Nicodemus stand in marked contrast to one another:

The Story of Nicodemus (3.1-15)	The Story of the Samaritan woman (4.4-42)
takes place in Jerusalem	takes place in Samaria
the context is the city	the context is the countryside
happens at night	happens at noon
focuses on a man	focuses on a woman
the man is a Jew	the woman is a Samaritan
the man is socially respectable	the woman has a history of immorality
Nicodemus initiates dialogue	Jesus initiates dialogue
Nicodemus descends into misunderstanding	the woman comes to faith
Nicodemus fails to see Jesus as the world's Saviour (3.16)	the woman and her village see Jesus as the Saviour of the world

This is the first narrative in John's story which portrays women in a more favourable light than men. The Samaritan episode focuses on a female not a male character. *gunē* (woman, wife) and related words occur throughout the story while the vocabulary of masculinity is decidedly less visible:

Words suggestive of femininity		*Words suggestive of masculinity*	
7.	*gunē*		
9.	*gunē/gunaikos*		
11.	*gunē*		
15.	*gunē*	16.	*andra*
17.	*gunē*	17.	*andra* (×2)
19.	*gunē*	18.	*andras, anēr*
21.	*gunai*		
25.	*gunē*		
27.	*gunaikos*		
28.	*gunē*		
39.	*gunaikos*		
42.	*gunaiki*		

Other narratives which present women as faithful disciples are:

Martha and Mary	(11.1-44)
Martha and Mary	(12.1-8)
The women at the cross	(19.25-27)
Mary Magdalene	(20.1-3)
Mary Magdalene	(20.11-18)

Structure

The structure of the story is again based on inverted parallelism or the literary technique of chiasmus.

A^1	4-9	The Samaritan woman comes to Jesus.
B^1	10-15	Jesus speaks of spiritual water.
C	16-26	Jesus teaches about true worship.
B^2	27-38	Jesus speaks of spiritual food.
A^2	39-42	The Samaritan men come to Jesus.

The whole piece is most carefully planned. Notice how the first and last sections echo each other in terms of vocabulary. In both sections, there is a coming to Jesus (*erchetai*, v. 7; *ēlthon pros auton*, v. 40) from the town (*polin*, v. 5; *poleōs*, v. 39) by a Samaritan or Samaritans (*Samareias*, v. 5; *Samaritōn*, v. 39). However, in the first section the approach is made by a woman while in the last it is made by many townsfolk (*anthrōpois*, v. 28; *polloi*, v. 39). Notice also the contrast between the theme of water in B^1 and the theme of food in B^2. The centrepiece is the section devoted to true worship.

Themes

A number of familiar themes appear in this story: water (vv. 7, 10, 11, 13, 14 [×3], 15, 28); knowledge (vv. 10, 22 [×2], 25, 32, 42); life (vv. 10, 11, 14, 36); truth (vv. 18, 23 [×2], 24, 37, 42); sight (vv. 19, 29, 35); faith (vv. 21, 39, 41, 42); the hour (vv. 21, 23); the Spirit (vv. 23, 24 [×2]); seeking

(vv. 23, 27); coming to Jesus (vv. 30, 40); sending (vv. 34, 38); the work of Jesus (v. 34); witness (v. 39); and remaining with Jesus (v. 40 [×2]).

The new theme of worship is raised in the central section of the story. There is a very condensed cluster of references to worship (*proskuneō*) in vv. 21-26 (×7). Here Jesus continues to introduce the new order of things appropriate to the messianic era by saying that true worship will no longer be confined to the holy places revered by Samaritans and Jews. True worship of God as Father will be in Spirit and in Truth. Since Spirit is personal in John's story (14.26) and since Truth is also personal (14.6), Jesus is here talking about worship based on a relationship with a person rather than worship based on a relationship with a place. True worship is paternal in focus (the Father), personal in origin (the Son), and pneumatic in character (the Spirit).

In this theme of the new and true worship of God, we return to the theme of Jesus' replacement of the existing religious institutions and beliefs begun in the wine miracle in 2.1-11. The insistence of Jesus in 4.21-26 that true worship must be in Spirit and in Truth (i.e. in *his* pneumatic presence) recalls his statement in 2.13-22 that his risen body will become the new Temple. The reader should also note the binary opposition between the fathers of the Samaritans (*pateres*, v. 20) and the Father of Jesus (*patēr*, vv. 21, 23 [×2]). The new age which Jesus inaugurates here is a worship based on trust in the Father, not in trust in the fathers.

Literary Devices

The narrator again uses the device of *double entendre* in 4.10. The phrase 'living water' can also be translated 'running water'. This results in the misunderstanding of the Samaritan woman who interprets the phrase at the literal level. Hence her mystification, for how can a well have running water?

The literary device of *misunderstanding* is evident in Jn 4.4-42. This device is especially visible towards the end of the story when the disciples interpret Jesus at a literal rather than a spiritual level, this time in relation to food (*brōsis*, v. 32). The contrast between the woman's misunderstandings about water and the disciples' misunderstandings about food is another sign of artful construction. It again reveals John's predilection for contrasts.

Another device used is that of *dual stage-setting*. This technique is employed with particular poignancy in the passion narrative; there the narrator describes the denials of Peter on one stage, and the trial of Jesus before Annas on another (18.15-27). In Jn 4.4-42 the dual stage-setting is created when the Samaritan woman leaves her water jar to return to the town (v. 29). This creates a front-of-stage, rear-of-stage effect (rather than two stages side by side, as in 18.15-27): front-of-stage is Jesus, having conversed with the Samaritan, and now teaching his disciples about the ripe harvest; rear-of-stage, as if to illustrate the time of harvest, are the Samaritans, who pour out of the town towards Jesus to become disciples.

Related to this dual stage-setting technique is the ironical use of *juxtaposition*. It is important to note the juxtaposition between the woman's journey to and from the town, and the journey to and from the same town undertaken by the disciples. The irony consists in the fact that the male disciples go to the town but they do not bring any-one back to Jesus. Theirs is a fruitless harvest. The one woman in the story makes the same journey but brings many people to Jesus, and they confess Jesus as the Saviour of the world. Hers is an undeniably fruitful harvest.

Notice also the presence of *proverbs*. Looking closely at vv. 27-38, we can see that Jesus quotes two agricultural aphorisms: 'Four months more and then the harvest' (v. 35), and 'One sows and another reaps' (v. 37). These are obviously proverbs because the one is introduced by *ouch humeis legete* ('Do you not say...'), and the other by *en gar toutō ho logos estin al ēthinos hoti* ('Thus the saying is true that...'). However, Jesus uses these proverbs as a basis for revealing the radical difference between natural harvesting and the supernatural harvest of the messianic era. The harvest Jesus is referring to is the reaping of unbelievers—the bringing into the kingdom of the many people who are ready to accept Jesus as Saviour of the world. This harvest is happening in the now of his ministry, as is evident from the conversion of the Samaritans. What is radically different about this new harvest is the fact that the disciples do not have to wait for it. Unlike the natural harvest, which is cyclical and therefore something to wait for (four months), the supernatural harvest is permanently present.

Characterization

The following characters appear in the story: Jesus, the Samaritan woman, the disciples, the people of Sychar.

a. Jesus. In 4.4-42, the divinity and humanity of Jesus are portrayed. The divinity of Jesus is expressed in a number of ways. First, Jesus goes into Samaria because of divine necessity (note the 'must' [*edei*] in v. 4) and teaches the divine necessity of true worship (note the 'must' [*dei*] of 4.20, 24). This implies Jesus' unhindered access to God's plan and will. Secondly, Jesus reveals himself as God in the giving motif. He refers to the living water as the gift of God in v. 10. He then says that he is the one who can give this gift in v. 14. This amounts to an implicit equation of himself with God. Thirdly, Jesus reveals his knowledge of the human heart. Through supernatural knowledge, he perceives that the woman has had five husbands and is living *de facto* with a sixth. Since this quality of knowledge is a characteristic of divine omniscience in the OT, it further indicates Jesus' divinity. Fourthly, the titles used of Jesus suggest his divine status. There is a definite progression in these: *Ioudaios* (v. 9), *kurie* (vv. 11, 15), *prophētēs* (v. 19), *messias/christos* (implicit, v. 25), *ho sōtēr tou kosmou* (v. 42). Finally, Jesus' self-designation underlines the divinity of his character. In v. 26, when the woman says that she knows that the Messiah is coming, Jesus replies, 'I am he'. The words here are *ego eimi*, the divine name.

   Alongside these indications of Jesus' divinity, there are also signs of his humanity. Jesus in Jn 4.4-42 is not a phantom, nor a fleshless deity. Thus, in 4.6, the narrator tells us that Jesus, because he was tired (*kekopiakōs*) from his journey, had to sit down and rest by Jacob's well. More than that, when the Samaritan woman comes by, he is evidently thirsty, for he asks her for a drink. These signals of the tiredness and thirst of Jesus speak of a real, human saviour, not of some proto-gnostic, superhuman redeemer.

b. The Woman of Samaria. Two aspects of John's characterization of the Samaritan woman need to be highlighted. The woman in John 4 is first of all presented *realistically*; she is certainly no cardboard stereo-type. When Jesus asks her for a drink of water, she responds with indignation: 'How can you, a Jew, ask me for a drink'. When Jesus points out that she is acting in ignorance, that she does not recognize the living water which Jesus has to offer, she replies with sarcasm (paraphrased): 'Where are you going to get this kind of water from? This well's too deep! How would you get at such water anyway? You haven't even brought a pitcher!' When Jesus describes the kind of water he has to offer, she responds with pragmatic celerity: 'Sir, give me this water'.

   What happens next reinforces this sense of character. Jesus now asks the woman to go back into the town and fetch her husband so that both can enjoy this new life. The woman's garrulousness now turns to a reluctant and laconic confession: 'I have no husband'. Jesus reveals that he knows already, and the woman's spiritual eyes are opened. Having interpreted all Jesus' words about living water at the literal, physical level, she now begins to see things 'from above'. She confesses Jesus as 'prophet' and begins to speak of worship from the point of view of Samaritan tradition. Jesus points her to a new form of worship. She responds with a statement of faith: 'I know that Messiah (called Christ) is coming. When he comes, he will explain everything to us.' Jesus reveals that he is the Messiah.

   At this point, John now moves into a second kind of portrayal. Having portrayed the woman as a *realistic* character—with personality, vitality and character development—he now portrays her as a *representative* character. It is vital from now on to watch the woman's movements and actions and to interpret them symbolically. First of all, she leaves her water jar (v. 28). This action symbolizes the prerequisite of disciple-ship. If a person is to follow Jesus he or she must leave everything. Secondly, she goes back to the town and says to the people, 'Come and see!' (vv. 28-29). This action symbolizes the development of the woman into a witness for Jesus (*marturousēs*, v. 39). Having become a disciple, she now invites others to come to Jesus. Thirdly, she testifies to the people of Samaria, and through her word (*dia ton logon*, v. 39) many come to faith. This process symbolizes the woman's development from disciple to disciple-maker. Having become a witness, she helps others to become disciples.

Narrative Echo Effects

In order to understand the richness of the woman's representative role, we need to identify the narrative echo effects in the story. There are, first of all, a number of analepses between the call and mission of the Samaritan woman, and the call and mission of the first disciples in 1.35-51. Particularly obvious is the parallel between Philip's 'Come and see!' in 1.46, and the 'Come and see!' of the woman in 4.29. In setting up this analepsis, the storyteller indicates that the woman of Samaria has become a true disciple of Jesus. She conducts her mission as Philip does. More than that, both Philip and the Samaritan woman conduct their mission as Jesus does, for Jesus says 'Come and see!' in 1.39. Since the pupil imitates the master, the woman's words prove her credentials as a true *mathētēs*.

Secondly, there are proleptic echoes between the word of the woman in v. 39 and Jesus' high priestly prayer in John 17, where he is praying about the continuation of his mission through the disciples. In Jn 17.20, Jesus says: 'My prayer is not for them alone. I pray also for those who will believe in me through their message.' The phrase, 'through their message', is *dia ton logon*. This is exactly the same phrase as in 4.39, where the narrator says that many of the Samaritans believed (*pisteuō*, as in 17.20) through the woman's message (*dia ton logon*). The fact that many come to faith through her word also proves her credentials as a true *mathētēs*.

Thirdly, the narrator informs us that the result of the woman's testi-mony was that the Samaritan men urged Jesus to stay with them. So Jesus stays two days. The verb used for 'stay' in both cases in 4.40 is *menō*, which we have already examined. It is a favourite thematic word in John, connoting permanence of relationship (between Jesus and the Father, Jesus and the Spirit, and Jesus and the disciple). Thus it has symbolic value in the context of the Samaritan villagers, for it implies a permanent relationship between Jesus and these new believers. The 'staying' of Jesus therefore speaks not only of an extended visit but also of a lasting master–pupil relationship.

What has this to do with the characterization of the woman? In Jn 15.8, Jesus says, 'This is to my Father's glory, that you bear much fruit, showing yourselves to be my disciples'. In 15.16, this thought is developed when Jesus says, 'You did not choose me, but I chose you and appointed you to go and bear fruit—fruit that will last'. These two pronouncements form a vital commentary on 4.4-42 for anyone *rereading* the Gospel. In 15.8 and 16, Jesus speaks of fruit (*karpos*). In 4.36 Jesus speaks about fruit (*karpos*). In 15.8, Jesus speaks of the disciple bearing *much* fruit (*polun*). In 4.39, we see many (*polloi*) believing in Jesus on the basis of the woman's word. In 15.16, Jesus speaks of the disciple bearing fruit that lasts (*menē*). In 4.40, Jesus stays (*emeinen*) with the people whom the Samaritan woman has brought to faith. All these echo effects can imply only one thing: that the Samaritan woman represents the true disciple (15.8) because she bears much fruit, and fruit that lasts.

Literary Form and Implicit Commentary

John 4.4-42 focuses on a dialogue and evolving relationship between a woman and Jesus. What is the literary form used here? John 4.4-42 centres on a man meeting a woman at a well. In Jewish literature, such meetings are betrothal scenes. The fundamental plot ingredients of the betrothal type-scene have been identified as:

1. The bridegroom journeying to a foreign land
2. He meets a girl (or girls) at a well
3. Someone draws water from the well
4. This leads to the girl running home to announce the stranger
5. The man and the woman are betrothed, generally in the context of a meal

This pattern is visible in Jn 4.4-42. Jesus is the bridegroom (3.29) and here he is portrayed travelling into the foreign land of Samaria (4.4). He meets a Samaritan woman who comes to the well. This woman draws water from the well. Jesus speaks to her, and she runs home to tell the people of Sychar that a stranger has arrived who is the Messiah. Jesus teaches about his true food or meal as the woman returns to the well with the villagers. Though a literal betrothal is not indicated between the two, there is marital imagery in the exchange in vv. 16-18 (paraphrase):

Jesus: Go, call your husband (*andra*).
Woman: I have no husband.
Jesus: You're right. The fact is, you've had five husbands, and the man you're living with at present is not yours by marriage.

These words point to a symbolic betrothal. If the woman has had five husbands and is living *de facto* with a sixth, then Jesus is the seventh man in her life. Since seven is the perfect number in Judaism, the implicit commentary must be that the Jesus is the man which she has been waiting for, the man in whose presence she will find wholeness (*sōtēria*, v. 22).

There are three details which support such an interpretation of the generic form and implicit commentary of this story. First of all, the fact that this encounter takes place at Jacob's well reminds the reader of the classic betrothal scene in Gen. 29.1-20, where Jacob journeys to the eastern peoples, meets Rachel at a well and becomes betrothed to her. Secondly, the fact that the Samaritan woman is unmarried (she is living with a sixth man, but not married to him), indicates her availability for symbolic betrothal. Thirdly, the marital symbolism in Jn 2.1-11 (the arrival of the eschatological wedding) and in 3.29 (the Baptist as the best man and Jesus as the messianic bridegroom) places precisely this kind of expectation in the mind of the reader.

Plot-Type

Using Northrop Frye's terminology (1983; see the introduction), we can see that the dominant *mythos* or plot-type here is romance. This narrative reconstruction of an historical encounter between Jesus and a Samaritan woman is based on the *mythos* of summer (note the sense of 'high noon' in 4.6). There are, to be sure, elements of the comic *mythos* in the feistiness of the woman and the misunderstanding of the disciples. These touches of humour probably mean that it is more accurate to speak of Jn 4.4-42 as comic romance. However, it is the romantic note which predominates. After the introduction of the eschatological bridegroom and the best man in John 3, the expectation of an eschatological bride is now satisfied. The surprise, of course, is the fact that this bride is a Samaritan and not a Jew. The eschatological wedding between Yahweh and his people is therefore not to be as narrowly nationalistic as was anticipated by the Jews. Jesus is the Saviour of the world (4.42), not just the Saviour of the Jewish people.

However, in delineating the deeper function of the Samaritan woman we must be careful not to reduce her to a mere symbol. Too often sermons, articles and books do one of two things with this woman: they either idealize her as a bride or they condemn her as a whore. Both are forms of inexcusable exploitation. In the final analysis, such interpretations of the woman of Samaria achieve the very opposite of the author's intention. Whoever the author of the Fourth Gospel really was, this person had a profoundly positive appreciation of the fruitfulness of female discipleship. The woman of Samaria brings many people to Christ. Martha confesses Jesus as the Christ (11.27) and acts as deacon at the meal table where Jesus reclines (12.2). Mary of Bethany anoints Jesus' feet (12.3) and Mary of Magdala announces the news of the resurrection and of Jesus' return to the Father (20.10-18). These narratives portray women as paradigmatic disciples, often in stark contrast to the male disciples in the relevant episodes. As such, the Fourth Gospel is a liberating narrative for Christian women oppressed by patriarchal systems. It is also a convicting word for those men who are complicit in such systems. As always, reading John's story of Jesus presents the reader with a *krisis*, a critical judgment or decision. Reading John is not always the most comfortable experience.

John 4.43-45

Comment
The narrator now addresses the reader, providing information about Jesus' itinerary (as in 2.12) and providing an explanation concerning Jesus' movements. We are informed that Jesus spent the two days with the Samaritans mentioned in 4.40. This is seemingly all the time he can spare because he is quickly on the move again, this time away from Jerusalem and Samaria to Galilee. The rationale for the celerity of Jesus' movements is provided in the narrator's aside in 4.44: 'Now Jesus himself had pointed out (*martureō*) that a prophet has no honour in his own country'. Here there is a distant analepsis of the Prologue, where the narrator says that Jesus came to his own (*ta idia*) but his own did not receive him. The *ta idia* of 4.44 picks up the *ta idia* of 1.11. Since Jesus has not been welcomed by his own (the Jews and Pharisees in Jerusalem), he moves from Judea back to Galilee where he is welcomed (*edexanto*, v. 45). Those who welcome him are the Galilaeans who had travelled to Jerusalem for the passover (2.13) and who had seen the things he had done during the feast.

John 4.46-54

Context
Jesus now completes the first itinerary of the Gospel. Having begun at Cana in 2.1, he now returns to Cana. His travels have taken him from Cana to Jerusalem, from Jerusalem into Judea, from Judea into Samaria, and from Samaria back to Cana. The circle of his first missionary journey is now complete.

It is important to note the echoes with the first Cana miracle. The basic form of the two narratives is the same:

First Sign in Cana (2.1-11)		Second Sign in Cana (4.46-54)	
Request:	mother to Jesus, about wine	Request:	father to Jesus, about son
Rebuke:	'what has this to do with me'	Rebuke:	'unless you see signs and wonders...'
Response:	miracle	Response:	miracle

Furthermore, the narrator draws our attention to the first sign in v. 46 ('Once more he visited Cana in Galilee where he had turned the water into wine') and in v. 54 ('This was the second miraculous sign that Jesus performed'). Also worth mentioning is the appearance of servants (*hoi douloi*) in 4.51, which reminds us of the *diakonoi* in 2.5.

The similarities between 2.1-11 and 4.56-54 are important. They are evidence again of John's technique of inclusio. By having details of this second miracle recall aspects of the first sign, John portrays the second sign as an act of closure in this section of the Book of Signs.

Themes

This sense of closure is strengthened by the way in which the themes of the story recapture some of the leading, organizing concepts of the whole section. The emphasis on signs in vv. 48 and 54 reminds the reader of the theme of Jesus 'doing signs'. The mention of believing (*pisteuō*) in vv. 48, 50 and 53, reminds the reader of the theme of faith. The threefold use of *zaō* in vv. 50, 51 and 53 ('Your son will live') reminds the reader of the allusions to Jesus as the giver of life (3.16, 36; 4.14).

Notice that the main theme of this second Cana miracle is life. In v. 47 the official's son is said to be close to death. In v. 49 the official begs Jesus to heal his son before he dies. Jesus says that his boy will live (v. 50), a pronouncement echoed in vv. 51 and 53. The binary opposition between death and life, mediated by the ministry of Jesus, will be a leading theme in the next section of the Book of Signs, from 5.1–10.42. Thus this second Cana miracle functions not only as a closure to section one but as an introduction to section two (see the commentary on Jn 2.13-25).

Structure

The formal arrangement of this episode is as follows:

A^1	46a	The visit to Galilee, reference to first sign
B^1	46b-50a	'Your son will live'
C	50b	The faith of the official
B^2	51-53	'Your son will live'
A^2	54	The visit to Galilee, reference to signs

What is clear from this structure is the importance of movement. In B^1 the official moves towards Jesus to ask him to perform a sign. This part ends with 'Your son will live'. In B^2, the official goes from Jesus believing in Jesus' word and the sign is duly performed. This part ends (as B^1 does) with the words, 'Your son will live'. The story is based on a chiastic structure, with an inclusio between the introduction and the conclusion, and with the theme of the royal official's faith acting as the centrepiece and focus of the reader's attention.

Characterization

Yet again the narrative focus is upon an encounter between Jesus and an individual, this time a *basilikos*, a servant to King Herod, tetrarch of Galilee. This royal official is portrayed from a number of different angles. He is first of all introduced in terms of his status. He is an administrator to a king. His social standing is strengthened by virtue of the fact that he has servants (v. 51). Secondly, he is given a representative function. When the official hears Jesus' words, 'Your son will live', the narrator tells us that 'the man (*ho anthrōpos*) took Jesus at his word and departed' (v. 50). The importance of the phrase *ho anthrōpos* to describe the official should not be missed. The narrator wants us to see in this man who believed and obeyed a paradigm of true faith. Thirdly, the official is characterized in terms of his fatherly love. He is called *patēr* by the narrator in v. 53, and throughout the story his love for his son is stressed (note the use of *ērōta* ['begged'] in v. 47).

The characterization of Jesus in this story is complex. In v. 48, the rebuke seems heartless in the light of the official's predicament: 'Unless you people see miraculous signs and wonders you will never believe' (v. 48)—though this is again behaviour appropriate to Christ's elusiveness. However, it is most important to note that this statement is not a critique of the official. Even though the statement is addressed at him (*pros auton*, v. 48), the addressees are the Galilaeans in general, not the official in particular. The verb 'see' is with you-plural, not you-singular. Thus Jesus' polemical outburst against faith based on signs and wonders is not a heartless condemnation of the anxious father before him, but of a social group who persist in pestering him for faith evoking miracles.

Another important observation to make is the way in which a development from condemnation to compassion in Jesus is indicated through the art of reticence. Up until v. 49, the narrator has referred to the official's offspring as *ho huios*, as his son. After the outburst from Jesus in v. 48, however, the official refers to his offspring as *to paidion mou*, 'my little boy' (*paidion* is the diminutive of *pais*, boy). Though the narrator does not intervene to offer an insider's view of Jesus' thought processes, it is probable that the word *paidion* is to be taken as a catalyst for Jesus' change of attitude. A son could be a male of any age. A little boy is something altogether different. The official is therefore quickly told, 'Your son will live'.

Implicit Commentary

The reader should note the use of *katabainō* in v. 49: 'Sir, come down (*katabēthi*) before my child dies'. There is a subtle and nuanced use of the verbs *anabainō* and *katabainō* in John's story (see the commentary on Jn 2.12). We know from John 3 that these words are used to portray the ascent and descent of Christ the Redeemer. However, the narrator also uses these verbs at strategic points to describe Jesus' geographical movements (see the use of *anabainō* in 11.55 and 12.20—appropriately enough, near the point of Jesus' return to the Father). The father's request for Jesus' *katabasis* to Capernaum helps to keep the overall U-shaped plot of the Gospel (the descent and ascent of Jesus) in the mind of the reader.

John 5.1-15

Context

The first section of the Book of Signs from 2.1–4.54 is now over. The second section from 5.1–10.42 begins with the healing of a crippled man at Bethesda in 5.1-15. This story is important for the reader's appreciation of the itinerary of Jesus and the author's intention in section 2.

a. The Itinerary of Jesus. Both of sections 1 and 2 of the Book of Signs depict a discernible itinerary in the ministry of Jesus. In section 1, Jesus travels in a circular movement from Cana through Jerusalem and back to Cana (2.1–4.54). Now in section 2, Jesus undertakes a circular journey from Jerusalem, through Galilee, back to Jerusalem. This itinerary is established through the narrative settings specified by the narrator. These locate Jesus on a journey which is the exact reverse of his journey in section 1, in which Jesus' movements are from Galilee, through Jerusalem, back to Galilee. In section 2, the itinerary begins in Jerusalem, going through Galilee and back to Jerusalem. The circle is not perfect, because some sort of journey towards Jerusalem is implied in 5.1 and away from Jerusalem in 10.40-42. However, the main itinerary seems to be as follows:

1.	5.1	Jerusalem
2.	6.1	Galilee (with emphasis on Capernaum)
3.	7.14	Jerusalem (with emphasis on the Temple courts)

b. Author's Intention. If the narrative setting ('There is in Jerusalem near the Sheep Gate a pool') initiates a Jerusalem-to-Jerusalem itinerary, the indication of time (v. 1, Jesus was in Jerusalem 'for a feast of the Jews') initiates the symbolism of section 2. The theme of the Jewish feasts is prominent in Jn 5.1–10.42. Passover is mentioned in 6.4, Tabernacles in 7.2 and Dedication in 10.22. In each of these contexts, Jesus' relationship to the various feasts is explored. At Passover, Jesus takes a symbol of the feast (bread) and declares himself to be the Bread of Life. At Tabernacles, Jesus takes symbols from the feast (light and water) and declares himself to be the Light of the World and the one who satisfies spiritual thirst. At Dedication, Jesus takes the central liturgical element of the feast (the consecration of the Temple) and applies it to himself (10.36). The narrator's statement in 5.1 that Jesus went up to Jerusalem for a feast of the Jews is of symbolic importance. It announces the intention of the storyteller, which is to show Jesus as the one who replaces existing religious feasts with his own person.

Form and Structure

A point worth noting is the difference in form and structure between this healing at Bethesda and the two signs described in 2.1-11 and 4.46-54. In the Bethesda miracle, there is no reference to signs and there is no request–rebuke–response structure. In Jn 5.1-15 we have a wholly different kind of storytelling. Here there is an actual description of the moment of healing, whereas in the two Cana miracles, the moment of transformation is merely implied. Furthermore, in the Bethesda miracle, the structure of the piece is clearly divided into a miracle followed by an interrogation pattern. In vv. 5-9a, the miracle is performed by Jesus. In vv. 9b-13, the healed man is interrogated by the Jews. We shall see in 9.1-42 a similar pattern of miraculous healing followed by interrogation, controversy and dialogue. This suggests that the miracle stories in John 5 and John 9 are of a different form from the two Cana miracles in John 2 and John 4.

Characterization

This story introduces the theme of conflict in the plot of John's Gospel. There are three characters: the crippled man, Jesus and the Jews.

a. The Crippled Man. Again we see the narrator's ability to create a full and individualized character with a few words. It should be noted from the outset that this man is one of two people in John's story who are on the margins of society (the other is in ch. 9). The social climate of the Gospel so far has been decidedly aristocratic (the abundant feast at Cana in 2.1-11, the ruler of the Pharisees in 3.1-15, the royal official at Cana in 4.46-54). Now we come face to face with a representative of the socially marginalized—a feature supported by the word John uses for his mat (*krabattos*, the Koine Greek word for the mattress used by the poor as bedding). In Jn 5.1-15 the love of God comes face to face with the poverty of humanity. By the end of the story, the man has gone from being carried on his *krabattos* to carrying it himself.

If the man's poverty is stressed, so is the pathos of his situation. It is said that he has been visiting the pool regularly because local superstition suggested that the first person into the waters when they were stirred (supposedly by an angel) would be miraculously healed. However, the man's chances of getting there first are seriously hampered by his disabilities. The pathos of his predicament is suggested by his own words: 'I have no one to help me into the pool when the water is stirred. While I am trying to get in, someone else goes down ahead of me'.

If the man's poverty and pathos are confronted by Jesus, so is his dependency. The narrator tells us that he has been sick for 38 years. People who have been sick for that length of time often become so dependent on others that the very idea of healing, which of course means relinquishing such dependence, is threatening. It is for this reason that Jesus approaches the man and asks: 'Do you want to get well?' This question shows deep insight into the man's dependency, a dependency which must be broken by an authoritative word of command: 'Get up! Pick up your mat and walk!'

It should be noted that this character is not given an entirely positive treatment by the narrator. Not only is there a hint of dependency, there is a hint of disloyalty in him. By the end of the story he appears to be informing on the one who healed him.

b. The Jews. The Jews emerge now as the *theomachus*, the enemies of God. A number of character traits are revealed about them. First of all, the Jews referred to in v. 10 are hostile authorities. The very fact that the crippled man is distinguished from 'the Jews', when he himself must be a Jew, suggests as much. Secondly, these authorities are evidently more concerned about the observance of the Law than about the man's well-being. Any joy they might have felt at the man's miraculous recovery is superceded by their obsession with Sabbath regulations (cf. the Mishnah, whose tractate on Sabbath regulations explicitly forbids the carrying of mattresses). In short, the Jews begin to emerge as the antagonists of Jesus in ch. 5.

c. Jesus. This episode marks a turning point in John's story. The plot develops, as does Jesus' characterization. As far as the plot is concerned, the emergence of the Jewish authorities as active enemies of Jesus means that the period of unrestricted movements and unhampered ministry which Jesus enjoyed in 2.1–4.54 is now at an end. From now on, Jesus will necessarily be evasive. As far as Jesus' characterization is concerned, traits which we have already seen in 2.1–4.54, such as his supernatural knowledge, are still visible (as in 5.6), but what appears much more forcefully is John's portrayal of Jesus as the elusive Christ.

Focalization

In the story before us, the narrator uses focus to highlight this theme. In 5.1-9a, Jesus is the focus of the action. It is Jesus who approaches the pool and it is Jesus who heals the crippled man. However, in v. 9b Jesus disappears and it is now the crippled man who is centre of the attention. Jesus slips out of the narrator's focus just as he slips out of the Temple precincts. His elusiveness is indicated in v. 13 when the narrator says that Jesus had slipped away into the crowd. Jesus' physical movements are portrayed as secretive. Similarly, his identity is described as elusive. The Jews ask, not for the last time in the story, 'Who was/is this man?'

Reality Effects

There is an unusual amount of specific detail in Jn 5.1-15. This creates the effect of the real and suggests (as in the case of Jn 9) an eye-witness tradition. Notice in particular the detail given to the narrative setting. There is a definite progression in the narrator's description in v. 2: Jerusalem–Sheep Gate–a pool–named Bethesda–surrounded by five colonnades. Notice also the specific notation of time ('a Sabbath', v. 9). Other examples of specificity are the length of time which the man had been paralysed (v. 5) and the kind of mat on which he was lying (vv. 8-9).

Implicit Commentary

The reference to Jesus 'going up' to Jerusalem is pregnant with double meaning. Here again the verb is *anabainō* (see 2.13), which is used for the ascent of Jesus into heaven. The use of this verb keeps the main plot alive in the mind of the paradigmatic reader.

John 5.16-47

Form

Throughout John's story, an ironic trial is in progress, a trial in which Jesus is in the dock. So strong is the forensic imagery in the Gospel (*marturia/martureō, krisis/krinō*) that many have thought of the whole story as an extended trial narrative. This feature of John's style is not an original invention. Deutero-Isaiah is composed artistically around a number of trial scenes which suggest a kind of cosmic law court (Lincoln 1993). In these scenes, Yahweh is the presiding judge as well as being one of the parties in dispute. The antagonists of Yahweh are the pagan deities worshipped by other nations, from whom Yahweh requests evidence of existence and activity. These gods are revealed as fictions by their silence. Yahweh then provides a concluding judgment in which the gods are condemned as false. The five clear-cut examples of Isaianic trial scenes are Isa. 41.1-5, 41.21-29, 43.8-13, 44.6-8 (with 21-22), 45.20-25.

We have already noted how John has created an atmosphere in his story which is suggestive of the law court. The metaphors of witness and judgment obviously contribute to this. The constant use of questions throughout the Gospel also suggests the kind of continuous barrage of interrogations germane to the law court scenario. In the law court of John's story, Jesus is both the judge and one of the parties in dispute. In this respect, he takes on the role of Yahweh in Deutero-Isaiah. His accusers, 'the Jews', are by implication the equivalent of the pagan deities who set themselves up against God. In Jn 5.16-47, the author creates the first of these trial scenes in which the judge is, ironically, on trial, falsely accused by the Jews. The dominant form in this text is discourse.

Structure and Analysis

The passage is composed of five carefully related and sequential blocks of material. All of them are unified by the legal symbolism of the Gospel. The overall structure of 5.16-47 is as follows:

1. 16-18   The Prosecution, Defence, charge and desired sentence
2. 19-25   First Defence of Jesus—Realized Eschatology
3. 26-30   Second Defence of Jesus—Future Eschatology
4. 31-40   Four witnesses for the Defence
5. 41-47   The Defendant turned Prosecutor

In 5.16-18, four important premises are established. First of all, the Jews set themselves up as the prosecutors of Jesus. Secondly, two charges are brought by them: that Jesus performed the miracle on a Sabbath, which broke the Law, and that he was calling God his Father, thereby implying equality with God (v. 18). The charge of 'equality with God' is the paramount one. Thirdly, Jesus establishes himself as the defendant. His defence against the Sabbath charge is that his Father works every day, so why should he not work. His defence against the charge of equality with God follows in vv. 19-47. Fourthly, the desired sentence of the prosecution is announced by the narrator in v. 18a: 'For this reason the Jews tried all the harder to kill him'. The sentence is death.

In 5.19-25, Jesus begins his defence. Here, as in the Isaianic trial scenes, Jesus is both the judge and a party in the dispute. That Jesus is involved in this informal trial is evident from the introduction in vv. 16-18. That he is in reality the judge rather than the defendant emerges in vv. 19-25.

Jesus' defence begins with a domestic proverb which he elaborates into a statement of his oneness with God. Originally, v. 19 probably looked like this: 'A son can do nothing by himself. He can only copy what he sees his father doing, and repeat what he hears his father saying. This is because whatever a father does, his son does also.' As elsewhere in the Gospel (4.35-38), a well-known proverb becomes the basis for theological elaboration. In this instance, an aphorism taken from the context of the family is elevated into a saying with the strongest possible christological implications. Here Jesus is the Son and God is his Father. Jesus is claiming that he copies what God the Father is doing, and he repeats what God the Father is saying. This is because the Son cannot help but imitate the Father.

The stumbling block for the Jews is Jesus' description of God as Father. This much is suggested by v. 18, where the narrator tells us that it was this fact which caused controversy, because it indicated oneness with God. Neither the reader nor the characters within the narrative world are allowed to forget Jesus' emphasis on his filial relationship with God. Correspondingly, the word *patēr* occurs throughout the Gospel.

In 5.19-47 we see Jesus referring to God as his Father 14 times. In 5.19-25, Jesus claims that he imitates the Father (v. 19), he is loved by the Father (v. 20), that he raises the dead as the Father raises the dead (v. 21), that he has been given authority to judge by the Father (v. 22), that he has the same honour as the Father (v. 23), and that he is the Giver of Life (v. 24), even life to the dead (v. 25). In 5.19-25, the emphasis is on realized eschatology. The things expected of God at the end of time (such as judgment, eternal life) are ministered to humanity through Jesus in the here-and-now of his ministry. Jesus' defence of himself centres on the realization of Jewish eschatological hopes in his own words and works.

In 5.26-30, however, Jesus' second defence is that these eschatological hopes will finally be fulfilled by him in the future. If the emphasis in 5.19-25 is on the evidence of the 'now' (v. 25), then in 5.26-30 it is on the 'not yet'. In 5.19-25, the hour of life and judgment has come. In 5.26-30, the hour of these things is coming (v. 28, and note the future tenses). Notice how the themes of vv. 26-30 parallel those in vv. 19-25:

19 // 30   The Son can only do what he sees the Father doing
20 // 28   The amazement of the Jews at the Son's works
21 // 26   The power to give life is given by the Father to the Son

22 // 27   The right to judge is given by the Father to the Son
25 // 28   A time is coming when the dead will hear the voice of the Son
25 // 29   Those who will rise to life

The defence of Jesus in vv. 19-30 is therefore as follows: 'The Father and the Son are one. The Father has given the Son power and authority in the world's today and in God's tomorrow.'

In 5.31-40, Jesus now brings in four witnesses for the defence, witnesses who will confirm his testimony. These four witnesses are all aspects of the one testimony provided by 'another', God (v. 32):

1.   John the Baptist (vv. 33-35), who testified to the truth and who was a lamp which drew attention to the light. The Baptist therefore testified to Jesus' oneness with God.
2.   The works the Father has given to Jesus (v. 36). Note how the narrator refers to Jesus' miracles as *erga* rather than *sēmeia* throughout ch. 5. The miracles of Jesus testify to Jesus' oneness with God.
3.   The Father himself (vv. 37-38). However, the prosecution does not hear God, nor see him, nor have his word in their hearts. All the same, the Father testifies to Jesus' oneness with himself.
4.   The Scriptures (vv. 39-40). The Hebrew Scriptures, much loved by the prosecuting Jews, also testify to Jesus' oneness with God.

By bringing into the dock these four different aspects of the witness of his Father, Jesus proves that he is not his own witness (v. 31). Jewish law stated that a person's own testimony could not be verified (v. 31), so Jesus supports his defence plea (concerning equality with God) with four witnesses.

In 5.41-47, Jesus ends his defence with judgment. If the prosecuting Jews thought that they had Jesus in the dock, and that they were the presiding judges, the paradigmatic reader knows that it is really Jesus who is the judge and that the Jews are in reality in the dock. As such, one of the oldest ironies in storytelling is played out before us: the irony which comes from role reversal. In 5.16-47, the judges become the judged, and the judged is revealed as eschatological Judge. In vv. 41-47, Jesus therefore passes judgment on his accusers. He tells them that he knows their hearts (compare 2.25), that they do not accept him, that they make no effort to obtain the praise which comes from God. He concludes his summing up with the warning that Moses will be their prosecutor in the law court on the Last Day. The very Scriptures which the Jews search will be used to condemn them, because Jesus is the *sensus plenior*, the deeper meaning, of all that Moses wrote.

In closing vv. 41-47 with a reference to the Scriptures, Jesus rests his case on the same theme with which he concluded vv. 31-40 (the

Scriptures that testify to Jesus, vv. 39-40 // vv. 46-47). This again provides evidence of literary design within these discourses.

Themes

As so often in John's story, there is a superabundance of themes in 5.16-47. Various keywords reappear: works, life (eternal), sending, believing, the hour, truth, sight, glory, love, seeking. The most important thematic words relate to the trial motif. There is a large cluster of words rooted in *krisis* in vv. 19-30, and an equally large number rooted in *marturia* in vv. 31-47:

krisis (judgment)		*marturia (witness)*	
22	*krinō* (×2)	31	*martureō/marturia*
24	*krinō*	32	*martureō* (×2)/*marturia*
27	*krinō*	33	*martureō*
29	*krinō*	34	*marturia*
30	*krinō*	36	*marturia/martureō*
30	*krisis*	37	*martureō*
		39	*martureō*

Added to these forensic metaphors is the concept of the 'accuser' or 'prosecutor' in 5.45. Jesus says he will not accuse the Jews (*katēgoreō*). Moses will be their accuser (*katēgoros*). It is interesting to note that the office of accuser (*katēgoros*) is the opposite of the office of advocate. The advocate figure in John's story, as we shall see, is the Holy Spirit (*paraklētos*, defence counsel).

Narrative Echo Effects

There are a number of analepses and prolepses in this trial scene. The most important prolepsis points to the Lazarus story in 11.1-44. The promise in vv. 28-29 that the time is coming when the dead in their graves will hear the voice of Jesus and come out is an anticipation of the raising of Lazarus in John 11.1-44.

John 6.1-15

Context

Jesus' critique of the Jews in 5.31-47 involves a condemnation of them as *readers*. In 5.39-40, Jesus claims that the Jews study the Scriptures without recognizing that they testify to Jesus. In 5.45-47, Jesus again criticizes them for their blindness when he points out that they have failed to see that Moses was really writing about him. The failure of the

Jews is a failure of reading. If true reading means moving beneath the surface sense of a story to the secret sense hidden within the text, then the Jews have truly failed. They have, according to Jesus, spent centuries delving into the details of the surface meaning without ever reaching the real depths of their writings. In relation to the Moses stories, they have failed as readers because they have been blind to the fact that Moses was pointing to someone greater than he (1.17) and to a salvation far greater than that wrought through the raised serpent in the wilderness (Jn 3.14). They have been blind to the hidden subject of their narratives: Jesus Christ and the cross.

In exposing the Jews as inadequate readers, the narrator woos the paradigmatic reader into a desire for the *sensus plenior* of the story of Jesus. The paradigmatic reader can see from the overt allusions to Moses in 1.17 and 3.14 that Moses is a key to the secret sense of John's narrative. Just as Jesus is the secret sense within the Moses story, so Moses is the secret sense within the Jesus story. If the Jews had penetrated the hidden subject of their writings, they would have escaped the judgment of Jesus. If the paradigmatic reader of John's Gospel is to escape judgment, then he or she too must penetrate the hidden subject within John's story. The challenge is first of all to live within the over-arching story-world centred on Moses and the Exodus, and secondly, to see how the narrator makes sense of Jesus, using the motifs, imagery and plot of that same narrative canopy. The words of Jesus immediately prior to John 6 alert the reader to this challenge.

There is evidence, then, that the narrator is using Moses as a hermeneutical key to our understanding of the second section of the Book of Signs, 5.1–10.42. Just a cursory glance at the overall themes of chs. 6, 7 and 8 reveals this to be so. In ch. 6, Jesus speaks of the Bread of Life which he has come to give to a humanity which is spiritually hungry. A direct comparison is made with the manna given by God to Moses in the wilderness. In ch. 7, Jesus goes to the feast of Tabernacles and announces that there is a new stream of living water available to a humanity which is spiritually thirsty. Indirect allusions are made to the rock from which water sprang, by God's supernatural intervention, in the wilderness. In ch. 8, Jesus is still at Tabernacles and proclaims that he himself is the Light of the World. Indirect allusions are again made, this time to the pillar of light which God gave to guide Moses and the Israelites during the Exodus. Clearly Moses is the *sensus plenior* of the Jesus story, just as Jesus is the *sensus plenior* of the Moses story. A true reading of John's narrative must therefore penetrate the hidden 'Mosaic' of Jesus' words and actions, otherwise the reader will be subject to the same critique as that levelled against the Jewish readers: that they study without belief (5.45-47).

Structure

The author uses a fivefold design for Jn 6.1-15 (as often elsewhere):

A^1	1-4	Jesus goes to a mountain to minister to the crowds
B^1	5-9	The lack: 'How can we feed so many with so little?'
C	10-11	The eucharistic actions
B^2	12-13	The provision: 'enough left over for twelve baskets'
A^2	14-15	Jesus goes to a mountain to escape from the crowds

Form

The reader should note the introduction of a new kind of miracle story in 6.1. So far in John, we have seen two different forms of miracle story. In 2.1-11 and 4.46-54, the narrator presents us with two Cana-based signs with a request–rebuke–response structure. In 5.1-15, we are presented with a Jerusalem-based miracle with a miracle-interrogation structure. This form of miracle story is repeated in ch. 9, where the miracle in Jerusalem (again related to a pool, this time Siloam), leads to another trial. This leaves four miracles in John's story: the feeding of the five thousand (6.1-15), the walking on the sea (6.16-21), the raising of Lazarus (11.1-44) and the miraculous catch of fish (21.1-14). The raising of Lazarus represents a unique form (see the commentary on Jn 11.1-44). However, the other three all stress that their context is Lake Galilee (Tiberias, 6.1; 21.1), they all happen close to or on the sea, and in at least two cases have close parallels (6.11; 21.13). This would suggest John's use of four different forms of miracle story in his Gospel:

1.   Signs at Cana (2.1-11; 4.46-54)
2.   Jerusalem miracles (5.1-15; 9.1-41)
3.   Lake Galilee miracles (6.1-15; 6.16-21; 21.1-14)
4.   Resurrection miracles (11.1-44)

The Narrator

In 6.1-15, the narrator's voice becomes audible once again. We have been aware of Jesus speaking from 5.19-47. Now in 6.1-15 we become aware of the voice of the narrator. Literary theorists have shown that the presence of a narrator in a narrative can be anything from mani-festly *overt* to apparently *covert*. The signs of overtness, in ascending order of visibility, have been identified as: 1. the narrator's description of setting; 2. the identification of characters; 3. the accounts of time-passage; 4. the definition of character; 5. the reports of what characters do not think or say; and 6. the interpretative commentary. In 6.1-15, all six of these signs of overt narration are present.

The narrator first of all describes settings (vv. 1, 3, 10, 15). He or she secondly identifies characters (Jesus, v. 1; the crowd, v. 2; the disciples, v. 3; Philip, v. 5; Andrew, v. 8). Thirdly, the narrator gives an account of the passing of time (v. 4). Fourthly, he or she defines characters by summing up their motives (note v. 2 and v. 14, and the comments about the crowd's dependence on signs). Fifthly, the narrator shows what Jesus deliberately conceals in v. 6: 'He asked this only to test Philip'. Finally, he or she interprets the behaviour of Jesus in vv. 6 and 15 (note the narrator's inside knowledge of Jesus' thought processes in these two verses). Clearly there is a transition from 'showing' (Jn 5.16-49) to 'telling' in Jn 6.1-15.

Characterization

Jesus is the protagonist of 6.1-15. His elusiveness is evident again. Note the vital difference which Jn 5.16-18 has made to the plot of John's story. Before ch. 5, Jesus is in no danger. He moves about openly and freely. He teaches without any controversy. However, after the healing on the Sabbath in 5.1-15, the narrator not only says that the Jews persecute Jesus, but that they are now out to kill him. From this point onwards, Jesus is evasive and secretive. His actions and movements are those of the *hidden* Messiah. His dialogue is characterized by a discontinuity which utterly mystifies his listeners. From ch. 5 onwards, Jesus is quintessentially the elusive Christ.

This elusiveness is evoked by Jesus' movements. In 6.1, we suddenly go from Jerusalem (ch. 5) to the far shore of the Sea of Galilee. The usual care which the narrator has taken to describe Jesus' itinerary is now absent. In fact, there is a curiously dislocating effect in 6.1; it is almost as if the protagonist has slipped supernaturally from Jerusalem to Galilee without effort. If this kind of transference and movement enhances Jesus' elusiveness, the deliberate evasiveness of Jesus reinforces it even more. The reader should note the narrator's words in 6.14-15: here it is said that the crowd saw the sign which Jesus performed and identified him as 'the Prophet who is to come into the world'. Realizing this, Jesus withdraws to a mountain by himself. As we have seen in the introduction, the motif of Jesus' withdrawals is connected with the primary theme of his elusiveness.

Individual disciples are named in Jn 6.1-15: Philip (vv. 5-7), Andrew (vv. 8-9) and Simon Peter (v. 8). Philip and Andrew are paired together in vv. 5-9, as they are in 12.20-22. Here they are foils for Jesus' multiplication miracle. Philip manifests inadequate faith and understanding in his complaint in v. 7. Andrew reveals more faith in pointing to a small boy with food. However, his question in v. 9, 'how far will that go among so many?' shows that he is far from a true appreciation of Jesus' divine resources.

Literary Devices

We should notice the literary device of *reality effects* here. There are a number of these in 6.1-15. The details which create the effect of 'the real' are: 1. the names of Jesus' addressees in vv. 5-9 (Philip and Andrew); 2. the notice of Andrew's relationship with Simon Peter (v. 8, compare 1.40); 3. the mention of the little boy in v. 9 (*paidarion*, a double diminutive of *pais*, boy); 4. the specific reference to five barley loaves (*artous krithinous*, the bread of the poor); 5. the double diminutive of *opsos* in v. 9 (*opsaria*, dried or preserved fish); and 6. the description of plentiful grass on which to sit in v. 10. All these reality effects contribute to the history-like quality of John's story.

John 6.16-24

Structure and Form
There are two narratives in this next stage in the development of John 6. The first, vv. 16-21, describes the journey of the disciples by boat from one side of Lake Galilee to the other. The second describes a similar journey undertaken by the crowds. The structure of these two stories is similar. At the most basic level, both stories begin with a process time-shape ('When evening came', v. 16 // 'The next day', v. 22), a reference to the lake (v. 16 // v. 22), to the boat trip of the disciples and the absence of Jesus (v. 17 // v. 22), a description of need (the disciples' fear in v. 19 // the crowds' need for boats in v. 22), the provision for the need (v. 20 // v. 23) and the arrival (v. 21 // vv. 24-25). The form of these two narratives is, however, markedly different. The first is a miracle story and the second an itinerary narrative.

Characterization
The principal rationale for including these stories is the fact that they add significantly to the portrayal of Jesus as the elusive Christ. From 6.15 until 6.25, a game of hide-and-seek is played out in the plot. Jesus begins by crossing the sea supernaturally. He appears out of the darkness, walking on the water. He reveals his true, divine identity to the disciples in the words 'I am', whereupon the boat suddenly arrives at the intended destination. The immediate arrival of the boat on the far shore seems to be as miraculous to the narrator as the walking on the water. Once Jesus is on board (v. 21), the disciples find that the normal constraints of movement against wind and water are mysteriously eradicated.

Later, in v. 22, the crowd who had witnessed the multiplication miracle are still on the opposite shore, near where the bread had been distributed. They perceive that Jesus is absent and that a boat is missing, and they infer that Jesus and his disciples have crossed the lake. More people join them in boats from Tiberias, and the newly formed mass of people climb into boats and leave for Capernaum, seeking (*zētountes*) Jesus. When they arrive at Capernaum they are bewildered, asking, 'Rabbi, when did you get here?' Again Jesus' elusiveness is stressed.

John 6.25-71

Structure and Form

From 6.25 onwards, speech or discourse material predominates. In vv. 25-71, Jesus speaks of himself as the Bread of Life, the new and life-giving manna in the wilderness of the world. The sections of this longer discourse material are marked by the use of questions (vv. 25, 34, 41-42, 52, 60) and by a certain parallelism in themes:

A	25-34a	Introduction: the true bread from heaven
B	34b-40	Coming to Jesus, part 1
C	41-51	Coming to Jesus, part 2
D	52-59	Staying with Jesus, part 1
E	60-71	Staying with Jesus, part 2

A number of points need to be made about the discernment of a literary structure in 6.25-71. First of all, the questions of various character-groups mark the beginnings of sections. Thus, A begins in v. 25 with the question of the crowd: 'Rabbi, when did you get here?' B, v. 34, 'Sir... from now on give us this bread?' (a request); C, v. 41, 'How can he say, "I came down from heaven?"'; D, v. 52, 'How can this man give us his flesh to eat?'; and E, v. 60, 'This is a hard teaching. Who can accept it?' Secondly, there is an obvious connection between B and C through the theme of coming to Jesus (v. 35, 37 in B and v. 44, 45 in C). There is also a connection between D and E through the theme of staying or remaining with Jesus. This is manifested in D, when Jesus states that anyone who eats his flesh and drinks his blood will remain in him, and he in them. It is visible in E in the way in which many cease to remain with Jesus because of this flesh-and-blood teaching but some stay with him.

The form of the speech material is one favoured by John throughout the Gospel. It is essentially the interrogation–response form. Here the interrogators are the crowds (v. 25 and v. 34), the Jews (v. 41 and v. 52) and the disciples (v. 60); the defendant is always Jesus. Within this basic form, John has also made use of the homiletic techniques of first-century rabbinic Judaism. Many scholars now show how 6.25-51 reveals marked similarities with the homilies in Philo and Palestinian *midrashim* (Lindars 1990: 36-37).

In synagogue preaching, the speaker first took a text (usually from the Pentateuch) which he then paraphrased. A homily would then follow in which the text was scrutinized word for word. Often this would be accompanied by a subordinate quotation from the Prophets, before the homily was concluded with the statement with which it began. Jesus follows this pattern in 6.25-50. There is first of all a text from the Pentateuch in 6.31 (Exod. 16.4, 15), which Jesus then paraphrases and redefines in a typically rabbinic style in vv. 32-34. He then preaches the main homily on eating bread from heaven in vv. 35-50 (notice the subordinate quotation from the Prophets in v. 45), before repeating v. 35 in vv. 48-51, towards the end of the homily. In support of this, we should note the narrator's intrusion at v. 59: 'He said this while teaching in the synagogue in Capernaum'. The context of Jesus' teaching in John 6 is a clue that there is a homiletic pattern within the words of Jesus.

Themes
Discipleship is a dominant idea in vv. 25-71. From v. 25 onwards, the narrator is concerned with what is involved in coming to Jesus, and then in remaining as a follower. However, the most potent theme in John 6 (one which unites the chapter) centres on the idea of bread. Bread figures prominently in the feeding of the five thousand in 6.1-15 (vv. 5, 7, 9, 11, 13). Here Jesus distributes a miraculous supply of physical bread to the five thousand on the mountain. In vv. 25-59, the discourse material takes up the theme of bread but elevates it to a much higher, spiritual and symbolic level. Here the bread on the mountain is recalled and used as a foil for discussion of the bread from heaven: 'You are looking for me, not because you saw miraculous signs but because you ate the loaves and had your fill. Do not work for food that spoils, but for food that endures to eternal life.' From here on, it is spiritual bread which is the subject of the story (vv. 31-35, 41, 48, 50, 51, 58). There is a subtle progression in John 6 from feeder (Jesus as giver of bread) to food (Jesus as bread; see Crossan 1980: 246). In John 6, the feeder becomes the food.

Characterization
Character traits are revealed in four main ways in most storytelling: through the actions performed by the characters; through their speech (either direct or indirect speech, or the thought-processes reported by the narrator); through external appearance (physiognomy, body language and the like); and through physical surroundings (a stormy climate implying a stormy character, for example). In John 6, the character traits of Jesus are revealed primarily through action and through speech. In Jn 6.1-24, action is the primary means by which the narrator reveals aspects of Jesus' character. From v. 25 onwards,

speech replaces action as the primary means of disclosing character.

From v. 25, Jesus' elusiveness is indicated by his use of language. Now the technique of discontinuous dialogue comes to the fore. The discontinuity between Jesus and his listeners arises from the fact that he teaches heavenly realities which are misunderstood by his listeners. The Jews find Jesus' language obscure. They cannot understand Jesus' claims to heavenly origins. Being literal interpreters, they complain that they know Jesus' parents (vv. 41-42). When Jesus proceeds to speak of himself as the object of spiritual sustenance, they again misunderstand: 'How can this man give us his flesh to eat?' The whole nature of Jesus' discourse is summed up in the description of the murmuring disciples of 6.60; it is *sklēros...logos*, 'hard teaching'.

Settings

We should observe the narrator's creative use of settings in the chapter as a whole. In John 6, we see the protagonist in three settings: the mountain (6.3-15), the sea (6.16-21) and the synagogue (6.59). In literature, these three settings are used as archetypes (Ryken 1979: 85-90). The mountain top (like the fertile valley or hill) is an archetype of ideal heavenly experience. The sea is a chthonic (underwordly) archetype; it is associated with chaos, with monsters, with evil. The synagogue (a sacred building) is an archetype of humanity's quest for God. The Jesus of John 6 is one who moves in all three contexts. He sits on the mountain top, close to heaven. He walks on the sea, where evil seems to rule. He teaches in the sacred place, where humanity seeks after God. Truly Jesus of Nazareth is the one in whom heaven and earth, the land and the sea, religion and revelation are mediated.

Implicit Commentary

In the comments on context in the commentary on Jn 6.1-15, I drew attention to the narrator's challenge to the reader. This challenge is essentially to move beneath the surface qualities of the text to its deeper levels of communication. Here we come to the implicit commentary taking place in John 6, a commentary which is only heard if the reader is prepared to acknowledge narrative echo effects with the Moses story. The following represents a list of many of these intertextual echoes with the Exodus story:

Transtextual (Direct) Allusions

31	'Our forefathers ate manna in the desert' (Num. 11.7-9).
32	'It is not Moses who has given you the bread from heaven.'
49	'Your forefathers ate the manna in the desert.'
58	'Your forefathers ate manna and died.'

Intertextual (Indirect) Allusions

	John's story	Moses' story
3	The mountain	Sinai
4	Passover	Exodus 12
5	'Where shall we buy bread for these people to eat?'	'Where can I get meat for all these people?' (Num. 11.13)
9	The two small fish	'Would they have enough if all the fish in the sea were caught for them?' (Num. 11.22)
16	The crossing of the sea	The crossing of the Red Sea
41	The grumbling of the Jews and disciples (see vv. 43, 61)	'Now the people grumbled about their hardships' (Num. 11.1).
51	'This bread is my flesh.'	'Give us meat/flesh to eat' (Num. 11.13).

The secret sense deriving from these echo effects is as follows: in John 6, there stands among the Jews one who is far greater than Moses, Jesus of Nazareth. This Jesus has bread to offer which is far more precious than the manna which God gave to Moses, for it is the life-giving bread of his own body. The tragic irony is this: that even though these Jews study the Scriptures of Moses, they have not recognized the one about whom Moses was really writing. As a result, when they hear the revelatory teaching of Jesus in this story, all they can do is murmur and grumble like their ancestors of old.

John 7.1-52

Context

Four points should be made about the context of ch. 7: first of all, the reader will recall that John's story in 2.1–4.54 depicts a circular itinerary. Jesus begins in Cana of Galilee in Jn 2.1, travels to Jerusalem (2.13), before returning to Cana (4.43) via the Judaean countryside (3.22) and Samaria (4.4). In Jn 5.1–10.42, Jesus also travels on a circular journey. This time the beginning and the end of the journey is Jerusalem (5.1 // 7.1) while the middle of the journey is spent in Galilee (Capernaum, 6.17, 24, 59). The itinerary in this second section (chs. 5–10) is the exact reverse of the one taken in the first section (chs. 2–4).

This second itinerary ends with Jesus' arrival in Jerusalem for the feast of Tabernacles in ch. 7. Until 10.40 there will be no mention of

Jesus' travels. The implied picture is of Jesus at Jerusalem throughout chs. 7–10. This is in marked contrast with the Cana-to-Cana cycle where the narrator is eager to depict Jesus as on the move through Galilee, Judea and Samaria. From ch. 7 onwards, the focus is very much on Jesus' more localized movements in Jerusalem, particularly in the area of the Temple courts (7.14, 28; 8.20, 59; 10.23).

Secondly, the reader should also note the connectedness of chs. 5 and 7. This is Jesus' third visit to Jerusalem in the story (2.13; 5.1; 7.14); there is a clear sense of sequence and causality between the second and third visits. In his second visit (ch. 5), Jesus goes up to Jerusalem for an unspecified 'feast of the Jews'. Here he heals a crippled man at Bethesda on the Sabbath, invoking the hostility of the Jewish authorities. In his third visit (7.14), Jesus finds that the same authorities have not forgotten the controversy which he caused in ch. 5. In 7.19-24, Jesus refers back to the healing at Bethesda ('I did one miracle and yet you are all astonished'), to the legal debate over the Sabbath ('Why are you angry with me for healing the whole man on the sabbath?' 7.23; see 5.9-10), and to the Jews' desire to kill him because of it (7.19, 25; see 5.18).

Thirdly, notice the importance of the narrator's references to the feasts for our understanding of the passing of process time. It is evident from the references to the two Passovers in 2.13 and 6.4 that chs. 2–6 cover a period of just over one year (running from about April to April). In chs. 7–10, a period of well under a year is described. Jesus celebrates the feast of Tabernacles in late September or early October (7.1–8.59), then presumably stays in or around Jerusalem for the feast of Dedication in late December (10.22-39). Thus the process time in John's story is beginning to slow down. If chs. 2–4 depict a period of one year, chs 5–10 depict a period of about four months. As we shall see, chs. 11–12 depict a period of about two weeks, while chs. 13–19 cover only 24 hours at the most.

Fourthly, as the process time decreases in speed from 7.1, so the intensity of the conflict increases. There are a number of points in chapter 7 where the narrator alerts the reader to the hostility of the Jews towards Jesus:

11   Now at the Feast the Jews were watching for him and asking, 'Where is that man?'
30   At this they tried to seize him, but no-one laid hands on him because his time had not yet come.
32   Then the chief priests and the Pharisees sent Temple guards to arrest him.
44   Some wanted to seize him, but no one laid a hand on him.

These narratorial descriptions are crucial for the development of John's plot. In the introduction (ch. 1) and first section (chs. 2–4) of the Gospel there has been no overt hostility towards Jesus. In the second section of the Gospel, all this changes. Here in chs. 7–10, Jesus will face a number of attempts to arrest and kill him.

Structure

There is a discernible, literary structure to the chapter as a whole. As so often, there are five sections in a chiastic arrangement:

A^1	1-13	Jesus' elusive movements thwart the authorities
B^1	14-24	Jesus' first dialogue, halfway through the Feast
C	25-36	Jesus' second dialogue
B^2	37-44	Jesus' third dialogue, on the last day of the Feast
A^2	45-52	Jesus' elusive movements thwart the authorities again

Of particular interest here is the ring composition. A^1 and A^2 have some obvious parallels, not least the theme of the Jewish authorities searching for Jesus. Beyond this, notice that the first verse of A^1 focuses on Galilee: 'After this, Jesus went around in Galilee', while the last verse of A^2 highlights the same region: 'Are you from Galilee too? Look into it, and you will find that a prophet does not come out of Galilee.' Also worthy of note is the theme of deception in A^1 and A^2. In 7.12, some people in the Jerusalem crowd say, 'No, he deceives (*plana*) the people'. In 7.47, the Pharisees ask, 'You mean he has deceived (*peplanēsthe)* you lso?' Since these are the only two occasions in the Gospel when *planaō* (deceive) is used, the inclusio should be seen as intentional. Finally, there is an inclusio between 7.5 and 7.48 in the phrase 'believing in him'.

If there are parallels between A^1 and A^2, there are also similarities between B^1 and B^2. B^1 begins with: 'Not until halfway through the Feast' (7.14). B^2 begins: 'On the last and greatest day of the Feast' (7.37). Furthermore, the structure of these two sections is similar:

B^1 14-24		B^2 37-44	
1.	Introduction: 14-15 (Halfway through the Feast)	1.	Introduction: 37 (On the last day of the Feast)
2.	Jesus' speech: 16-19 ('If anyone...')	2.	Jesus' speech: 37-39 ('If anyone...')
3.	The reaction of the crowd: 20	3.	The reaction of the crowd: 40
4.	A final speech involving Scripture: 21-24	4.	A final speech involving Scripture: 41-44

Though the narrator is more involved in B^2, the similarity is noticeable.

This leaves C (7.25-36) as the central section of the chapter. This section has a structure which is identical to the structure of the whole chapter. That is to say, it is composed of five units in a chiastic arrangement:

A^1	25-27	People asking each other questions about Jesus
B^1	28-29	Jesus' words: 'I am from him and he sent me'
C	30-32	'Will the Christ do more miraculous signs than these?'
B^2	33-35	Jesus' words: 'I go to the one who sent me'
A^2	35-36	The Jews asking each other questions about Jesus

Each unit is approximately the same length (as is the case with each section of the chapter as a whole). The theme of 7.25-36 is the central issue of the Gospel: 'Is Jesus the Christ?' (Note the word *christos* in 7.26, 27 and 31). We know from Jn 20.31 that the main purpose of John's story is rhetorical; it is to persuade the reader that Jesus is the Christ. In the central section of ch. 7, John's story rehearses the arguments for and against this confession: the origins of Jesus (7.27, 29); the miracles of Jesus (7.31); the future return of Jesus to the Father (7.33-34, 35-36).

Form

The discourse form has been introduced in ch. 5. In 5.19-47, Jesus delivers a long speech in the style of a legal defence. In ch. 6, Jesus delivers an equally long speech, this time in the didactic style of the rabbinic homily (6.26-58). In the discourse material of 7.14-44 there are didactic elements (notice the *didaskō* in 7.14, 28, 35, and *didachē* in 7.16, 17). However, the forensic overtones of this material mark it out as yet another trial scene (note especially the informal 'trial' in 7.45-52). We are alerted to the legal character of the conflict by the repeated appeals to the Law (7.19, 23, 51) and by legal terminology (*krisis/krinō* in vv. 24 and 51). Much of the material in ch. 7 is constructed to suggest the progress of a trial which has begun in ch. 5. The fact that a death sentence hangs precariously over Jesus' head shows that the outcome of the argument here is a matter of life and death.

Characterization

a. **Jesus.** In ch. 7, Jesus' elusiveness is again explored. Whereas there is only a suggestion of it in chs. 2–4, in chs. 5–10 the portrayal of Jesus as the elusive Christ now becomes the primary and dominant aspect of his characterization. In ch. 7, he is elusive, first of all, in the *present tense* of his ministry. As far as his language is concerned, Jesus' meaning is difficult throughout (see in particular 7.33-36). As far as his movements are concerned, we should note that Jesus is urged by his brothers to go openly to Judea. However, he leaves later than they do, and in secret (7.10). When Jesus arrives, he waits until half way through the feast until he appears publicly. Up until that point the Jews have been looking for him in vain (7.11). From then on, Jesus slips from their grasp every time the Jews attempt to arrest him. The narrator says: 'At this they tried to seize him, but no one laid a hand on him, because his time had not yet come' (7.30).

If Jesus is elusive in the present tense of the narrative world, he also proves elusive in relation to its *past and future*. The whole question of Jesus' past origins prove utterly evasive to all the social groups represented in ch. 7. Some of the people in Jerusalem state: 'We know where this man is from'. However, their knowledge concerns Jesus' native town, not his heavenly descent. The same is true for the group mentioned in 7.41-42 and for the Pharisees in 7.52. As for his future, Jesus states in 7.33: 'I am with you for only a short time, and then I go to the one who sent me. You will look for me, but you will not find me; and where I am, you cannot come.' Jesus is here referring to his future return to the glory of the Father. However, his meaning is again misinterpreted; the Jews think he is talking about a future ministry to diaspora Jews and Greeks.

Thus, throughout ch. 7, Jesus is elusive in relation to his past origins, his present language and movements, and to his future destiny in glory (7.39).

b. Social Groups. Chapter 7 explores the reactions of various social groups to Jesus, and again the important thing to note is the varying faith-responses represented by each. Five such groups can be discerned: the brothers of Jesus, the crowds in Jerusalem, the Jews, the chief priests/Pharisees, and the Temple guards. The last of these (the Temple guards) are the arrest party in John's narrative. They are sent out at v. 32 but return frustrated and without Jesus at v. 45. They fail to bring Jesus in because they are impressed by Jesus' authority: 'No one ever spoke the way this man does' (v. 46). We shall see a similar dynamic in 18.6 when the Temple police are floored by Jesus' majestic, 'I am he!' In John's story these temple attendants fulfil the narrative function of arrestors.

The Pharisees/chief priests are depicted as the instigators of the opposition against Jesus. They operate behind the scenes. They have to send the guards to arrest Jesus (v. 32). The same guards return to the chief priests and Pharisees in v. 45. This idea of sending and returning underlines the suggestion that they are destructive, backstage instigators. Their characteristics as a group are explored in the last section of the narrative. In 7.47 they accuse the guards of having been deceived when they fail to bring Jesus in (ironically, it is they who are deceived). They openly pride themselves as people who do not believe in Jesus ('Has any of the rulers or of the Pharisees believed in him?' v. 48), thereby condemning themselves. They criticize the crowd for being an ignorant and accursed mob (v. 49) and they point an accusing finger at Nicodemus when he tries to expose the illegality of their proceedings. This social group is the subject of satire throughout John's story.

The group identified as the Jews in 7.11, 13 and 33 is hard to distinguish from the chief priests and the Pharisees. The fact that they are taking an up-front role in looking for Jesus in 7.11, as well as their presence with the crowds in 7.35, would seem to indicate that they are not identical with the backstage hierarchy. Indeed, the narrator shows that the crowd are afraid to say anything positive about Jesus in public 'for fear of the Jews' (v. 13). This suggests that the Jews are a spear-head representative of the backstage, hostile authorities. Furthermore, it seems almost as if it is 'the Jews' who hear the whispering of the crowd in 7.32 and who report the contents of these rumours to the Pharisees. Their chief characteristic is misunderstanding. In 7.15 they demonstrate their ignorance concerning the source of Jesus' wisdom. In 7.35-36 they openly reveal their inability to discern anything deeper than a literal interpretation of Jesus' words.

The crowds in ch. 7 are a diverse and lively community. Their diversity is suggested by the division of opinion about Jesus within their ranks. On a number of occasions in ch. 7, this diversity is described by the narrator:

12-13   Among the crowds there was widespread whispering about him. Some said, 'He is a good man'. Others replied, 'No, he deceives the people'.

30-31   At this they tried to seize him, but no one laid a hand on him, because his time had not yet come. Still, many in the crowd put their faith in him.

40-41   On hearing his words, some of the people said, 'Surely this man is the Prophet'. Others said, 'He is the Christ'. Still others asked, 'How can the Christ come from Galilee?'

What the narrator presents in this social group identified as 'the crowd' (also 'the people of Jerusalem', v. 25) is a wide spectrum of faith-responses to Jesus. At the negative end, the crowd are capable of describing Jesus as a deceiver (v. 12) and as 'demon-possessed' (v. 29). Some of them are even depicted as trying to seize Jesus (v. 30). However, there are elements in the same community who are capable of a response which is nearer the mid-point of the spectrum: 'He is a good man'. On the way to the positive end are those who assert that Jesus is 'the Prophet' (v. 40). Nearer still to this end of the spectrum are the many people who 'put their faith in him' (v. 31) and who confess Jesus as 'the Christ' (v. 41). Overall, the crowds are characterized in a less negative way than the Jews. However, the fact that they are afraid of the Jews (v. 13), as well as the fact that their confessions are whispered (vv. 12, 32), shows that the portrayal of them is not entirely positive either.

The fifth group mentioned in ch. 7 is described by the narrator as 'the brothers of Jesus'. They appear in 7.3 as those who encourage Jesus to move about openly in Judea rather than elusively and secretly. In saying this, they manifest unbelief. When they say to Jesus, 'Show yourself to the world!' (v. 4), the narrator states that 'even his own brothers did not believe in him'. The background to this evaluation lies in ch. 2 where the brothers of Jesus were present at the wine miracle in Cana (see 2.12). There Jesus criticized his mother's request because the time for an open demonstration of his power had not yet come (2.4). Here the brothers of Jesus are seen, like their mother, making a similar bid for a public manifestation which will prove Jesus' credentials. Jesus again reproves members of his family for not understanding that there is a preordained time for such public revelation (7.6-8). Jesus' brothers are therefore characterized as unbelievers in John's story.

c. **Nicodemus.** When the Pharisees retort, 'Has any of the rulers (*archontōn*) or the Pharisees (*Pharisaiōn*) believed in him?' (v. 48), narrative echos are immediately felt with the Nicodemus story in Jn 3.1-21. At the outset of that story, Nicodemus is introduced as 'a man of the Pharisees' (*anthrōpos ek tōn Pharisaiōn*) and as 'one of the rulers of the Jews' (*archōn tōn Ioudaiōn*) (3.1). In 3.1-15, Nicodemus appears as a man who is attracted to Jesus yet incapable of complete understanding, faith and commitment. In 7.50, Nicodemus is portrayed in a favourable light. He is not prepared to see the Jewish hierarchy, in which he is a vocal member, ignore the protocols of justice by condemning Jesus without a fair hearing (v. 51). Though it is reading too much between the lines to say that he is standing up for Jesus here, it is not incorrect to say that he is standing up for justice. In doing this, he is roundly criticized by his peers. They are working with certain messianic assumptions ('a prophet does not come out of Galilee') which have prejudged the case. Nonetheless, the reader is certainly meant to view Nicodemus as 'the best of a bad bunch'. He is the only character in the chapter (besides Jesus) who elicits any support from the reader.

Plot

These comments on the characterization pave the way for some important insights concerning the plot structure of ch. 7. Up until now, the main plot has been established as follows: God the Father sends his Son into the world in order to give life to those who believe. Jesus is depicted as alone in this mission except that the Spirit is said to remain on him. Pitted against him are the Pharisees and the Jews (the latter understood as the Jewish leadership) who are portrayed as agents of Satan, the prince of this world, the source of darkness. This plot outline can be summarized using Greimas's actantial model:

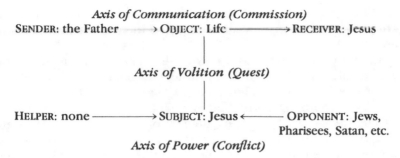

Axis of Communication (Commission)
SENDER: the Father ———→ OBJECT: Life ————→ RECEIVER: Jesus

Axis of Volition (Quest)

HELPER: none ————→ SUBJECT: Jesus ←——— OPPONENT: Jews,
                                                Pharisees, Satan, etc.
Axis of Power (Conflict)

In ch. 7, the outline of a different perspective on this plot emerges. The reader should recall that the word 'plot' not only denotes the story shape in a narrative but also a conspiracy, as in the phrase 'Gunpowder Plot'. The plot of John 7, understood in the sense of a conspiracy, can now be drawn up as follows:

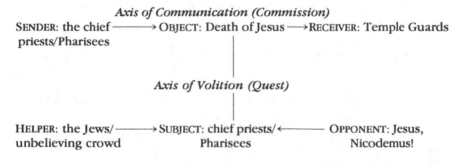

Axis of Communication (Commission)
SENDER: the chief ———→ OBJECT: Death of Jesus ——→ RECEIVER: Temple Guards
priests/Pharisees

Axis of Volition (Quest)

HELPER: the Jews/ ———→ SUBJECT: chief priests/ ←——— OPPONENT: Jesus,
unbelieving crowd   Pharisees   Nicodemus!

Axis of Power (Conflict)

Justification for this outline is not least provided by the narrator's highly ironic use of the 'sending' motif in connection with the Pharisees. Just as Jesus is sent by the Father as an agent of life, so the Temple guards are 'sent' by the Pharisees (7.32) as agents of death.

Time-Shapes

Important to the plot are the narrator's notations of time. There are indications of process time in John 7—'Not until halfway through the Feast' (v. 14) and 'On the last and greatest day of the Feast' (v. 37) are two of them. These help to keep the story moving. Much more important are the barrier time-shapes. Into the narrative at John 7, the narrator inserts references to the prescribed time limit or barrier in the story. In 7.9-8, Jesus is depicted as a man who waits on God's appointed time for action. In the narrator's aside in 7.30, the barrier time-shape is brought into sharp focus in the concept of the hour: 'No one laid a hand on Jesus because his time (*hōra*) had not yet come'. The use of barriers gives suspense to the action but it also provides a sense of control in Jesus' behaviour. Though attempts will be made to arrest and to kill Jesus, these will only succeed when the pre-ordained hour has come.

Alongside these process and barrier time-shapes, the reader should also note the use of the polytemporal time-shape in 7.39. Here the narrator speaks to the reader from the perspective of the end of the story. The narrator explains that the Spirit was later to be given by Jesus after he had been glorified (lifted up on the cross). In 7.39, there is consequently a mixing of temporal horizons as the narrator takes the reader out of the story world for a moment in order to interpret a Jesus saying from a post-resurrection point of view.

Themes

In John 7, many of the characteristic Johannine themes are present: faith (vv. 5, 31, 48); sending (vv. 16, 18, 28, 29, 32, 33); truth (vv. 18, 28); signs (vv. 3, 21, 31); Moses (vv. 19, 22); judgment (vv. 24, 51); knowledge (vv. 28-29, 49); coming to Jesus (v. 37); water (v. 38); the Spirit (v. 39); glorification (v. 39).

We should detect the importance of the image of water in Jesus' discourse in 7.37-38. As nearly all the commentaries point out, behind this text there lies a ritual connected with the feast of Tabernacles. This consisted of a procession to the fountain of Gihon where a priest filled a golden pitcher with water. At that moment, singers would chant words from Isa. 12.3: 'With joy you will draw water from the wells of salvation'. The procession then left the fountain, proceeded through the Water Gate, and into the Temple where the priest poured the water into a silver funnel on the Altar of Sacrifice. All this is significant for our understanding of Jesus' words in John 7. Jesus, on the last and greatest day of the feast of Tabernacles (Jn 7.37), stands up and shouts out the truth that it is he, not an ancient religious ritual, that is the source of living water. The narrator then explains that this living water is the Spirit which Jesus will give to his disciples after he is glorified (7.39).

John 8.12-59

Context

Chapters 7 and 8 of John's story form a unit within this section of the Gospel. This is first of all suggested by the inclusio between 7.1-13, where Jesus goes secretly (*en kruptō*, v. 4) to the Temple, and 8.59 where Jesus is said to slip away (*ekrubē*) from the Temple grounds. It is also suggested by the fact that the two chapters share an identical narrative setting: in the Temple grounds at the feast of Tabernacles.

Jesus' statement 'I am the light of the world' is prompted by the ceremony of lighting the four golden candlesticks in the Court of Women. This took place during Tabernacles and reveals that Jesus is still employing the same strategy as at 7.37-39, where he applies aspects of the Temple ceremony to himself. Finally, the unity of the chapters is suggested by thematic parallels: note the echoes between 7.33b and 8.21a ('I am going away'); 7.34a and 8.21a ('You will look for me'); 7.34b ('Where I am, you cannot come') and 8.22 (the misunderstanding of the statement by the Jews); 7.36 and 8.22 (where the Jews repeat what Jesus has said).

These three features show the fundamental connectedness of chs. 7 and 8. However, there is progression as well as coherence here. In John 8, the conflict between Jesus and the Jewish hierarchy reaches its most intense point. Throughout ch. 8 the issue is paternity. Who is the real spiritual father of the Jews? Who is the real spiritual father of Jesus of Nazareth?

Structure

8.12-59 is divided into five parts (as is ch. 7). The divisions in the unit are not as obvious as those in 7.1-52; the predominance of discourse material disguises the beginnings and endings which are generally more visible in the narrative material. The unit seems to be structured as follows:

A^1	12-20	The relationship between Jesus and the Father
B^1	21-30	The Jews' misunderstanding about Jesus' Father
C	31-41	The Jews claim that God is their Father
B^2	42-47	The Jews' misunderstanding about their own father
A^2	48-59	The relationship between Jesus and the Father

Within this structure there are some interesting points to notice. For example, A^2 concludes in a way which is reminiscent of A^1:

8.59	'At this, they picked up stones to stone him, but Jesus hid himself, slipping away from the Temple grounds.'
8.20	'He spoke these words while teaching in the Temple area near the place where the offerings were put. Yet no one seized him, because his time had not yet come.'

There is a further inclusio between the use of the divine name in 8.12 ('*I am* the light of the world') and its appearance again, in the absolute usage, at 8.58 ('Before Abraham was born, *I am*').

A further important observation concerns the way in which this speech material in 8.12-59 often follows a tripartite pattern of statement–misunderstanding–explanation. There are five instances of this literary pattern (Leroy 1968: 45-47, 53-67):

1. 32-37

Statement:	'You will know the truth, and the truth will set you free.'
Misunderstanding:	'...How can you say that we shall be set free?'
Explanation:	The parable of the slave and the son

2. 38-40

Statement:	'You do what you have heard from your father.'
Misunderstanding:	'Abraham is our father.'
Explanation:	'If that were so you would behave like Abraham.'

3. 41-47

Statement:	'You are doing the things your own father does.'
Misunderstanding:	'We are not illegitimate children.'
Explanation:	Your misunderstanding shows that the devil is your father.

4. 51-55

Statement:	'If a man keeps my word, he will never see death.'
Misunderstanding:	Abraham and the prophets died. Who do you think you are?
Explanation:	'My Father...is the one who glorifies me.'

5. 56-58

Statement:	'Abraham rejoiced at the thought of seeing my day.'
Misunderstanding:	'You are not 50 years old...and you have seen Abraham!'
Explanation:	'Before Abraham was born, I am.'

Form

John 8.12-59 is another example of a 'trial scene' (Lincoln 1993). This description derives from form-critical studies of Deutero-Isaiah (a text which has many intertextual resonances with John's story). In Deutero-Isaiah, trial scenes are used at 41.1-5, 41.21-29, 43.8-13, 44.6-8, 44.21-22 and 45.20-25 (Whybray 1983: 34-41). Their function is to answer the question, 'Who is the true God?' Isa. 43.8-13 is a good example:

8   Lead out those who have eyes but are blind, who have ears but are deaf.

9   All the nations gather together and the peoples assemble. Which of them foretold this and proclaimed to us the former things? Let them bring in their witnesses to prove they were right, so others may hear and say, 'It is true'.

10   'You are my witnesses', declares the Lord, 'and my servant whom I have chosen, so that you may know and believe me and understand that I am he. Before me no god was formed, nor will there be one after me.'

11   'I, even I, am the Lord, and apart from me there is no saviour'.

12   'I have revealed and saved and proclaimed—I, and not some foreign god among you. You are my witnesses', declares the Lord, 'that I am God'.

13   'Yes, and from ancient of days I am he. No one can deliver out of my hand. When I act, who can reverse it?'

There are several intertextual resonances between this trial scene and Jn 8.12-59. The following parallels with Isa. 43.8-13 are interesting:

a   The speaker takes on the role of judge (Yahweh in Isa. 43 and Jesus in Jn 8).

b   The context takes on the character of a law-suit.

c   The speaker's opponents are deemed to be blind and deaf (see Jn 8.43, 47, and see 9.35-41).

d   There is a concern to use 'former things' as evidence of the speaker's credentials (see Jn 8.56-58 and Jesus' use of Abraham).

e   The speaker identifies himself with the divine name, 'I am' (see Jn 8.12, 24, 28, 58).

f   There is a concern for truth (see Jn 8.32, 45-46), understanding (8.27), belief (8.30, 31) and knowledge (8.14, 19, etc).

g   There is a strong emphasis upon the importance of witnesses (see Jn 8.14-18).

If the form of Jn 8.21-59 is really that of the trial scene, then the implicit commentary throughout this text supports the narrator's defence of the divinity of Jesus and the concomitant satire of the diabolism of the Jews. Jesus takes on the role of Yahweh while the Jews take on the role of the false, pagan gods. This accounts for much of the irony in the chapter.

Rhetorical Analysis

A text which is so obviously forensic in character really calls for a rhetorical-critical as well as a narrative approach. Aristotle wrote that there are three species of rhetoric (*Rhetorica* 1.3.7-8): forensic (the legal oratory of the law court), political (also known as 'deliberative' oratory —used in parliamentary assemblies) and epideictic (the ceremonial oratory of display, used to praise or vilify someone). John 8.12-59 can be classed as judicial rhetoric because the language and imagery is thoroughly forensic in character. Aristotle wrote that 'Forensic speaking either attacks or defends somebody' (*Rhetorica* 1.3.10-11). This is clearly happening in Jn 8.12-59. Jesus is both defending himself and attacking his accusers.

There are three essential elements to rhetoric in general and judicial rhetoric in particular: a speaker, a person addressed and a subject or discourse (*Rhetorica* 1.3.2). In Jn 8.12-59, the speaker is Jesus, and he takes on the role of the defendant. The hearers are the Jewish social groups who take on the role of prosecutors. The subject is the paternity of Jesus.

The key thing about the speaker is what Aristotle calls *ethos*—the personal credibility which he or she establishes. In Jn 8.12-59, Jesus uses the following arguments to enhance his credibility:

12	'I am the light of the world.'
14	'I know where I came from and where I am going.'
16	'My decisions are right.'
18	'I am one who testifies for myself.'
21	'I am from above.'
24	'I am.'
28	'I am.' 'I speak what the Father has taught me.'
29	'I always do what pleases him.'
38	'I am telling you what I have heard in my Father's presence.'
40	I am 'a man who has told you the truth that I heard from God.'
42	'I came from God.'
45	'I tell the truth.'
49	'I honour my Father.'
51	'If a man keeps my word, he will never see death.'
54	'My Father...glorifies me.'
55	'I know him...and I keep his word.'
58	'Before Abraham was born, I am.'

In these assertions, Jesus establishes his credibility as defendant by stressing his dependence on God ('I speak what the Father has taught me'), his obedience to God ('I always do what pleases him'), his proximity to God ('I am from above'), his origin from God ('I came from God'), his unity with God (the use of 'I am'), and his likeness to God ('Before Abraham was born, I am').

Of critical importance are the absolute and predicative uses of the divine name, *egō eimi*. There are seven predicative 'I am' sayings in John's Gospel:

6.35, 51	'I am the bread of life.'
8.12 (9.5)	'I am the light of the world.'
10.7, 9	'I am the gate.'
10.11, 14	'I am the good shepherd.'
11.25	'I am the resurrection and the life.'
14.6	'I am the way, the truth and the life.'
15.1, 5	'I am the true vine'.

8.12 is the second of these. Furthermore, three of the four absolute uses of 'I am' are in ch. 8:

24	'If you do not believe that I am, you will indeed die in your sins.'
28	'When you have lifted up the Son of Man, then you will know that I am.'
58	'Before Abraham was born, I am.'

The fourth instance of the absolute use is in 13.19. The use of the divine name establishes, more than anything else, the *ethos* of Jesus' character.

The hearers whom Jesus is endeavouring to persuade are three hostile Jewish groups. These are the Pharisees (v. 13), the Jews (vv. 22, 48, 52, 57) and the Jews who had believed him (v. 31—presumably the group identified in 2.23-25). These three groups take on the role of prosecutors, as can be seen by the use of questions and accusations throughout the chapter. In all cases these are put forward by the three groups just mentioned:

19	'Where is your father?'
25	'Who are you?'
33	'How can you say that we shall be set free?'
48	'Aren't we right in saying that you are a Samaritan and demon-possessed?'
53	'Who do you think you are?'
57	'You are not yet fifty years old and you have seen Abraham!'

The irony of the chapter is the fact that Jesus himself becomes the prosecutor. Having begun a process of questioning and prosecuting Jesus, the three Jewish groups find themselves almost imperceptibly taking on the role of defendants. The old irony of the judged becoming the judge is played out here. This can be seen if we identify the judgments and accusations made by Jesus against the groups:

Pharisees

14	'You have no idea where I come from or where I am going.'
15	'You judge by human standards.'
19	'You do not know me or my Father.'
21	'You will die in your sin. Where I go you cannot come.'

The Jews

23	'You are from below.'
24	'You will indeed die in your sins.'
55	'You do not know the Father…you are liars.'

The Jews who had believed in him

37	'You have no room for my word.'
41	'You are doing the things your own father does.'
43	'You are unable to hear what I say.'
44	'You belong to the devil.'
45	'You do not believe me.'
47	'You do not belong to God.'

No wonder Jesus' hearers are depicted as experiencing what Aristotle called *pathos*, an emotional response to the speaker's forensic rhetoric. While the Pharisees show no visible response to the charges made against them, the Jews who had believed in Jesus are said to 'protest'

(v. 41). The Jews reveal a variety of responses. Some put their faith in him (v. 30). However, the text concentrates on the emotional response of those who reject Jesus. Theirs is one of misunderstanding (v. 27), indignation (v. 53) and violence (v. 59).

The reaction of the Jewish groups is largely traceable to the third aspect of the judicial rhetoric used by Jesus, his discourse. The critical feature of discourse, in Aristotle's view, is its *logos*, its logical argument. Jesus' use of logic in Jn 8.12-59 is forceful in its clarity and dogmatism. Jesus uses *paradeigmata* (examples) from Jewish history (Abraham, 8.33-58) and everyday life (for example, the short parable in 8.35) to support his argument. He uses the *gnōmē* or 'maxim' (e.g. 8.34) and some of his reasoning takes on the form of the syllogism (*epicheireme*—see the relentless progression from premise to conclusion in 8.31-41 and 8.42-47). Of importance to the *logos* of Jesus' arguments are his use of laws and witnesses. In the *Rhetorica*, Aristotle identifies five non-technical means of persuasion in forensic oratory: 'laws, witnesses, contracts, tortures, oaths' (1.15.3). While Jesus certainly avoids 'contracts, tortures, oaths', he does use 'laws' (8.14-18) and 'witnesses' (8.18, 56) throughout to make his case. These help to convince the reader of the truth of his claims.

Plot

If a rhetorical-critical approach uncovers some of the literary qualities in this chapter, so also does a structuralist approach. In the commentary on John 7 I used Greimas's actantial analysis as a means of illuminating the deep structure of the chapter. In John 8, an actantial approach to the narrative reveals the extent to which there is a development in the counter-plot in the Gospel (the conspiracy against Jesus). In John 7 we noted that the Sender figure was the chief priests and Pharisees, the Receiver figure was the Temple guards (who are sent to arrest Jesus). The Subject of the plot was the chief priests and the Pharisees and the Object of their quest was, at the very least, the interrogation of Jesus. The Helper figure was occupied by the Jews (who seemed to be taking on the role of 'fifth columnists' in the crowds), and the Opponent was of course Jesus himself. In John 8, what is worthy of note is the way in which the storyteller develops and clarifies this counter-plot. In John 8 a much wider perspective on the counter-plot develops, one which serves well the satirical purpose of the author.

In John 8 the Sender or Originator is no longer the chief priests and Pharisees, it is the devil. He is the 'originator' of the plot to kill Jesus. This emerges very clearly in 8.31-59 where Jesus tells the Jews who had believed in him that they are trying to kill him only because they are doing what their true father, the devil, has been doing since the beginning of the world.

If the devil is the Originator or Sender, the Jews (who had believed in him) are the Receivers. They are the ones who hear what their father, the devil, is saying and who attempt to put that 'commission' into effect. The Subject of the counter-plot is therefore now these Jews and the Object is the destruction of Jesus.

In the power struggle of this chapter, the Opponent of the Jews is quite obviously Jesus. The Helper figure does not emerge as yet. However, when we move into the Book of the Passion at the start of John 13, we shall see that Judas fulfils this function. As the Helper of the Jews he too will be seen as both prompted and possessed by the powers of darkness.

Seen as a whole, the counter-plot of the Gospel now looks like this:

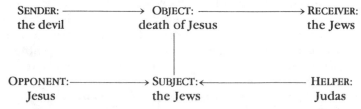

Seen in this light, we can detect something of the subtlety of John's satire of the Jews in his Gospel. What John has achieved in his counter-plot is a grim parody of what takes place in the main plot. The main plot involves a positive quest: the Father sending Jesus into the world to bring life. The counter-plot involves a negative quest: the devil (also depicted as a 'father') sending the Jews to kill the Giver of Life (note the paradox here). The ironic purpose of the author is revealed in this structuralist analysis. Such an approach to the text shows that the relationship between the devil and the Jews is a sinister imitation of the relationship between the Father and the Son. That is why the Jews only do what they hear their father, the devil, saying (8.38). Such a relationship mimics in a most sinister manner the Son's desire to hear his Father and to do only what he sees his Father doing (5.19).

John 9.1-41

Context

The progression from ch. 8 to ch. 9 is a smooth one. In ch. 8, Jesus declares, 'I am the light of the world' (8.12). Now, in ch. 9, that thought is developed as he provides two forms of illumination. At the literal and physical level, Jesus brings light to the eyes of the man born blind. In 9.6, Jesus spits on the ground, makes some mud with his saliva and puts it on the man's eyes. The man is told by Jesus to go and wash in the pool of Siloam. The narrator then laconically remarks: 'So the man went and washed, and came home seeing'. After many years of blindness, the man for the first time rubs his eyes and blinks in the sunlight.

At the metaphorical and spiritual level, Jesus brings illumination to the man's understanding. John 9 is an artfully constructed study of growing insight (the man born blind) and growing unbelief (the Pharisees/Jews). By the end of the story, the healed man has not only had his eyes literally opened, he has also experienced the ultimate vision of the eyes of faith. He has seen that Jesus of Nazareth is more than just a man, more even than a prophet. He has seen that Jesus is Son of Man and Lord. After many years of spiritual darkness, the man for the first time sees the light of God's revelation.

There is a subtlety about John's ordering of material. Narrative sections are ordered according to a thematic rationale. In other words, John is more interested in the juxtaposition of material which has thematic correspondences, and less interested in placing everything in an accurate chronological sequence. Thus, one reason for placing John 9 after John 8 is because the latter focuses on the theme of light. Another reason is because it picks up several of the themes in the implicit commentary of chs. 7 and 8. These chapters describe debates during the feast of Tabernacles. As we have seen, this feast contained rituals to do with water and light. Both these images re-emerge in ch. 9. Jesus repeats that he is the light of the world. Furthermore, the setting of the miracle itself is the pool of Siloam, whose waters were used in the daily liturgy at Tabernacles. The literary context of John 9 is therefore established according to an artistic design.

Form

The form of ch. 9 is very similar to that of ch. 5. As we have already noted, there seem to be a number of different literary forms of miracle story used by the author. There are the Cana signs, the Galilean sea miracles and the Jerusalem 'works'. The two Jerusalem 'works' are closely related as the following parallels reveal:

	Chapter 5		Chapter 9
5	The man's history (38 years)	1	The man's history (blind from birth)
8	The man is one of the socially marginalized	8	The man is one of the socially marginalized
6	Jesus initiates the healing	6	Jesus initiates the healing
2	The setting of the miracle is a pool (Bethesda)	7	The setting of the miracle is a pool (Siloam)
2	The setting is Jerusalem	7	The setting is Jerusalem
9	The miracle happens on the Sabbath	14	The miracle happens on the Sabbath

9b	Jesus slips out of the picture	8	Jesus slips out of the picture
10	Sabbath-violation charge	16	Sabbath-violation charge
12	The Jews interrogate the man	15	The Jews interrogate the man
13	Jesus' whereabouts are unknown by the man	12	Jesus' whereabouts are unknown by the man
14	Jesus reappears to find the man	35	Jesus reappears to find the man
14	The relationship between suffering and sin is explored	3	The relationship between suffering and sin is explored
16	The miracle results in a kind of trial (of Jesus)	13- 34	The miracle results in a kind of trial (of the man)
17	The miracle is described as a 'work' (*ergon*)	4	The miracle is described as a 'work' (*ergon*).

Structure

There are few chapters in John's Gospel composed with more structural expertise than this one. Here the author departs from the fivefold structure which we have seen so often (frequently in a chiastic arrangement) and creates more variety with a sevenfold plan. John 9 is composed as follows (Duke 1985: 118):

A^1	1-7	The dialogue between Jesus and the disciples
B^1	8-12	The dialogue between the blind man and his neighbours
C^1	13-17	The dialogue between the Pharisees and the blind man
D	18-23	The dialogue between the Jews and the blind man's parents
C^2	24-34	The dialogue between the Pharisees and the blind man
B^2	35-38	The dialogue between Jesus and the blind man
A^2	39-41	The dialogue between Jesus and the Pharisees

The chiastic pattern emerges once we recognize the thematic parallels between the related units. For example, A^1 and A^2 share the themes of blindness, sin and the world. These words (*tuphlos, hamartia, kosmos*) create a sense of inclusio involving the beginning and the end of the narrative. B^1 and B^2 are related: in B^1 Jesus disappears from the scene; in B^2 he reappears on stage. Both units are concerned with narrative focus and the presence of Jesus. C^1 and C^2 are obviously parallel: they form the first and second interrogation of the blind man by the Pharisees. In both units the overarching issue is whether or not Jesus is a sinner (because he has performed the miracle on the Sabbath). This leaves unit D as the centrepiece of the chapter.

Why should D be given the greatest structural emphasis? Here we need to bear in mind the social function of John's narrative. Johannine scholars since the 1960s have been proposing that the Fourth Gospel was completed towards the end of the first century after John's original readers had been expelled from the synagogues because of their Christology. After about 85 CE, Jewish Christians were banned from the synagogues if they openly confessed Jesus as the Messiah. The process of excommunication probably took the form of a trial and resulted in

alienation from non-Christian family members. It almost certainly made
Christian discipleship a fearful experience.

The author places 9.18-23 at the centre of his story because it echoed
the recent, traumatic experience of the original readers of the Gospel. In
this unit, the family members of the man born blind are summoned by
the Jews as witnesses. They refuse to answer the question, 'Who healed
your son?' The reason given by the narrator is as follows: 'His parents
said this because they were afraid of the Jews, for already the Jews had
decided that anyone who acknowledged that Jesus was the Christ
would be put out of the synagogue'.

This is the only point in the chapter where the narrator's voice
becomes intrusive, where the narrative turns for a moment from
'showing' to 'telling'. This is a sure sign that the unit is the focal point.
Notice the word 'already' in v. 22. The narrator is saying, to his ostra-
cized readership, 'Even in Jesus' ministry itself you could be excommunicated from the synagogue (*aposunagōgos*) for confessing Jesus as
the Messiah. Even in Jesus' ministry people were afraid of the Jewish
hierarchy.' In the light of these remarks, we can begin to see why 9.18-
23 forms the structural centre of the chapter.

Characterization

a. The Man Born Blind. The protagonist of the story is the man born
blind. As far as the original readers of the story are concerned (the
Johannine community), his character takes on heroic proportions. Once
he is thrown out by the Pharisees (*exebalon auton exō*) in 9.34, he
becomes the paradigmatic Christian—the epitome of the original readers'
experience of expulsion from the synagogues.

The greatest part of the narrative is given to the development of the
protagonist's character. Over one quarter of the chapter is the direct
speech of the man born blind (Resseguie 1979: 296). Note the progression in the man's confessions of faith (Brown 1966: I, 377). In 9.11
he refers to Jesus as 'the man they call Jesus'. In v. 17 he confesses that
Jesus is 'a prophet'. In v. 33 he emphasizes that Jesus must be 'from
God'. In v. 38 he confesses Jesus as 'Lord' and indirectly as 'Son of
Man'. Like the Samaritan woman in 4.4-42, the reader is witness to a
growth of faith and understanding in a minor character.

Most impressive of all is the vitality of the blind man. His stubborn
refusal to give way to the perverse denial on the part of his accusers is
noteworthy: 'Whether he is a sinner or not, I don't know. One thing I
do know. I was blind, but now I see!' (v. 25). His sarcasm in v. 27 is also
suggestive of vitality: 'Why do you want to hear it again? Do you want
to become his disciples too?' The manner in which he reminds the
authorities of some basics of Jewish theology ('We know that God does
not listen to sinners', v. 31) is heavily ironic. Notice also the use of

parody in the 'we know' of v. 31. Here the blind man mimics the use of the same verbal construction on the lips of the Pharisees in v. 24. All these aspects of his character add to the heroic stature of a man who should have been the 'underdog'. One can almost hear the original readers cheering as the narrative progresses from v. 24 to v. 34.

In evaluating this portrait, it is interesting to use some categories of E.M. Forster. It has become customary in recent years for literary critics of the Gospels to use Forster's theory of characterization from his *Aspects of the Novel* (1962). I have alerted readers to two problems with this in my book *John as Storyteller* (1992: 8, 11, 24-25). First of all, we should remember that the characters of John's story are historical, not fictional. This meant that it is not always easy to use 'aspects of the novel' in analyzing them. Secondly, Forster's clear-cut distinction between 'flat characters' (cardboard cut-outs with no development) and 'round characters' (characters with depth of personality, life and development) does not take into account a peculiar feature of John's minor characters: the fact that some of them are simultaneously 'flat' and 'round', stereotypical and developed.

The characterization of the protagonist in John 9 provides a good example of the difficulties with Forster's terminology. The man born blind is, in some senses, a 'flat character'. He only appears here and seems (as we shall see later) to be a stereotype of the Christian in John's community whose situation is summed up in the word *aposunagōgos*. However, the traits which I have outlined above, coupled with the character development implied within his confessions of Jesus, give us some grounds for calling the blind man a 'round character'. Readers of John's story should therefore be cautious of using categories from novelistic literature when evaluating subjects such as the man born blind. Here is a character who exhibits life and depth without any of the psychological insights provided by the narrator of modern novels.

b. Jesus. We have already spotted the tendency in John's story to have Jesus as the centre of controversy (see Jn 5.1-15) even when he is off-stage. This is certainly the case here. The narrative focuses on the role of Jesus in vv. 1-7 where he plays the part of miracle worker. From v. 8 onwards it is the man born blind who is in the centre of the action. Jesus does not enter on stage again until v. 35. However, in all the time between his unannounced exit and his highlighted reappearance, Jesus is the subject of the controversy. In v. 11 he is referred to as 'the man they call Jesus'. In v. 14 the narrator refers to him. In vv. 15-17 he is the subject of the dialogue between the Pharisees and the blind man. In vv. 24-34 he is the subject of their second dialogue. Clearly the narrator is employing the device of 'focus' in such a way as to leave Jesus in the centre of the reader's thinking even when he is not physically present in the narrative world of the Gospel.

The two major facets of Jesus' characterization in John 9 are his elusiveness and his function as judge. Concerning the former, notice the interesting juxtaposition between 8.59 and 9.1:

8.59	At this, the Jews picked up stones to stone him, but Jesus hid himself, slipping away from the Temple grounds.
9.1	As he went along, Jesus saw a man blind from birth.

The startling contrast between the necessary furtiveness of Jesus' behaviour in 8.59, and his open movements (*kai paragōn*) in 9.1 highlight that mysterious ability which Jesus has throughout the story to walk in and out of situations of danger without difficulty. This enigmatic evasiveness is further emphasized by the way in which Jesus slips in and out of the focus of both characters and readers in John 9. When the neighbours ask, 'Where is this man?' this elusiveness becomes apparent again.

The main purpose behind John's portrait of Jesus here is to present him as judge. There is a sense in which Jesus is on trial with the blind man in vv. 13-34. Though it is the blind man who is accused and thrown out, it is Jesus' status as 'a man from God' or 'a sinner' which is the issue at stake. However, the by now customary role reversal in which the judged is revealed as judge takes place in vv. 39-41. In the *dénouement* of the story, the accused states: 'For judgment (*krima*) I have come into this world' (v. 39). Jesus then pronounces judgment on his accusers: 'Your guilt remains' (v. 41). Much of the irony of the story derives from Jesus' ability to function as judge even when he is apparently in the dock.

c. The Pharisees and Jews. The antagonists are referred to as 'the Pharisees' in v. 13, 15, 16 and 40, and as 'the Jews' in v. 18 and 22. It is interesting that the narrator switches to *hoi Ioudaoi* in the narrative unit which resonates most powerfully with the real readers' historical circumstances. This may indicate that the hostile use of phrase 'the Jews' functions as a signal in the text that the author is addressing contemporary issues in the Johannine church.

The characteristic of both these groups (who are intimately related to each other, as we have noted in chs. 7 and 8) is unbelief. Their judgment about Jesus is that he is a sinner because he has broken various Sabbath regulations in healing the blind man. The first words of v. 18 sum up their mind-set. The narrator says, *ouk episteusan*—'they did not believe'. This unbelief is expressed in a number of statements which they make about Jesus. Just as there is a progressive nature about the blind man's confessions, so there is a progressive nature about those made by the Pharisees/Jews. This time, however, the progression is negative rather than positive. While the blind man's eyes are gradually opened to the real identity of Jesus, the Pharisees/Jews become progressively blind about him. They begin with, 'This man is not from God, for he does not keep the Sabbath' (v. 16). They then proceed to call him 'a sinner' (v. 24). Finally, they proclaim, 'We don't even know where he comes from' (v. 28). These statements mark them out as the truly blind people in the story (v. 41) and as the true sinners, because the essence of sin in John is unbelief about Jesus.

d. The Disciples. The group called *hoi mathētai* here are not the Galilaean followers of Jesus but rather the Judaean disciples mentioned by the brothers of Jesus in 7.3. There the brothers say, 'You ought to leave here and go to Judea, so that your disciples may see the miracles you do'. Since Jesus goes to Judea secretively and on his own, the disciples mentioned in 9.2 must be seen as this Judaean group. The fact that Jesus in John 9 fulfils the very function urged by his brothers in 7.3 (performing a miracle for the encouragement of the Judaean disciples) seems to support this identification.

This Judaean group of disciples has been absent between 7.3 and 9.2. Between chs. 7 and 9 there are no references to the disciples of Jesus. Here in 9.2 the disciples function as the foils for the action of Jesus and one of the subsequent arguments of the chapter ('who or what is a sinner?'). They ask, 'Rabbi, who sinned, this man or his parents, that he was born blind?' From this moment, the Judaean disciples disappear from the chapter. This shows how they merely function as foils to Jesus.

e. The Parents. The only other characters in the story are the parents of the man born blind. They feature in the central section of the narrative. Their main character traits are their fear of the Jews and their lack of love for their son. In v. 22, the parents abdicate their responsibility to stand by their son because, to quote the narrator, 'they were afraid of the Jews'. Thus they reject their son. In depicting the parents in this way, the author reminds the original readers that faith in Jesus involves, in extreme cases, alienation not only from the synagogue but also from the family.

Themes

Not surprisingly, the principal thematic words in John 9 all contribute to the main question of the story: 'Will the characters *see* who Jesus really is?' Thus we find many occurrences of the adjective 'blind' (*tuphlos*, vv. 1, 2, 13, 17, 20, 24, 25, 32, 39, 40), of the noun 'eye' (*ophthalmos*, vv. 6, 10, 11, 14, 15, 17-19, 21, 26, 30, 32), and of the verb 'see' (mainly *blepō*, vv. 7, 8, 15, 18, 19, 21, 25, 37, 39, 41). What is significant about these words is the way in which they are used to describe physical and spiritual realities. Thus, in v. 1 the narrator says that Jesus saw a man born blind (*tuphlos*). Here the word denotes physical blindness. In

v. 40, however, the Pharisees ask Jesus, 'What? Are we blind (*tuphloi*) too?' The same adjective now denotes spiritual blindness.

Other thematic words appear (works, vv. 3, 4; revelation, v. 3; sending, vv. 4, 7) but the remaining significant themes are knowledge, faith and sin. These are significant because they are closely related to the overarching theme concerning true sight. The verb 'to know' is found at vv. 12, 20, 21, 24, 25 and 29-31. Throughout the story knowledge and ignorance are related to sight and blindness. The verb 'believe' is found at vv. 18, 35, 36 and 38. Here again belief and unbelief are connected to sight and blindness. Perhaps the most noticeable theme related to the idea of 'true sight' concerns sin. The verb 'sin' and noun 'sinner' occur at vv. 2, 3, 16, 24, 25, 31, 34 and 41. Indeed, there is more discussion about sin in ch. 9 than in the entire Gospel so far. The point being made is that the Pharisees/Jews see sin as breaking (in this instance) Sabbath laws, whereas the protagonist and the narrator see sin as unbelief about Jesus.

Contrasts

Throughout the Gospel, the narrator presents bold antitheses to the reader. In structuralist terms, he or she is constantly weaving significant binary oppositions into the text. This formal technique could be described as *schisma*. This is the word translated 'division' in v. 16 ('there was a division in them'). In this instance, the contrast is between the Pharisees who say, 'This man is not from God', and those who say, 'How can a sinner do such miraculous signs?' However, the most obvious *schismata* are between sight and blindness, light and darkness, day and night. These divisions are established as the foundational symbols of the story in 9.1-5. They are represented to the reader in character form in the antithesis between the man born blind (a symbol of those who see, know and believe) and the Pharisees/Jews (a symbol of those who are blind, ignorant and unbelieving).

Irony

John 9 provides us with some fine examples of irony. Throughout the story, the continuing irony is that the blind man, professing his ignorance, is really the character 'in the know', while the Pharisees/Jews, parading their knowledge, are in reality ignorant. Closely related to this is the ironic truth that the man born blind has more sight by the end of the story (certainly at the spiritual level) than those characters born with unimpaired vision.

These ironies are developed in the satire of the Pharisees in vv. 24-34. This satire derives entirely from the statements made by the Pharisees in their interrogation of the man born blind. When they summon the man a second time, they say, 'Give glory to God'. It is likely that the phrase,

'Give glory (*doxa*) to God' was originally an oath sworn by a witness. However, its meaning in John 9 is deeply ironic. We have learnt as early as 2.11, that the signs (*sēmeia*) of Jesus reveal God's glory (*doxa*). In 9.16, the author departs from the normal word for miracles in ch. 9 (*erga*) to describe the blind man's healing as a sign (*sēmion*). When the Pharisees say, 'Give glory to God', the reader is supposed to notice that glory has already been witnessed through the miracle itself.

Perhaps the most savage irony is reserved for the very end of the story where the Pharisees ask, 'Are we blind too?' Here the author uses the literary technique of the unanswered question, used with great ironic effect already in the Gospel (Culpepper 1983: 176):

1.46	Can anything good come from Nazareth?
4.12	Are you greater than our father Jacob?
6.42	Is this not Jesus, the son of Joseph, whose father and mother we know?
6.52	How can this man give us his flesh to eat?
7.20	Who is trying to kill you?
7.26	Have the authorities really concluded that he is the Christ?
7.35	Where does this man intend to go that we cannot find him?
7.42	Does not the Scripture say that the Christ will come from David's family and from Bethlehem, the town where David lived?
7.48	Has any of the rulers of the Pharisees believed in him?
8.53	Are you greater than our father Abraham?

The irony of these questions is the fact that, in most of the instances, the speaker is expecting the answer 'no', while the reader knows that the answer is 'yes'. This is particularly true of Jn 9.40, 'Are we blind too?'

Implicit Commentary

This analysis of John's use of themes, symbolism and irony show us something of the secret communication going on between the narrator and the reader. Perhaps the richest aspect of the implicit commentary in this chapter relates to the symbolic identity and function of the man born blind. At the level of carnal sense (Kermode 1979: 1), the man is the recipient of a healing miracle, followed by a trial, followed by a faith-encounter with Jesus. However, at the level of secret sense, he is far more than that. He is presented as a narrative hero with some of the characteristics of Jesus himself. Thus, when the blind man's identity is questioned by the neighbours, he insists, 'I am the man' (v. 9). The Greek here is '*egō eimi*', which we have already identified as the divine name, when found on the lips of Jesus. Obviously the reader is not supposed to think of the blind man as divine, as possessing a status similar to that of Jesus. However, the phrase on the lips of the blind man is a surprise to the reader. It shows that the man is speaking, like the narrator, in the same idiom as Jesus.

This identity between the blind man's idiom and that of Jesus is brought out in vv. 24-34. Here we see the blind man doing to the Pharisees what Jesus in John 3 did to Nicodemus. First of all, the blind man imitates the sarcasm of Jesus. In the Nicodemus narrative, Jesus says, 'You are Israel's teacher, and do you not understand these things?' In 9.30 the blind man says, 'You don't even know where he comes from, yet he opened my eyes'.

Secondly, the blind man imitates Jesus' rhetorical tactics in confounding Nicodemus; in particular, the way Jesus takes hold of Nicodemus's way of speaking and uses it for satirical effect. In ch. 3 we heard Nicodemus confidently assert, 'We know you are a teacher come from God' (v. 2). Jesus then uses the expression 'we know' in order to expose Nicodemus: 'We speak of what we know'. In John 9, we see the blind man doing the same thing. The Pharisees confidently assert, 'We know this man is a sinner' (v. 24). The man then uses the expression 'we know' to expose the Pharisees: 'We know that God does not listen to sinners' (v. 31).

It is crucial to sense the narrative echo effects between John 3 and John 9 if we are to perceive the close identification between the blind man and Jesus. The purpose of this identification is to indicate that he is a model disciple. The essence of rabbinic discipleship can be summed up in the word 'imitation'. The pupil was expected to imitate the master. Here we see the blind man imitating the words of Jesus. We also see him experience the same things as Jesus (trial and rejection at the hands of the Pharisees/Jews). In portraying the blind man as like Jesus, the narrator is able to underline the authentic and paradigmatic nature of the blind man's discipleship.

But there is more than just this. We have suggested already how important it is to penetrate the communication going on in this story between the author and the original readers. Once we do that, we begin to see the man born blind as a representative of those who have been rejected by their family and by their culture for faith in Christ. The blind man, forsaken by his parents and expelled by the Jews, is a symbol of the Jewish element in John's readership, the *aposunagōgoi* (those excommunicated from the diaspora synagogues). The fact that he is portrayed with Christlike characteristics must have been a source of consolation for John's readers. It shows that their costly discipleship has been an authentic, Christian path. To use the terminology of the social sciences, it acts as a social legitimation of their past and present history.

Perhaps the most consoling feature of the story for the real readers must have been the sight of Jesus coming back to the man, indeed 'finding' (*heurōn*) him in 9.35. Here the reader is supposed to detect an antithesis between Jesus' acceptance of the man and the Pharisees' rejection of him. Indeed, the reader should recall Jn 6.37: 'Whoever comes to me I will never drive away' (*ekballō exō*, as in 9.34-35). This action helps to reinforce the sense of religious belonging in the community. John's readers, witnessing Jesus' return to the man, can know that they too will be embraced by the returning Jesus even if they are rejected by Judaism (see 14.3).

John 10.1-21

Context
In spite of appearances, there is a sense of sequence between the story of the man born blind and the shepherd discourse in John 10. There is an analepsis with John 9 in 10.21: 'Can a demon open the eyes of the blind?' Less obvious is the link between the characters in the *paroimia* in 10.1-19 and the characters in John 9. The conduct of Jesus in ch. 9 is that of the *kalos poimēn* (model shepherd). Having been ejected from the fold of Judaism, the blind man is sought and found by one who will even lay down his life for his sheep (10.14-19). Thus, Jesus in ch. 9 represents the epitome of true pastoral commitment. The behaviour of the Pharisees/Jews, however, is anti-pastoral. Having been given the privilege of pastoring the people of God, they show how incapable they are of acting out the role of 'shepherd' by ejecting a socially marginalized person from the synagogue. As such they invoke the polemic of Jesus in John 10: 'All who ever came before me were thieves and robbers, but the sheep did not listen to them' (v. 8).

Form
The form of the passage is predominantly discourse. There are minimal intrusions into this direct speech by the narrator. The intrusions are:

6   Jesus used this figure of speech, but they did not understand what he was telling them.
7   Therefore Jesus said again...
19   At these words the Jews were again divided.
20   Many of them said...
21   But others said...

The narrator's comments in v. 7, 20 and 21 are intended merely to identify speakers in the debate. The intrusion at v. 19 is significant for thematic purposes, as we shall see in a moment. Most important of all is the narrator's aside in v. 6 because it identifies the form of the discourse as a 'figure of speech' (*paroimia*). A *paroimia* is to be understood as a symbolic word-picture with a cryptic meaning. It is essentially elusive discourse. Consequently 10.1-19 should be regarded as an enigmatic word-picture while vv. 19-21 function as a summary statement, describing the reactions of the Jews.

Structure

10.1-21 is carefully constructed. Like every other literary unit of the Gospel which we have so far analysed, it shows evidence of artistic design. 10.1-21 has a tripartite pattern. The first unit is vv. 1-6, which presents the basic *paroimia* and its characters (shepherd, thief, robber, watchman, sheep, stranger), setting (sheepfold, gate) and action (the thief and robber climb over the wall of the fold; the shepherd passes freely in and out of the gate; the watchman opens the gate for him; the sheep follow him; they do not follow a stranger). The unit ends with the narrator's aside in v. 6.

The second unit begins with the first 'I am' saying in v. 7: 'I tell you the truth, I am the gate for the sheep'. Verses 7-10 form the first of two sub-sections in this second unit. The theme of this sub-section becomes evident in the repetition of the 'I am' saying at v. 9: 'I am the gate'. Jesus is the gate to life in all its fulness.

The second sub-section of this second unit embraces vv. 11-18. The metaphor now changes focus. Having highlighted his function as the 'gate' for the sheep in vv. 7-10, Jesus now focuses on his role as the model shepherd of the sheep. Again there are two 'I am' sayings in this sub-section, as in vv. 7-10. At v. 11 and v. 14, Jesus says, 'I am the good shepherd', and the recurrent theme of this unit is the voluntary self-sacrifice of the shepherd. Four times (vv. 11, 15, 17, 18) Jesus says that he lays down his life for the sheep.

The third unit is vv. 19-21. These verses portray the responses of the Jews to the *paroimia*. Verse 20 depicts the negative reaction: 'He is demon-possessed and raving mad. Why listen to him?' Verse 21 gives the positive response: 'These are not the sayings of a man possessed by a demon. Can a demon open the eyes of the blind?'

Overall the structure looks like this:

Unit 1	1-6	The shepherd *paroimia*
Unit 2	a. 7-10	Development of the *paroimia*, Jesus as gate
	b. 11-18	Development of the *paroimia*, Jesus as good shepherd
Unit 3	19-21	Responses to *paroimia*: a. negative, b. positive

Characterization

Jesus' character is indicated entirely by direct speech in 10.1-21. Jesus describes himself as the gate through which his sheep can find pasture and at the same time the good shepherd who will lead them in and out of the gate. The reader should note the prominence of boundaries in Jesus' imagery here. Jesus is the threshold to life in all its fullness (Jn 10.10). He is the shepherd who is prepared, of his own volition, to cross the threshold of death. The focus on boundaries in Jesus' pastoral language indicates that he is a Saviour who lives at the limits of human experience for the sake of those who follow him.

Jesus is again portrayed as the elusive Christ, this time in two respects: his use of the *paroimia* indicates his evasive use of language—if Jesus is trying to promote his own pastoral role, and to condemn the Jews for their lack of pastoral care, this is an indirect and oblique way of doing it; secondly, Jesus' statement in v. 18 that no one can take his life from him partly explains why his enemies have not been able to kill him up until now. His elusiveness is due to his authority (*exousia*, v. 18).

Consistent with the presentation of Jesus' elusiveness is the portrayal of the misunderstanding of the Jews in v. 6. Jesus delivers the *paroimia* and the Jews are said not to understand it. His language is much too elusive for them. They cannot penetrate its secret sense and, unlike the reader, they are deaf to its implicit commentary. Their confusion is further indicated by the *schisma* or division (v. 19) in their ranks. Many make the perverse claim that Jesus is demonized. Others, baulking at the logic of this, object that demons do not open blind peoples' eyes.

Themes

These remarks about the Jews highlight one of the main themes in this passage, the division among the Jews. This is the third time in the second section of chs. 1–12 that the narrator has alerted us to the *schisma* among the Jews:

7.43   Thus the people were divided because of Jesus.
9.16   So they were divided.
10.19   At these words the Jews were again divided.

10.19 reminds the reader of the divisive nature of God's revelation in Christ.

Other themes in 10.1-21 are: following Jesus (*akoulotheō* in vv. 4, 5), knowledge (*ginōskō/horaō*, vv. 4-6, 14, 15), listening (*akouō*, vv. 3, 8, 16), voice (*phōnē*, vv. 3-5, 16), life (*zōē*, v. 10), 'his own' (*ta idia*, vv. 3, 4, 12; recalling the *ta idia* of 1.11). The reader should also note the thematic *entolē* (command) in v. 18. This is a favourite word of John's occurring eleven times, particularly in the farewell discourses (chs. 14–17). There are two main uses of *entolē* in the Fourth Gospel, one referring to the command given by the Father to the Son, the other referring to that given by the Son to his disciples. In 10.18 we have the first reference to the Father's commandment to the Son.

Prolepsis

The entire section strikes an ominous note in the plot of the Gospel. The hostility of the Jews has reached the point where Jesus' life is in danger.

The narrator has made repeated allusions throughout chs. 7–8 to the attempts of the Pharisees and Jews to seize or stone Jesus. On each occasion Jesus has proved elusive because, as the narrator has reminded us, Jesus' appointed hour has not yet arrived. Now, in 10.1-21, the reader senses the imminence of the hour of Jesus. Much in this section seems to act as a proleptic warning of the passion. The characters in the *paroimia*, as we shall see in our approach to Jn 18.1-27, perform actions which will be enacted by characters in the arrest and trial of Jesus. The fourfold reference of Jesus to the voluntary laying down of his life also functions as a narrative prolepsis of the passion. Truly, the wolf (*lukos*, v. 12) is at the door.

John 10.22-39

Context

The mood of the story has now changed. The sense of impending doom in 10.1-21 is now heightened by the atmospheric statement of the narrator in v. 22, *cheimōn ēn*, 'it was winter'. From the springtime of Passover (ch. 2 and ch. 6) and the autumn of Tabernacles (ch. 7) we now come to the winter of Dedication.

All this points again to the importance of the feasts in John's story. Here the context is the feast of Dedication, the fifth of six references to the Jewish feasts in the plot of John's story:

2.13	When it was almost time for the Jewish Passover...
5.1	Some time later, Jesus went up to Jerusalem for a feast of the Jews.
6.4	The Jewish Passover feast was near.
7.2	But when the Jewish feast of Tabernacles was near...
10.22	Then came the feast of Dedication at Jerusalem.
11.55	When it was almost time for the Jewish Passover...

(Notice the additional references to the sixth feast at 11.56; 12.12, 20; 13.1, 29).

The reader should note three other important features concerning the context. First of all, there is a close link with 10.1-21 in that the pastoral metaphor is carried over into 10.22-39. Here again Jesus uses the diction of the shepherd discourse. In v. 26 he says to the Jews, 'you are not my sheep'. In v. 27 he repeats aspects of the *paroimia*: 'My sheep listen to my voice; I know them, and they follow me'.

Secondly, the theme of Jesus' elusiveness (a characteristic of chs. 5–10) is continued in 10.22-39. In v. 31 the narrator states, 'Again the Jews picked up stones to stone him'; in v. 39 he or she says, 'Again they tried to seize him, but he escaped their grasp'. The key word in these two statements is the word 'again'. The narrator is establishing a continuity between these two attempts on Jesus' life and the ones that have preceded them (5.18; 7.30, 32, 44; 8.20, 59).

Thirdly, the setting of the story in 10.22-39 is the Temple, specifically the Temple courts (*en tō hierō*, v. 23). 10.22-39 describes the last occasion in the Gospel on which Jesus teaches in the Temple area. Previously we have seen similar settings at 2.13-22; 5.14; 7.14-44; 8.12-59. There is an inclusio intended between the first unit of the second section of the Book of Signs (chs. 5–10) and this concluding unit. In 5.2 we have an architectural allusion to 'colonnades' near the pool of Bethesda in Jerusalem. In 10.23 we have an architectural allusion to the 'colonnades' of Solomon in the Temple courts. Yet again, the storyteller links the opening and closure of a narrative section in a most subtle way.

Form and Structure

The form of this passage is again predominantly forensic discourse. Trial features are suggested by the use of interrogation, by the use of *martureō* (to testify) in v. 25, by the legal evidence of the miracles and by the introduction of the blasphemy charge in 10.33 and 36—a charge which will feature in the passion narrative (19.7). The presence of legal overtones links this discourse particularly with 5.19-47, 7.14-44 and 8.12-59—the three trial scenes prior to 10.22-39.

Urban Von Wahlde has also suggested that there are formal and theological similarities between 10.22-39, 6.31-59 and 8.13-59 (1984: 575-77). All three discourses have the same form and content:

1. The Jews demand proof of Jesus' identity: 6.30; 8.25; 10.24.
2. Jesus tells them that they have already seen/heard but do not believe: 6.36; 8.25; 10.25.
3. Jesus gives the reason for their unbelief: 6.37; 8.47; 10.26.
4. Jesus speaks of those who do believe: 6.37; 8.47a; 10.27.
5. Jesus says that he does not lose any of those who are his: 6.39; 8.51; 10.28b.
6. Jesus says that those who do believe will have eternal life: 6.40; 8.35; 10.28a.

The important observation to make here is the fact that 10.22-39 has all six of these recurring elements in close succession. In many ways it functions as a summary of the arguments used in the discourses of section 2 of the Book of Signs.

Characterization

The elusiveness of Jesus is a dominant feature in John's characterization of his protagonist in chs. 5–10. In 10.22-39 this feature re-emerges in a forceful way. The Jews in v. 24 ask Jesus to speak 'plainly'. The word here is *parrēsia* which functions to emphasize both the elusiveness of Jesus' movements (he will not move about *parrēsia*, 'openly', 7.4) and the elusiveness of his language (Jesus does not always speak *parrēsia*, 'plainly', 16.29). In 10.24 it is the elusiveness of Jesus' language which is stressed. In 10.39 it is the elusiveness of his movements: 'Again they tried to seize him, but he escaped their grasp'.

In 10.22-39, however, it is the deity of Jesus which is the most evident charactcristic of his portrayal. The question which begins this narrative unit is, 'If you are the Christ, tell us plainly' (v. 24). After that, Jesus proceeds to give his legal defence. There is the evidence of the miracles which he does in his Father's name (v. 25), the evidence of the followers whom the Father has given him (vv. 27-29), the evidence of Scripture (vv. 34-36), the evidence of the unity of action between the Son and the Father (v. 37). All this gives him the right to make the most overt claim for his divine origin, identity and nature in v. 30: 'I and the Father are one!' That this is to be interpreted as a claim for ontological equality with God is evident from the reaction of the Jews in v. 31.

The Jews themselves are depicted as fulfilling the *theomachus* function in the narrative (the enemy of God). Throughout chs. 5–10 they have unwittingly been trying to commit deicide. Now in v. 31 they try again to stone Jesus. In 10.22-39 the perversity of their intense hostility is underlined through their lack of faith and their lack of knowledge. Their unbelief is stressed at vv. 25, 26, 37 and 38 (×2) through the verb *pisteuō*. Their ignorance is stressed at vv. 27 and 38 (×2) through the verb *ginōskō*. The latter is also highlighted by their lack of perception concerning the Law. They simply have not grasped the implications of their own Scriptures (in this case Ps. 82.6).

Implicit Commentary

The symbolism of the Temple is significant here. The feast is referred to as Dedication in v. 22. This immediately connotes the Temple because it was the Temple that was dedicated. Since the dedication of Jesus is a theme in 10.22-39, the implicit commentary is that Jesus is the ultimate fulfilment of OT ceremonial laws. In ch. 6 Jesus is revealed as the fulfilment of Passover ('I am the bread of life', 6.35). In John 7 and 8 Jesus is depicted as the fulfilment of Tabernacles ('If anyone is thirsty, let him come to me and drink', 7.37; 'I am the light of the world', 8.12). Now in 10.22-39 Jesus is depicted as the fulfilment of Dedication. As early as 2.13-22 the body of Jesus has been portrayed as the New Temple ('The Temple he had spoken of was his body', 2.21). Now in ch. 10 this symbolism is reinforced by Jesus' description of himself as 'the one whom the Father set apart as his very own' (10.36). Here the word 'set apart' (*hēgiasen*) denotes dedication, consecration. In the context of the Dedication of the Temple, this can only mean that Jesus is affirming that he is the absolute fulfilment of the Jewish cultus.

John 10.40-42

The second section of the Book of Signs now closes with Jesus withdrawing from Jerusalem to the place where the Baptist was ministering in the first chapter of the Gospel. This is a reference to the hitherto undiscovered Bethany of Perea (1.28), a rural village somewhere east of the Jordan river. Here Jesus stays (*menō*). Many people come to Jesus (*ēlthon pros auton*, a favourite Johannine periphrasis for conversion) and many are said to believe in him (*episteusan eis auton*).

It is important to uncover the contrast with the beginning of ch. 5, the first narrative unit of the section running to 10.42. The narrator pictures Jesus moving from the countryside (Cana, 4.46) towards Jerusalem in 5.1. In 10.40 he portrays Jesus moving away from Jerusalem back to the countryside. This should alert the reader to one of the major contrasts in John's story, between the country (place of faith) and the city (place of unbelief). It is particularly noticeable in 10.40-42 that we have faith in Jesus highlighted in a rural context. This is patently different from the unbelief which Jesus' opponents have manifested throughout chs. 5–10.

Throughout John's story so far, it has been the urban setting in which hostility, ignorance and unbelief have been the norm. In the city of Jerusalem, Jesus has stood alone against a backcloth of institutional religion which has become wholly opposed to him. In the rural contexts of Galilee, Judea, Samaria and Perea (10.40-42), however, the climate has been much more sympathetic:

Countryside				City	
1.19-51	Perea	Faith			
2.1-11	Galilee	Faith			
			2.13-22	Jerusalem	Unbelief
			3.1-21	Jerusalem	Misunderstanding
3.22-36	Judea	Faith			
4.4-42	Samaria	Faith			
4.46-54	Galilee	Faith			
			5.1-47	Jerusalem	Unbelief
6.25-70	Galilee	Faith of Twelve			
			7.1–10.39	Jerusalem	Unbelief
10.40	Perea	Faith			

In order to appreciate the narrator's conscious equation of rural settings with positive faith-responses, the reader should note the narrative echo effects between 10.40-42 (the conclusion of section 2 of the Book of Signs) and 4.40-41 (towards the conclusion of section 1). The two narratorial summaries, side by side, look similar:

10.41-42	*4.40-41*
Here he stayed and many people came to him.	So when the Samaritans came to him, they urged him to stay with them, and he stayed two days.
They said, 'Though John never performed a miraculous sign, all that John said about this man was true'.	They said to the woman, 'We no longer believe just because of what you said; now we have heard for ourselves, and we know that this man really is the Saviour of the world' (v. 42).
And in that place many believed in Jesus.	And because of his words, many more became believers (v. 41).

This parallelism further highlights the contrast between the country (Samaria in ch. 4, Perea in ch. 10) and the city. It also underlines what an important contribution is made by the short postscript in 10.40-42.

John 11.1-44

Context
The second section of the Book of Signs extends from Jn 5.1 to Jn 10.42. With the narrative of the raising of Lazarus beginning at 11.1, a new section commences. This is the conclusion to the first book of the Gospel and extends from Jn 11.1 to Jn 12.50. Thus, the Book of Signs is structured as follows:

1.1-51	The introduction
2.1–4.54	The Cana to Cana itinerary
5.1–10.42	The Jerusalem to Jerusalem itinerary
11–12	The conclusion

The raising of Lazarus in 11.1-44 is a fitting climax to the Book of Signs. The following table demonstrates how it functions as the seventh and therefore perfect miracle in the ministry of Jesus:

1.	2.1-11	The wine miracle at Cana
2.	4.46-54	The healing of the official's son
3.	5.1-15	The healing at Bethesda
4.	6.1-15	The feeding of the five thousand
5.	6.16-21	The miraculous sea crossing
6.	9.1-41	The healing of the man born blind
7.	11.1-44	The raising of Lazarus

Notice the sense of contrast between the first and seventh sign. The first, in Cana, was conducted in the setting of a rural wedding. There the mood was festive. Now, in the last sign, there is a marked contrast. The context is the aftermath of Lazarus' death. Here the mood is funereal. This shows that the Jesus of John's Gospel is a deity who enters into the rites of passage experienced by human beings. He is the deity whose incarnate existence takes him right into the liminal or threshold experiences of birth, marriage and death.

John 11.1-44 is therefore an important narrative for our appreciation of the characterization of Jesus. It is also important for the reader's understanding of the plot of the whole Gospel. While in the synoptics it is the cleansing of the Temple which proves to be the decisive factor in determining Jesus' fate, in John's story the same event is placed at the very beginning of the Gospel narrative. In John it is the raising of Lazarus which proves to be the last straw for the hostile Jewish hierarchy. The immediate aftermath of this narrative will see Caiaphas and the Sanhedrin formally convening in order to plot Jesus' death.

Form

The story of Lazarus is the only resurrection miracle in the Fourth Gospel. It is unique in many respects.

Miracle	Text	Formal Similarities with Other Miracles
The first sign at Cana	2.1-11	4.46-54: Request–rebuke–response structure, setting in Cana, description as *sēmeion*
The second sign at Cana	4.46-54	2.1-11: Request–rebuke–response structure, setting in Cana, description as *sēmeion*
The healing of the crippled man	5.1-15	9.1-41: Setting in Jerusalem, pool followed by trial scene
The feeding of the 5000	6.1-15	6.16-21: The setting (Sea of Galilee) and context (6.1-15 and 6.16-21 are juxtaposed)
The crossing of the sea	6.16-21	6.1-15: The setting (sea of Galilee) and context (6.16-21 follows directly after 6.1-15)

The healing of the man born blind	9.1-41	5.1-15: Setting in Jerusalem, pool followed by trial scene
The raising of Lazarus	11.1-44	No obvious parallels

Plot

Another feature which distinguishes this story is its plot. Looking at the beginning, the middle and the end of the Lazarus narrative, the following plot sequence is discernible:

Beginning: Jesus is told of Lazarus' illness but delays his journey to Bethany (vv. 1-16).

Middle: Jesus arrives at Bethany and speaks with Martha and Mary outside the village (vv. 17-37).

End: Jesus comes to the tomb and raises Lazarus from the dead (vv. 38-44).

The distinctive feature about the plot sequence here is the way in which the miracle itself takes place at the end of the story. In the two Cana miracles (Jn 2.1-11; 4.45-54) the miracles take place in the middle of both stories. The same could be said for the two Galilaean miracles (Jn 6.1-15, 16-21). In Jerusalem (Jn 5.1-15; 9.1-41) the two miracles take place at the beginning. The plot sequence of the Lazarus narrative is unique in John's Gospel because the miraculous resuscitation of Lazarus is the final act in the story.

Another characteristic of the plot of Jn 11.1-44 is the way in which the narrator uses process time. The emplotment of narrative events involves placing them in a temporal sequence. In the case of the Lazarus episode, the first part of the story involves a period of about four days (11.1-16). The second and third parts of the story involve a period of minutes. There is thus a noticeable imbalance between the first part of the narrative, and the second and third parts. This imbalance, interestingly, is true of the Gospel as a whole. The first book (chs. 1–12) depict a period of between two and three years. The second book (chs. 13–21) depict a period of under two weeks. Consequently, something of the overall plot shape of the Gospel is imitated in the temporal emplotment of the Lazarus episode.

This is further borne out if we submit the Lazarus narrative to an actantial, structuralist analysis. Using structuralist terminology, we can see that the Sender figures in the story are the two sisters Mary and Martha, who literally *send* for Jesus. He is the Receiver, and the Object of the narrative 'commission' given to him is to bring health and life to their brother Lazarus. The Opponent of Jesus in the story is not easy to discern. The Jews are remarkably non-confrontational in 11.1-44 and even seem to participate with sincerity in the mourning process. From the reaction of Jesus outside the tomb, however—where he is visibly troubled and even angry—it would appear that the Opponent role of the narrative is not a person but rather that which has destroyed Lazarus and saddened his loved ones, namely death. The Helper figure in the narrative is also unclear. The mourners help Jesus to find the tomb but they do not help him to perform the miracle. The Father could be said to be Jesus' Helper, and yet the prayer which Jesus prays seems to be for the benefit of the bystanders and not a request for help. Altogether, the deep structure of Jn 11.1-44 looks like this:

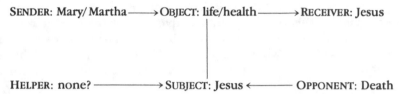

What is important about this deep structure is the way in which it has some parallels with the deep structure of the Gospel as a whole, where Jesus is also the one sent, where he is also apparently short of helpers, and where the object of his mission is to bring life into a world of sin and death. This reinforces the impression noted above that something of the shape and character of the whole Gospel is being intimated in the plot of the Lazarus episode.

Plot-Type

A final indication of this sense of 'hologrammatic' conformity (the part imitating the whole) is the way in which the plot-type of the Lazarus narrative reflects the plot-type of the whole Gospel. The Gospel as a whole has a U-shaped plot. It begins on a comic and romantic note (John 2–4), proceeds into a satirical phase (John 5–10), then on into a tragic sequence (the farewell of Jesus and his death in John 13–19) before returning to the comic and even romantic note with which we started (the resurrection in John 20–21). In Northrop Frye's (1971) terminology, the U-shaped plot of the Gospel (from happy beginning to happy ending) represents the *mythos* of spring.

If we begin in 10.40-42, we can see that the plot of Jn 11.1-44 begins on a very high note. Here the narrator reports that many believed in Jesus. Subsequently, there is a sense of descent into something far darker, much more tragic, as Jesus returns to a place of great danger (Judea) to weep over his friend's death. However, the story ends with a definite ascent into the comic (signalled by the theme of resurrection) as Jesus raises Lazarus and once again, many are said to believe in him (11.45). This U-shaped sequence functions as a microcosm of the plot structure of the story in its entirety.

Settings

Related to the creation of this plot sequence is the narrator's subtle use of narrative settings. At the beginning of the plot, Jesus is outside Judea. The challenge in vv. 1-16 is to go back to Judea (v. 8, 16). In the middle of the plot, Jesus is now outside Bethany. In vv. 17-37, this is made clear by the way in which Martha and Mary have to go out to Jesus (v. 20), and by the narrator's comment: 'Now Jesus had not yet entered the village, but was still at the place where Martha had met him'. At the end of the plot, Jesus is now outside the tomb. In v. 38, the narrator tells us that 'Jesus...came to the tomb'. By v. 38, the two objects of the focalization (Jesus and the tomb) are now fully 'in focus'.

Each phase of this plot sequence is dynamic; it includes a sense of movement from one place to another. The initial stance of Jesus in each phase is 'outside' somewhere. In phase 1, it is *outside Judea*. In phase 2, it is *outside Bethany*. In phase 3, it is *outside the tomb*. By means of focalization, the storyteller presents a progression from outside Judea, to outside Bethany, to outside the tomb. The tomb of Lazarus stands as the ultimate destination.

Characterization

a. Jesus. There are many aspects of Jesus' characterization in Jn 11.1-44 which are worthy of mention: his elusiveness (notice the way he delays his return to Judea), his humanity (weeping and the fact that he is 'deeply moved in spirit and troubled') and his divinity (by raising Lazarus from death, Jesus is seen doing something which, in traditional Jewish thought, only God had the authority and power to carry out). But one feature which has not been mentioned before is the way in which the characterization of Jesus has been designed in order to evoke what one might call a *liminal Christology*. The Jesus of John's Gospel is a Jesus who is prepared to stand at the limits. He is the God of the thresholds, the gateways. In Jn 10.7, one of the *egō eimi* sayings actually exploits this threshold imagery: 'I tell you the truth, I am the gate for the sheep'; then in 10.9: 'I am the gate; whoever enters through me will be saved. He will come in and go out and find pasture.'

In Jn 11.1-44, Jesus stands at the threshold of the tomb of his friend Lazarus. By standing at an entrance associated so obviously with suffering, mourning, sickness and death, Jesus is revealed as the God who is prepared to stand at the most extreme and painful of human experiences. Here Jesus stands at the threshold between life and death, between suffering and glory, pain and sleep. Something very important is being said about the incarnation in this gradual homing in on the tomb by Jesus. Through this artful use of plot, settings and characterization, John's Gospel shows that the Messiah is not aloof from the mystery and experience of human pain. He is not some mystical, neo-Platonic God who stands far beyond the harsh realities endured by those trapped within a frail mortality. This Jesus, the Son of God, is the deity who sheds tears, who feels anger, and who dares to look through the dark threshold of a place which he himself will have to enter. John's Gospel, in short, presents humanity with a potent, liminal Christology which consoles us in the face of our own human limits.

b. Disciples. Other characters in the story who should be mentioned are, first of all, the disciples. In chs. 5–10, it is always the Jews who are the victims of Johannine satire. It is they who come off the worst when the narrator uses the literary device of the *misunderstanding*. In 11.1-16, however, it is the disciples who manifest misunderstanding. They are portrayed as people who are unable to understand even the most transparent of metaphors. When Jesus uses the metaphor of sleep to talk about Lazarus' death (v. 11), the disciples respond with the same superficial literalism which the Pharisees and Jews have shown. They fail to understand a metaphor which was so common it was almost a cliché. They say, 'Lord, if he sleeps, he will get better' (v. 12). In what is essentially a comic story, the disciples function as the typical, ignorant buffoons.

c. Thomas. 11.16 is the first mention of Thomas in the Gospel. He is referred to as Thomas *Didymus* (twin). Thomas features in Jn 11.16, 14.5 and 20.24-29. His statement in 11.16 ('Let us also go, that we may die with him') reveals an element of misunderstanding. If Thomas really knew what kind of death was in prospect he would surely not have said this. His comments manifest naivete at best, insincerity at worst

d. Martha and Mary. The role of the two women in Jn 11.1-44 is crucial to the plot. Martha appears first. She goes out alone to meet Jesus and, like the Samaritan woman, is portrayed as one who grows in faith and understanding. In v. 21 she confesses an implicit faith in Jesus as healer by telling him that her brother would not have died if he had been present (v. 21). She then confesses her faith in Jesus as someone more than just a healer of the sick by saying, 'I know that even now God will give you whatever you ask' (v. 22). She goes on to assert, 'I know he will rise again in the resurrection at the last day' (v. 24). Jesus then guides her from a futuristic to a realized and personal eschatology by saying, 'I am the resurrection'. With this, traditional Jewish theology gives way to a true christological confession. Martha exclaims, 'I believe that you are the Christ, the Son of God, who was to come into the world'. With these words, Martha exhibits complete faith (20.31). She has moved from 'I know' (vv. 22, 24) to her climactic 'I believe' (v. 27).

At v. 28, Martha goes back and calls Mary. In performing these actions, she moves from confessor to witness. Like the Samaritan woman in 4.28, she begins to prove her discipleship by fetching some-one else and encouraging them to go to Jesus—in this case, Mary. Mary, Martha's sister, has been sitting at home. She gets up quickly and goes to the place where Martha had met Jesus. Jesus is still there. She falls at his feet and cries, repeating her sister's lament, 'Lord, if you had been here, my brother would not have died'. The pathos of her response is so intense that Jesus himself is said to weep. In portraying Mary's reactions in such an intense and natural way, the narrator shows a concern to depict characters not only as types of faith response but in the most realistic manner possible.

e. The Jews. The Jews appear in v. 33. The narrator refers to them as a group of people who have been mourning with Mary inside Lazarus' home. This comes as something of a shock to the reader after their rather unsympathetic behaviour hitherto. They show little concern for the crippled man in ch. 5 or the man born blind in ch. 9. Indeed, they expel the latter from the synagogue. Here, in complete contrast, they are portrayed alongside Mary in her grief. They are shown 'weeping' (v. 33). There seems, at last, to be something positive and distinctly humane about this portrait of the Jews. However, this impression is short lived. In vv. 36-37, the narrator returns to the now expected *schisma* of opinion among the Jews. Some say, 'See how much he loved him!' Others respond with sarcasm, 'Could not he who opened the eyes of the blind man have kept this man from dying?' (vv. 36-37).

f. Lazarus. Lazarus is one of those named individuals, like Nicodemus and Nathaniel, who are distinctive to John's story of Jesus. He is the focus of the action in John 11 even though he is dead! It is to his tomb that Jesus travels, risking his life. It is around Lazarus' death that the dia-logue revolves. It is his restoration to life which is the climax of the story. Within all this, Lazarus never says a word and only performs one action, his emergence from the tomb. His is an entirely passive role, yet much is made of him. He is the only character in the story thus far who is described in a positive, indeed intimate relationship with Jesus. Lazarus is beloved of Jesus. The narrator stresses this in v. 5. The Jews stress it in v. 36. Jesus himself stresses it in his description of Lazarus as 'our friend' (v. 11). Everywhere the narrator seems to be taking trouble to depict Lazarus as (to use an epithet which we shall see frequently in the Book of the Passion) the 'beloved disciple'.

Irony
The narrator uses the device of irony throughout the Lazarus story. The profoundest irony is the fact that Jesus' act of giving life leads to his life being taken away from him. The narrator is well aware of this irony

and woos the perceptive reader into this level of paradox by using the word *ekraugasen* in v. 43: 'Jesus called in a loud voice, "Lazarus, come out!"' This reference to Jesus shouting is a prolepsis of the passion, where the same word is used for the persistent shouting of the Jews for Jesus' death. In 18.40, the Jews are said to shout out (*ekraugasan*), 'Give us Barabbas!' In 19.6, we read that the chief priests and the officials see Jesus before Pilate. The narrator says, 'They shouted (*ekraugasan*), "Crucify him! Crucify him!"' In 19.12, Pilate tries to set Jesus free but is thwarted because, according to the narrator, 'the Jews kept shouting (*ekraugasan*)'. In 19.15, Pilate tells the Jews, 'Here is your king!' But 'they shouted (*ekraugasan*)..."We have no king but Caesar!"' These four shouts for death are intended by the reader as an ironic contrast with Jesus' shout for life in 11.43. They point to the paradox of the way in which Jesus' life-giving actions lead to his own death.

Symbolism

Another means by which the narrator addresses the reader at the level of implicit commentary is through symbolism. In John 11, the principal use of symbolism can be found in two enigmatic sayings. The first is in vv. 9-10: 'Are there not twelve hours of daylight? A man who walks by day will not stumble, for he sees by the world's light. It is when he walks by night that he stumbles, for he has no light.' Here again we have the archetypal symbols of light and darkness, day and night, used to represent the realms of faith and unbelief, knowledge and ignorance. What Jesus seems to be saying in 11.9-10 is this: 'I can return to Judea because the hour for my death (the hour of darkness) is not quite upon us. I will therefore not be killed ('stumble') at Bethany because I am still ministering in a season of pre-ordained security (daylight).'

This saying is illustrative of the two-level communication going on between narrator and reader. The saying can, after all, be easily interpreted at an entirely literal level. The challenge, however, is to understand the implicit commentary in these words, to ascend from the earthly meaning of Jesus' words to their spiritual, symbolic sense. This same challenge is thrown down in the second enigmatic saying of Jesus in 11.25-26. Here the language of Jesus moves without warning from the literal to the spiritual and back again, so that only the perceptive reader penetrates the complete meaning of what is said: 'I am the resurrection and the life. He who believes in me will live [spiritually], even though he dies [physically]; and whoever lives [physically] and believes in me will never die [spiritually].' The whole saying depends upon the reader's ability to discern the chiasmus linking spiritual life with physical life and physical death with spiritual death.

Narrator and Reader

These remarks about implicit commentary lead us to a closer evaluation of the relationship between narrator and reader in John 11. If the brief analysis above has shown anything, it has revealed how John's story has been constructed for rereading. This fact is indicated by the curious remark by the narrator in 11.2, that 'This Mary, whose brother Lazarus now lay sick, was the same one who poured perfume on the Lord and wiped his feet with her hair'. Here the game is given away. First-time readers will be mystified by this comment. They will interpret it as an analepsis of something which has already occurred in John's story. In vain they will search the previous chapters for a scene in which Mary of Bethany anoints the feet of Jesus. Giving up, they will read on and find the relevant episode in the next chapter, indeed at the very start of ch. 12! What the first-time reader interprets as an analepsis is really a prolepsis.

While the first-time reader can certainly enjoy the story for its suspense, the person rereading the text enjoys a different aesthetic pleasure: the pleasure of interconnectedness. This is the sense of complete satisfaction when parts of the Gospel are seen by the reader in their complex interrelations. This pleasure has to do with fulness and wholeness. The narrator has a paradigmatic reader in mind, one who can link microscopic parts into the panoramic whole of the story. Few features of John 11 show this intention more clearly than the way in which the narrator establishes proleptic echo effects with the resurrection of Jesus. When Lazarus emerges from the tomb wrapped with strips of linen and a cloth around his face (*soudarion*), the person rereading the Gospel is supposed to see in this a prolepsis of the empty tomb. In Jn 20.7, Simon Peter peers into the empty tomb and sees the head-cloth (*soudarion*) of Jesus lying there. The raising of Lazarus, in the paradigmatic reader's mind, is proleptic of the raising of Jesus.

The narrator therefore has a particular kind of reader in view: one who follows the beginning and the middle of the story always from the point of view of its end. In this respect, narrative form and christological claim are inseparable. What the narrator creates is a reader whose response is a matter of *realized eschatology*—that is, a matter of living in the end-time of the story even while it is still in progress. As such, form matches content, for in the content of the story Jesus Christ is depicted as the *eschaton* in person, the one who brings the end of history into the middle of time.

John 11.45-54

Context

John 11.45-54 is crucial to the plot of John's story. I have already indicated that chs. 11 and 12 form the conclusion to the Book of Signs. They also point forward to the kernel events of the Book of the Passion. As such, the theme of Jesus' death becomes particularly prominent, especially from 11.45 until the end of John 12. In the narrative section before us now, this theme is introduced in the unconscious prophecy which Caiaphas declares concerning Jesus' death. He says, 'It is better for you that one man die for the people than that the whole nation perish' (v. 50). This utterance forms the focal point of the story and acts as a prolepsis of the death of Jesus.

Structure

Again the material is arranged with care. There are five units in 11.45-54 composed in a chiastic sequence:

A^1	45-46	The reaction of the Jews to Jesus
B^1	47-48	The gathering together of the Sanhedrin
C	49-50	Caiaphas's prophecy
B^2	51-53	The gathering together of the children of God
A^2	54	The reaction of Jesus to the Jews

The inverted parallelism is evident in the relationships between A^1 and A^2, B^1 and B^2, and in the formation of C as the centrepiece. A^1 and A^2 are related in that there is a contrast between the Jewish response to Jesus (another *schisma* of opinion, vv. 45-46) and Jesus' response to the Jews (to withdraw, v. 54). These units are linked by the words 'therefore' and 'the Jews'. B^1 and B^2 are linked by the common theme of 'gathering together'. In B^1 the Pharisees and chief priests 'gather together' (*sunēgagon*) in the Sanhedrin. In v. 52, the narrator speaks of Jesus' death as the means by which the scattered children of God will be gathered together (*sunagagē*) and made one people. The reader should also recognize that B^1, C and B^2 are linked by the word *ethnos*, meaning nation (vv. 48, 50, 51). This helps to establish C, the Caiaphas prophecy, as the focal point.

Themes

The death of Jesus is the central theme. As I have suggested above, the present narrative marks a turning point in the plot insofar as it introduces a strong emphasis on the imminence of the passion. In vv. 51-52, the narrator helps to increase the profile of this theme by intruding into the storytelling in order to explain the significance of Caiaphas's words. The reader is addressed more obviously and directly than is customary.

> He did not say this on his own, but as high priest that year he prophesied that Jesus would die for the Jewish nation, and not only for that nation but also for the scattered children of God, to bring them together and make them one.

With these words the narrator intimates the unifying and reconciling effect of Jesus' death. Through Jesus' death, the Jewish nation and the scattered children of God will be brought together and made one. At this point the paradigmatic reader is supposed to hear analeptic echo effects with 10.16 and 6.13. In 10.16, Jesus spoke of laying down his life for the sheep. He added, 'I have other sheep that are not of this sheep pen. I must bring them also. They too will listen to my voice, and there shall be one flock and one shepherd' (note the oneness motif). In 6.12-13, Jesus commands that the pieces of bread left over (in the feeding of the five thousand) should be 'gathered together' (*sunagagete, sunēgagon*). Twelve baskets are filled with these 'gathered' remnants. When the narrator speaks of Jesus 'gathering people together' and making them 'one' through the cross (11.51-52), the paradigmatic reader recognizes from the analepses above how central this mission is from the start of John's story.

Characterization

In the commentary on the Lazarus story I highlighted the now stereo-typical division in vv. 45-46 between Jews who believe and Jews who do not. The present narrative focuses more on the role of those who go to the Pharisees. This group is depicted as playing the role of spies. Their action of going and telling functions as a negative and indeed ironic version of the 'going and telling' by Johannine witnesses in the story.

The Pharisees and chief priests in turn are portrayed as the hostile authorities behind the scenes who make the decision to arrest and kill Jesus. In this respect, they are consistent with their behaviour in 7.45-52. Indeed, there are some formal similarities between 7.45-52 and 11.45-54. In 7.45-52, the temple guards return to the Pharisees and declare, 'No one ever spoke the way this man does!' This is paralleled in 11.47 by the Pharisees' remark, 'Here is this man performing many miraculous signs!' In 7.47-49, the Pharisees reply that the guards have been deceived and that the crowds 'know nothing'. This is paralleled by the remark of Caiaphas in 11.49, 'You know nothing at all!' (note the theme of knowledge).

Caiaphas is brought into the centre of the stage in the dramatic narrative before us. This is the first time he has been mentioned in John's story. He is the victim of satire in 11.45-54. The critical weapon which the narrator uses to create this satirical effect is irony. Irony sets up a contrast between the understanding of a character within the narrative world and the much greater understanding of the reader, who is guided by the narrator into a more enlightened point of view. The fundamental contrast in 11.50-52 is between Caiaphas's understanding of his words and the reader's. Caiaphas understands his words to convey the notion that Jesus' death is politically expedient. The reader understands the same words more equivocally, as connoting the powerful effect of the cross in uniting the scattered children of God. The reader is guided into this higher level of meaning by the narrator, who is keen to present the inadequacies of the high priest ('He did not say this on his own', v. 51).

Finally, Jesus is absent from the narrative until v. 54. Two points should be made about the way he is characterized here. First, Jesus is again the centre of attention even when he is absent from the stage. Everything in 11.45-53 concerns Jesus even though he is not himself physically present. Second, the theme of Jesus' elusiveness is again brought into focus at v. 54. Here the keyword *parrēsia* alerts the reader to the motif of Jesus' secret movements. Jesus is portrayed in v. 54 withdrawing from the city (area of hostility) to the countryside (area of security), indeed to a region near the desert. Here he stays (*menō*) with his disciples.

John 11.55–12.11

Context
The *anabasis* or ascent to Jerusalem by the many people in v. 55 can be interpreted at a deeper level. The hour of Jesus' *anabasis*, his return and ascent to the Father via Calvary, has now arrived. The double mention of the third and final Passover of the Gospel in 11.55 prepares the reader for the sacrifice of Jesus at Golgotha. Indeed, the process time-shape in 12.1 ('Six days before the Passover') brings the imminence of the death of Jesus closer. What the narrator shows us now is another unconscious prolepsis of the passion by a character within the narrative world. Just as Caiaphas unconsciously prophesies the death of Jesus in 11.45-54, so now Mary performs an unconscious, enacted prophecy of the anointing of Jesus for burial.

Characterization
Judas is centre-stage in 12.4-6. Here the narrator departs from the normal reticence about the psychology of characters to explain what was going on in Judas' mind. Judas is first of all depicted as someone apparently concerned for the poor. He complains, 'Why wasn't this perfume

sold and the money given to the poor?' This appears to be a reasonable question. However, the narrator intrudes to elucidate Judas' motives: 'He did not say this because he cared about the poor but because he was a thief; as keeper of the money bag, he used to help himself to what was put in it'. Far from being a laudable statement, Judas' words in v. 5 are now seen as arising from a deep-seated and perverse avarice. Judas is really a 'thief' (*kleptēs*), a description used in 10.1-5 for those who climb over the wall into the sheepfold. Judas, like Caiaphas in the preceding narrative, is therefore the target of Johannine satire.

In stark contrast to the inadequacies of this male character, the female characters in 12.1-8 are portrayed in a very positive light. Martha is mentioned at v. 2. The narrative setting is a dinner at Lazarus' house in Bethany. Martha is described as 'serving' Jesus (*diēkonei*). This diaconal conduct marks Martha out as a paradigmatic character. She is a true disciple because she serves and follows Jesus (compare with *diakonē*, 12.26).

The central female character is not Martha but Mary. She is contrasted with Judas in Jn 12.1-11. She is seen at Jesus' feet in v. 3, pouring an expensive perfume on them and wiping them with her hair. This functions as an analepsis with 11.32, where Mary falls at Jesus' feet after her brother's death. It also functions as a prolepsis with the footwashing in John 13 and the burial in 19.38-42, where Nicodemus and Joseph bring expensive perfume to anoint Jesus' dead body. In 12.3 the weight of this expensive perfume is referred to (*litra*). In 19.39, the weight of the perfume is again mentioned (*litra*). What is emphasized in both passages is the expense of the aromatic spices. Thus Mary is presented as a woman who is prepared to give everything to Jesus.

Other characters mentioned in the narrative are the many people of 11.55-56 and 12.9, the Pharisees and chief priests of 11.57 and 12.10, the Jews in 12.11, Lazarus in 12.1-2 and 12.9-10, and of course Jesus. As far as Jesus is concerned, it is important to notice that he understands Mary's actions in terms of his death and burial, and commends her for her action. Indeed, it is noticeable that the principal female character in the narrative (Mary) comes in for Jesus' commendation while the principal male character (Judas) comes in for condemnation.

Lazarus's role in the story is significant. As we have seen, the narrative setting is a dinner party at his home in Bethany. He is described reclining at the table with Jesus (*anakeimenōn*) in v. 2. Is this detail concerning Lazarus' posture intended to heighten the verisimilitude of the scene? Or is there some deeper significance intended here? The reader should remember that Lazarus was described throughout John 11 as a man beloved of Jesus. Indeed, we proposed that he is the one character within the narrative world of the whole Gospel whom we could call 'the beloved disciple'. In this respect, it is important for us to observe the posture of the beloved disciple in 13.23. There the setting is a dinner (the last supper), and the anonymous disciple is said to be 'reclining next to Jesus' (*anakeimenos*, 13.23). Since exactly the same word is used in both 12.2 and 13.23, we should see the posture of Lazarus in 12.1-8 as a means by which the narrator prepares the reader to make this identification.

John 12.12-19

Context

Jesus is now at the entrance to Jerusalem, the urban setting which spells hostility, danger and unbelief. The large crowd mentioned in 12.9 is present again at 12.12. They are part of a great number of people who would have made the pilgrimage to Jerusalem for Passover. On the way, they may well have sung the Psalms of Ascent. Certain phrases from these psalms are now applied to Jesus by way of confession and acclamation. 'Hosanna!' is a cultic acclamation in Ps. 118.25, meaning 'Lord, save us!' 'Blessed is he who comes in the name of the Lord' is a quotation from Ps. 118.26. 'He who comes in the Lord's name' is a title applied to Jesus here and is reminiscent of the Baptist's 'He is the one who comes after me' in 1.27.

Implicit Commentary

A correct reader response to this brief narrative depends entirely on our appreciation of the intertextual dimensions of the piece. I have already shown how Ps. 118.25-26 lies behind the first two acclamations in 12.13. The reference to the palm branches is probably an allusion to Ps. 118.27b: 'With boughs in hand, join in the festal procession up to the horns of the altar'. These intertextual resonances with Psalm 118 link the entrance of Jesus into Jerusalem with the coming of the long-awaited Davidic King, considered in Jewish speculation to be the Messiah. This is supported by the fact that the author has added, 'Blessed is the king of Israel' to the citation from Ps. 118.25-27. (The title 'king of Israel' is also an analepsis of 1.49, Nathaniel's confession.)

The narrator tells us that Jesus found a young donkey and sat on it, an action which must have mystified the disciples. Indeed, the narrator says that they were baffled. However, he also explains Jesus' conduct by combining two OT texts: Zech. 9.9 and Zeph. 3.16 (Zeph. 3.15 may have supplied the 'king of Israel' confession in Jn 12.13). He omits statements suggestive of military honour and triumph, preferring to focus on Jesus' humility: 'See your king is coming, seated on a donkey's colt'. By doing so, the narrator reveals the symbolism in Jesus' actions. Jesus chooses to ride a donkey's colt as a corrective to the crowd's nationalism. He is a king, yes, but not the kind of king they are expecting. His kingship is not of this world, as we shall learn in the passion narrative.

Narrator and Point of View

The narrator plays an important part in shaping the reader's understanding of the implicit commentary in this story, providing descriptive statements, such as 12.12, 13a, 14, 17, 18, and indications of who is speaking, v. 19. The most important contribution is in v. 16: 'At first his disciples did not understand all this. Only after Jesus was glorified did they realize that these things had been written of him and that they had done these things to him.' These words give us a classic example of the narrator's use of the polytemporal time-shape. In v. 16, the narrator takes the reader outside the process of the story to a vantage point beyond the story's ending. Speaking from a post-resurrection point of view, the narrator informs the reader that the disciples only understood the full importance of what Jesus did, and what was said about him, once the resurrection had occurred. Then they remembered the events (*emnēsthēsan*), related them to OT Scripture, and understood their true significance. This same process has already been described in 2.17 and 2.22, where the remembrance motif is also used.

Characterization

A number of characters are mentioned in this section. They are mostly social groups against which the solitary, heroic figure of Jesus is silhouetted. The first character group is the 'great crowd' of 12.12-13. This crowd is depicted as influenced by strong nationalistic fervour. As such, it is also a group guilty of misunderstanding, because Jesus has not come as a political figure. The second character mentioned is Jesus. His humility is stressed. He is the only individual in the narrative and thereby becomes the 'focalized'. The third character group is the disciples. They are presented as prone of misunderstanding. However, the narrator also indicates that they will understand later. Another crowd is mentioned in v. 17—the crowd that witnessed the raising of Lazarus (note the way in which Lazarus gives unity to chs. 11 and 12). They are said to bear witness (*emarturei*) for Jesus. The final character group is the Pharisees. They exclaim, 'Look (*ide*) how the whole world (*kosmos*) has gone after him!' The key point about this confession is its universalism. The Pharisees see that Jesus is attracting the whole world, but they cannot make the step to seeing him as 'the Saviour of the world (*kosmos*)' (4.42). Their exasperation and exclamation has also been a feature of 11.47-48.

John 12.20-36

Context

Throughout chs. 11 and 12 the reader has become aware of the growing imminence of Jesus' death. In the Lazarus story, the disciples warn Jesus not to go back to Judea where the Jews have tried to kill him (11.7). In the subsequent narrative, the narrator tells how the Sanhedrin formally plot to kill Jesus (11.53). In the next story, Mary anoints Jesus' feet, an act which forms a prolepsis of his burial. In 12.12-19, Jesus enters Jerusalem publicly for the last time. Jesus announces in 12.23, 'The hour (*hōra*) has come!' The appointed time has arrived.

Characterization

a. Jesus. The humanity of Jesus is again suggested. 'Now my heart is troubled', he cries, as he sees the prospect of his passion (12.27). The verb translated 'troubled' is *tarassō*, last used in 11.33, where Jesus' heart was troubled by the death of Lazarus and the weeping of the mourners.

We also see a feature of Jesus' characterization which will become prominent in the passion narrative: namely, his sovereignty. Notice the way in which Jesus shows a mastery of his emotions here. He transcends his feelings of unease by focusing on the importance of his calling: 'It was for this very reason I came to this hour' (v. 27). More than that, instead of wilting before the prospect of his death he rejoices in its consequences. His death will result in a number of things: glorification (v. 23, 28), a fruitful harvest (v. 24; see 4.36), an example for those who follow him (vv. 25-26), judgment on the world (v. 31a), the expulsion of Satan (v. 31b), and the means by which all are drawn to him (v. 32).

The elusiveness of Jesus is stressed again in v. 36b. This is the last of the narrator's references to the hide-and-seek dynamic in the Book of Signs. The story before us begins with the Greeks seeking Jesus, and it ends with Jesus hiding from the crowd. The narrator says: 'When he had finished speaking, Jesus left and hid himself (*ekrubē*, as in 8.59) from them'. Having just warned his listeners to seek the light while they still have it, Jesus now withdraws and hides.

b. The Father. This is the only occasion in the Fourth Gospel when characters within the narrative world hear God speak. A voice is said to come from heaven in v. 28 in response to Jesus' words, 'Father, glorify your name!' The voice (clearly that of 'the Father' addressed) replies, 'I have glorified it, and will glorify it again'. What is noteworthy is the elusiveness of this voice. The crowd are divided as to what it really is

(v. 29). Thus, even when the heavens do open in John's story (and notice that they do *not* open at Jesus' baptism in 1.32-34), the hiddenness and transcendence of God are in no way compromised. The elusiveness of the Son is seen to be at one with the elusiveness of the Father, vindicating Jesus' assertion, 'I and the Father are one' (10.30).

c. The Greeks. The *Hellēnes* in 12.20 are the epitome of the true seeker in John's story. In the introduction I showed how the theme of seeking Jesus is pervasive in the Gospel. Since ch. 5, however, the seeking of Jesus has been done principally by the Jews (understood as the hostile authorities), whose intention has been to kill Jesus. Now, in 12.20-22, we see a complete contrast. We see Greeks (the antithesis of *Ioudaoi*) 'coming to' Philip (an action symbolizing incipient discipleship) and saying, 'Sir, we would like to see (*idein*) Jesus'. The use of the verb 'see' points to the depth of their seeking. Their religious quest is for true 'sight/insight' about Jesus. This cameo of sincere enquiry is an emotive incident in the Gospel. Jesus comes to his own people but they reject him. Those who are not ethnically and religiously 'his own' come to him and accept him.

d. Philip and Andrew. The reader needs to note the analepses with 1.35-51, the calling of Andrew and Philip. In ch. 1, Andrew and Philip, both from Bethsaida (1.44), are found by Jesus. Andrew is found first, then Philip. Both disciples are seen bringing another man to Jesus. Andrew leads Peter and Philip leads Nathaniel. In 12.21-22, the order is reversed. Philip is found first by the Greeks, then Andrew is found by Philip. The narrator forms an inclusio with 1.35-51 by reminding us that Philip was from Bethsaida in Galilee (12.21; see 1.44). Both disciples are depicted in the same positive light as in ch. 1, where they are seen as effective missionaries.

e. The crowd. The background clamour of the crowd's confusion is again audible. In v. 29 there is another *schisma* of opinion over the voice from heaven. They are uncertain whether it was thunder or the voice of an angel. This confusion is carried over into 12.34, where the crowd cannot work out how the Son of Man can be 'lifted up' (since the Christ was supposed to live forever), and who 'the Son of Man' is that is referred to by Jesus. The literary device of misunderstanding is exploited by the narrator again. The confusion of the crowd is in marked contrast to the genuine search for Jesus undertaken by the other social group in the narrative: the *Hellēnes*.

Intertextuality

I have tried to argue throughout this commentary that Deutero-Isaiah functions as a rich resource for the author. We can see this again in the specifically Johannine concepts of the lifting up and glorification of the Son of Man. With these words, the narrator provides the paradigmatic reader with intertextual allusions to the suffering servant song in Isa. 52.13: 'See, my servant will act wisely; he will be raised and lifted up and glorified'. The emphasis on the lifting up of Jesus in John (with its *double entendre*: elevate on the cross/ascend to heaven) shows that the reader is meant to see the death of Jesus as the sacrifice of the Servant of Yahweh, the one led like a lamb to the slaughter (see 1.29 and Isa. 53.7).

Implicit Commentary

The symbolism of light and darkness resurfaces in 12.35. Jesus warns his listeners that the light (a symbol of his presence in the world, 1.4-9) will be with them just a little longer. He warns them that the darkness is about to overtake them (*katalabē*, an analepsis of 1.5). His subsequent concealment in v. 36b ('he hid himself from them') symbolizes the withdrawal of this light. The narrator's terse statement in 13.30, 'it was night', reveals that the period of darkness has now come. The light has gone. If the Book of Signs is the period in which the light is prominent, the Book of the Passion will be, correspondingly, the period in which the world's darkness is most visible.

John 12.37-43

Context

For the last two units of the Book of Signs (12.37-43, 12.44-50), the two principal voices in John's story assert themselves. In the unit before us now, the voice of the narrator is prominent. In the ensuing unit, the voice of Jesus will be the sole, exclusive source of description. If 12.44-50 functions as the protagonist's concluding remarks, 12.37-43 functions as the narrator's closing address. Here the narrator looks at the heart and soul of the unbelief of the Jews.

Narrator

In 12.37, we move from *mimesis* (showing) to *diegesis* (telling). In other words, the presence of the narrator becomes obvious and indeed paramount. The theme which the narrator wishes to explore with the reader is the antithesis between unbelief and faith. The narrative unit begins with a comment about unbelief: 'Even after Jesus had done all these miraculous signs in their presence, they still would not believe in him' (v. 37). The unit ends on a note of faith: 'Yet at the same time many

even among the leaders believed in him' (v. 42). Between the opening
and closure of the narrative, the narrator examines the faith/unbelief
continuum through the lens of OT testimony.

Narrative Time

There is a perceptible deceleration in the pace of the plot now. The two
fairly lengthy interpretative pauses in 12.37-43 and 12.44-50 are mainly
responsible for slowing the pace of John's story as we come to the closure of the Book of Signs. Thus the narrator's intrusions in this unit are
partly intended to act as a brake upon (and a 'break' in) the tempo of
the narrative as a whole.

Intertextuality

The passage is notable for its analepses with the stories of the author's
heritage. In particular, there are transtextual references to the testimonies of Isaiah. John 12.38 is a verbatim reference to the LXX of Isa.
53.1. John 12.40 is a reference to Isa. 6.10. This is the first time since 1.23
that we have had a direct allusion to the book of Isaiah (which suggests
an inclusio between the introduction and conclusion to the Book of
Signs). The function of these historical analepses in 12.37-43 is to highlight the fact that all the great figures of the overarching OT story were
in fact testifying about Jesus. The secret sense of the OT story points to
Jesus. Thus, Moses wrote about Jesus (5.46). Abraham rejoiced at seeing
the day of Jesus (8.56). Isaiah saw the glory of Jesus and spoke about
him (12.41; note the echo effect with 8.56).

Point of View

There is no clearer example of the polytemporal time-shape in John's
story than here. The polytemporal time-shape involves a mixing of
temporal horizons: the present into the past, the eternal into the present,
and so on. Here the narrator does both of these. First of all, the eternal
is mixed with the present by guiding the reader into a kind of timeless
perspective on events. In vv. 37-41 the narrator shows how a person
centuries before the events of John 1–21 actually saw the future glory
of Jesus. In providing a point of view with the mind of Isaiah, the
narrator brings an eternal dimension into the present of the story.

In the second half of the narrative, however, the narrator does
something different. The present situation of the readers is brought into
the past of Jesus-history. In referring again to the fear of excommunication (*aposunagōgos*, 9.22), the situation of the Johannine community
(post 85 CE) is made to resonate with the situation of Jesus. The satire
on the Jewish authorities in 12.42-43 is a critique of Jesus' opponents
from the point of view of John's *own* historical circumstances. The reference to the Pharisees as the principal *bêtes noires* reflects the situation

late in the first century when Pharisaical Jews persecuted Christian Jews. The fear of some of the leaders concerning 'confession of Jesus' (v. 42) resonates with the fear caused by Jewish Christians' expression of open faith in the author's *Sitz im Leben*. The biting comment in v. 43, 'they loved praise (*doxa*) from men more than praise (*doxa*) from God', is the author's final indictment of the antagonists of the original readers. Thus, in vv. 42-43, the present of John's community fuses with the past of Jesus' history.

John 12.44-50

Comment

The Book of Signs has a clear sense of an ending. This sense of closure is first of all caused by the circularity between the introduction (ch. 1) and conclusion (particularly ch. 12). The parallelism between these two sections is unmistakable. In 12.20-36, there are a number of examples of ring composition: the reference to Andrew and Philip of Bethsaida (12.20 // 1.44); the references to the Son of Man (12.23, 34 // 1.51); the Son of Man raised up between earth and heaven (12.32 // 1.51); the mention of angels (12.29 // 1.51); the reference to voices (*phōnē*, 12.28, 30 // 1.23) and to hearing (12.29 // 1.37); and the symbolism of light and darkness (12.35 // 1.4-9).

This circularity between the two sections is carried over into 12.37-43 and 12.44-50. The direct allusion to Isaiah in 12.38 and 40, mirrors the direct allusion to Isaiah by the Baptist in 1.23. In 12.44-50, there is a sense of *inclusio* with the Prologue. See in particular the echo effects between 12.46 ('I have come into the world as a light, so that no one who believes in me should stay in darkness') and 1.9 ('The true light that gives light to every man was coming into the world'). These suggest that 12.44-50 functions as the epilogue to the conclusion of the Book of Signs, just as 1.1-18 functions as the prologue to its introduction.

A second factor which helps to create a sense of an ending in 12.44-50 is the fact that Jesus is here summarizing the main themes of chs. 1–12. The following themes have been ubiquitous in the story so far: believing in Jesus (vv. 44, 46); the description of God as 'the one who sent me' (vv. 44, 45, 49); sight (v. 45); coming into the world (v. 46); light (v. 46); darkness (v. 46); hearing (v. 47); judgment (vv. 47, 48); salvation (v. 47); accepting Jesus (v. 48); the Father (vv. 49, 50); the dependency of the Son upon the Father (vv. 49, 50); the commandment of God (v. 50); and eternal life (v. 50). Their reappearance indicates that 12.44-50 functions as a restatement of the leading concepts of the Book of Signs.

A third factor which elicits a sense of an ending from the reader is the historical prolepsis concerning 'the last day' in v. 48. Jesus says, 'I will condemn him at the last day'. This is a flash-forward to the conclusion of the real world and real time. The reference to the closure of history in a text which itself functions as a conclusion helps to create the sense of an ending. World and book are fused together.

However, 12.44-50 should not be seen exclusively in terms of closure. The prolepses or flash-forwards to the farewell discourses in John 13–17 are significant. Note the proleptic echo effect between 12.47 ('hearing and keeping my words') and 14.15-24. Most of all, notice the correspondence between the *form* of Jesus' address in 12.44-50 and what we find in chs. 14–17. There is a complete absence of spatio-temporal indicators in 12.44-50. There are no signals of a setting or the passage of time. The last reference to any movement or location was in 12.36: 'Jesus left and hid himself'. The reader must therefore suppose that Jesus is speaking from an unspecified place of concealment. This anticipates chs. 14–17.

A further point should be made about the way in which 12.44-50 prepares for the farewell discourses. Notice that the one contribution which the narrator makes in 12.44-50 is in v. 44, where he says, 'Then Jesus cried out'. The use of *ekraxen* here signals to the reader that he or she is about to hear heavenly truths. The last time this verb was used was in 7.37 where Jesus 'cried out' (*ekraxen*), 'If anyone is thirsty, let him come to me and drink'. However, in that context Jesus was depicted as speaking directly to an addressee (the people of Jerusalem referred to in vv. 40-43). John 12.44 differs from 7.37 insofar as there is no addressee mentioned in the entire passage. Jesus is simply depicted as 'crying out'. What we have in 12.44-50 is therefore much more like a dramatic soliloquy, a form of discourse in which the hero voices his thoughts on an empty stage. This again anticipates much of the farewell discourses, where the reader *overhears* the Revealer speaking or praying in apparent isolation. Perhaps such discourses as these are a kind of first-century version of what we find in modern novelistic fiction: the narrator's commentary on a protagonist's internal thought processes.

It is at this point that we can appreciate the helpfulness of Bultmann's description throughout his commentary of 'the hiddenness of the revelation'. What we are presented with in 12.44-50 is the paradox of revelation given in hiding, of disclosure from a place of concealment. The appeal of this kind of discourse consists of the fact that the reader is allowed to hear the revelation at all. He or she is given the privilege of hearing the secrets of the hidden Messiah. It is this kind of literary dynamic which we shall find time and again in chs. 14–17. In these chapters there will be virtually no spatio-temporal coordinates. The suggestion again will be of 'the hiddenness of the revelation'. As in 12.44-50, the appeal of these chapters will derive from the truth that the reader is given a confidential audience by the concealed Revealer, the elusive Christ. Thus 12.44-50 has a prospective as well as a retrospective orientation. It is, in a sense, both introduction and conclusion.

John 13–17

Introduction

We now come to the celebrated farewell discourses (Jn 13–17). Several comments need to be made about these chapters by way of introduction, before we look at the opening section in Jn 13.1-38.

The first of these relates to the story time of John 13–17. Alan Culpepper points out that John's Gospel depicts a period of about two and a half years in chs. 1–12 (indicated by the references to the three Passovers). John 13–19, on the other hand, covers a period of about 24 hours, from the evening meal on the eve of Passover (13.1) to the evening of the Day of Preparation (19.31). So while it takes the reader approximately one hour (narrative time) to read about a period of two and a half years in John 1–12 (story time), it takes the reader a similar length of time to read about a period of 24 hours in John 13–19. Culpepper's conclusion is that 'The "speed" of the narrative reduces steadily, therefore, until it virtually grinds to a halt at the climactic day' (1983: 72).

Gail O'Day has highlighted another important feature of the story time in John 13–17. She talks about the presence of the future in John 13–17, of the paradoxical feeling of 'the remembrance of things hoped for' (1991: 157). This is principally because Jesus speaks in the farewell discourses 'from a post-resurrection vantage point' (1991: 157). As O'Day puts it, 'These chapters bring the future and the present together in one narrative moment in ways that challenge conventional notions of time' (1991: 156). O'Day points to the following examples of polytemporal effect:

13.19   'I tell you this now, before it occurs, so that when it does occur, you may believe that I am.'

14.29   'And now I have told you this before it occurs, so that when it does occur, you may believe.'

15.11   'I have said these things to you so that my joy may be in you, and that your joy may be complete.'

16.1, 4   'I have said these things to keep you from stumbling (v. 1)... But I have said these things to you so that when their hour comes you may remember that I told you about them' (v. 4).

16.33   'I have said this to you, so that in me you may have peace.'

The vision of the future in John 13–17 embraces both the immediate future (prolepses of chs. 18–21) and a future beyond that future (events in the real time after the story, or 'external prolepses'). Thus, there are moments when Jesus describes the presence of the immediate future of his disciples. As O'Day says,

> In 16.32, what is still future in terms of the narration of events in the Gospel is the present reality of the discourse: 'The hour is coming, *indeed it has come*, when you will be scattered, each one to his home, and you will leave me alone' (O'Day 1991: 160).

This is a prolepsis of ch. 18. But there are other moments when Jesus points to the presence of a more long-term future, of the future that follows the events of the Gospel. These references encompass his return (14.3), the transformation of the disciple's sorrow into joy (16.22), the new relationship which they will have with the Father (14.14, 16.23-24) and their experience of the world's hatred and persecution (15.18-20, 16.2-3).

Another new feature in John 13–17 is the literary form of these chapters. By far the most obvious distinction between chs. 13–17 and what has preceded them is the prominence of the discourse form. In John 1–12 there are discourse sections but they are nothing like the length of John 13–17. As Werner Kelber puts it:

> The Farewell Discourse alone (John 13.31–17.26), a vast repertoire of speech materials, comprises approximately one-fifth of the Gospel. If we discount ch. 21 as a later redactional addition, three-fourths of chs. 1–20 consists of sayings, dialogues, and monologues (1991: 126).

Beyond the description of John 13.38–17.26 as 'discourse', Kelber suggests that the form of these chapters should be identified as 'the genre of the revelation discourse', a form of communication character-ized by 'self-disclosure among the privileged few' (1991: 128). However, Fernando Segovia has recently proferred a more precise description in the most thorough literary analysis of John 13–17 to date. In *The Farewell of the Word* (1991), Segovia argues that the form of the farewell discourses is to be located within the Graeco-Roman and Hebrew tradition of 'the testament or farewell of a dying hero' (1991b: 1)—one of the type-scenes identified in Robert Alter's influential book, *The Art of Biblical Narrative* (1981: 47-62).

A year earlier, William Kurz published a book on *Farewell Addresses in the New Testament* (1990). Like Segovia, Kurz describes John 13–17 as an example of the genre of farewell address to be found in both the pre-Christian Hellenistic and Jewish literature. Kurz summarizes this genre as follows: 'Within this genre of farewell address the form is somewhat elastic. The narrative framework of a farewell address provides its most defining characteristic, that of "a discourse delivered in anticipation of imminent death"' (1990: 19). The fact that Kurz and Segovia have both published books proposing a similar thesis at the same time further supports the view that John 13–17 belongs to the form of the farewell address.

Kurz writes, 'Though farewell addresses have many common elements, they do not follow a fixed pattern. They typically feature a father or leader addressing his or her sons or successors' (1990: 20). In an earlier essay, Kurz identifies twenty formal characteristics of this farewell genre (cited in Segovia 1991b: 16). The first four refer to the *context* of the farewell speech:

1.   The summoning of successors
2.   The blessing
3.   Farewell gestures
4.   The bewailing of the loss by the rest

The remaining sixteen refer to the *content* of the farewell speech:

1.   The speaker's own mission as example
2.   An account of the speaker's own life
3.   The announcement of impending death
4.   Exhortations
5.   Warnings and final injunctions
6.   Tasks for successors
7.   A theological review of history
8.   Revelations of the future
9.   Promises
10.   The question of successors
11.   Future degeneration
12.   The renewal of a covenant
13.   Care of those left behind
14.   Consolation of the inner circle
15.   Didactic speech
16.   *Ars moriendi*

Kurz shows that the classic farewell passages in the Old Testament are Jacob's farewell to his sons, the patriarchs of Israel's twelve tribes, in Genesis 49, and Moses' farewell in Deuteronomy 31–34 (1990: 24). Other examples could be added: 1 Samuel 12, 1 Kgs 2.1-10, Joshua 23–24. The classic examples in the extrabiblical sources are 1 Macc. 2.47-70 and Josephus, *Antiquities of the Jews* 12.6.3, 279-84. Other examples can be found in *The Testaments of the Twelve Patriarchs*, *The Testament of Moses*, and Jacob's farewell in *Jubilees* 22.10-30 (1990: 31-32).

The Graeco-Roman tradition is perhaps less rich. Apart from Socrates' farewell in Plato's *Phaedo*, the extant Graeco-Roman farewells are 'merely ornamented narratives with "last words" in the form of a short witty saying by their heroes' (Kurz 1990: 19). However, it is from these and other examples of the farewell that Kurz and Segovia establish the formal characteristics of the genre. In the present commentary, I shall follow their lead and base the literary analysis of John 13–17 on the view that these chapters belong to the farewell genre.

However, before we look at Jn 13.1-38 it is important to gain some understanding of the overall narrative structure and design of these chapters. In this regard I must express my indebtedness to Yves Simoens. Apart from Segovia, Simoens (1981) is the only scholar to have attempted a literary analysis of the structure of John 13–17. This analysis uncovers a chiastic structure for the farewell discourses as a whole:

A^1	13.1-38	The themes of glorification and love
B^1	14.1-31	The theme of Jesus' departure and the encouragement of the disciples
C^1	15.1-11	The themes of abiding and joy
D	15.12-17	The love command
C^2	15.18–16.3	The themes of hatred and exclusion
B^2	16.4-33	The theme of Jesus' departure and the warnings to the disciples
A^2	17.1-26	The themes of glorification and love

Notice the parallels between 13.1-38 and 17.1-26. These are set up right at the start of both sections (13.1, 'the hour had come' // 17.1, 'the hour has come'). The overall thematic parallels between B^1 and B^2 are also established right at the start of both sections (14.2, 'I am going there' // 16.5, 'I am going to him who sent me'). C^1 and C^2 are interesting; their connection is based on contrast rather than parallelism (abiding/ exclusion, joy/hatred). This leaves the love command in 15.12-17 as the centrepiece. This is very much what we would expect since the main theme of John 13–17 is the love of Jesus (13.1). In this commentary I agree with Simoens except in the matter of the ending of C^2. This unit begins at 15.18 and ends at 16.4a.

John 13.1-38

Context

John 13.1-38 begins with the words, 'It was just before the Passover Feast' (13.1). Here the narrator situates the footwashing just before the third and final Passover in John's Gospel. In 11.55 the narrator tells us that it was almost time for the Passover (*ēn de engus to pascha tōn Ioudaiōn*). In 12.1 we are told that it is now six days before the Passover. The passing of days in ch. 12 (12.12, *tē epaurion*) keeps this sense of anticipation alive. Now in 13.1 the narrator says that it is 'just before the Passover feast'. The more general term *engus* used in 2.13 and 6.4 is replaced by *pro*, a preposition which suggests a greater sense of imminence. From 13.1 until 19.42, we are dealing with the 24 hours prior to the start of the Sabbath (which began on the Friday evening at sunset).

Form

John 13.1-38 belongs to the genre of the farewell. As we have already seen, the context of farewell scenes has four characteristics: the summoning of successors, the blessing, the farewell gestures, and the bewailing of the loss by the rest. John 13.1-38 has all of these: Jesus gathers his disciples around him (the summoning of successors). He demonstrates his love by washing the disciples' feet (farewell gesture). He tells his disciples that this is to be an 'example' (*hupodeigma*, v. 15). This indicates that the footwashing is a symbolic farewell gesture; it is pregnant with soteriological and martyrological significance.

In the ensuing narrative, Peter objects to being washed but Jesus goes on to tell the disciples that they will be blessed if they follow his example. This *blessing* is another ingredient of the context for the typical farewell speech. Jesus then tells the disciples that one of them will betray him (v. 21). They are bemused (v. 22) but Peter ends up promising to follow his master even unto death (vv. 36-38). These two responses are signs of *the successors bewailing the loss of their leader*—another characteristic of the farewell genre.

Evidently Jn 13.1-38 has the four ingredients for the context of the typical farewell speech. The reader should also note the content of the farewell speech itself in 13.1-38. There are *exhortations* (vv. 14-17), *revelations of the future* (vv. 18-21), *promises* (vv. 31-33), *tasks for successors* (vv. 34-35) and predictions of *future degeneration* (v. 38). Even at this stage the *content* as well as the *context* of Jesus' words conforms to the conventional farewell scene.

Structure

F.J. Moloney has highlighted the literary unity of Jn 13.1-38 in his essay, 'The Structure and Message of John 13.1-38' (1986). He has shown how the double *amēn* formula (13.16, 20, 21, 38) occurs more in John 13 than in any other chapter of the Gospel. He has also shown how this expression functions as a structural marker, indicating the beginning and ending of units.

Thus there are three main units in John 13: vv. 1-17, which close with a double *amēn* in vv. 16-17; vv. 18-20 (the centrepiece of the chapter) which close with a double *amēn* in v. 20; and vv. 21-38, which open with the double *amēn* formula in v. 21 and close with the same expression in v. 38. The first and third units of John 13 are both composed of three sub-sections. Section 1 (13.1-17) has an introduction to the footwashing (vv. 1-5), a first dialogue (vv. 6-11) and an explanation by Jesus (vv. 12-17). Section 3 has three sub-sections as well: an introduction concerning the gift of the morsel to Judas (vv. 21-26a), the gift of the morsel and the words of Jesus to Judas (vv. 26b-30), and the interpretation by Jesus, involving a second dialogue with Peter (vv. 31-38). Moloney sees a number of parallels between these two main sections (1986: 6):

I. *The footwashing seen in the light of the betrayal (13.1-17).*

1.   The love of Jesus for his own comes to its perfection (v. 1)
      Allusion to the betrayal (v. 2)
2.   Simon Peter and Jesus (vv. 6a-10ab).
      Allusion to the betrayal (vv. 10c-11)
3.   The gift of example (vv. 12-17)

III. *The gift of the morsel as the continuation of the footwashing (13.21-38).*

1.   Jesus troubled in spirit and his witness (v. 21a).
      Allusion to the betrayal (vv. 21b-25)
2.   Judas and Jesus (vv. 26b-27)
      Anticipation of the betrayal (vv. 28-30)
3.   The gift of love (vv. 31-38)

This leaves the central unit in 13.18-20. Moloney argues that these three verses form the very centre of Jn 13.1-38 both materially and theologically. He provides the following structured presentation (1986: 6-7):

II. 18. I am not speaking to you all.
    I know whom I have chosen.
    It is that the scripture may be
        fulfilled.
    'He who *ate my bread*
    has lifted his heel against me.'

19. I tell you this now
    before it takes place
    that you may believe
    when it does take place
    that I AM HE.

20. Amen, amen I say to you,
    he who receives any one whom I
        sent receives me.
    And he who *receives me* receives
        him who sent me.

As Moloney writes in a later essay,

> Forming a central statement between the narratives of the foot-washing and the gift of the morsel, John reports Jesus' choosing and sending his disciples (vv. 18-20)... Read within the whole chapter, Jesus tells disciples who will betray him, that he is telling them these things before they happen, so that when the denials, betrayals, and the death of Jesus have been perpetrated by the very ones whom Jesus has chosen and sent, then they will come to belief in Jesus as 'I am he' (1991: 247).

The notion of revelation indicated by the *egō eimi* formula in v. 19 is central. After the resurrection the disciples will recall this incident and what Jesus said, and recognize that both were more revelatory than they knew at the time. In coming to this post-resurrectional *anagnorisis* (recognition), the disciples will also see that the foreknowledge of Jesus provides even more evidence for the christological belief that Jesus is the 'I am' (v. 19).

Characterization

a. Jesus and Peter. The elusiveness of Jesus is again stressed. In 13.1-11, this theme is focused upon Jesus' elusive actions as he washes the disciples' feet. The enigmatic nature of Jesus' act emerges in his dialogue with Peter. Jesus says to Peter, 'You do not realize now what I am doing, but later you will understand' (v. 7). As we shall see in a moment, Peter has failed to see that the footwashing is itself a kind of riddle whose soteriological significance will only emerge after the resurrection (see 2.22; 12.16).

Peter is again the victim of Jesus' elusiveness at the end of John 13. If Peter is the victim of Jesus' elusive actions in 13.1-11, he is the victim of Jesus' elusive language in vv. 31-38. In 13.31-38 Jesus says, 'My children, I will be with you only a little longer. You will look for me, and just as I told the Jews, so I tell you now: Where I am going, you cannot come.' This, like the footwashing, is a riddle concerning Jesus' death: 'I am about to go the way to the Father'. Peter again misunderstands. This forms an inclusio between 13.1-11 and 13.31-38. In both units the elusiveness of Jesus and the misunderstanding of Peter are highlighted.

More important than these indications of Jesus' elusiveness is the narrator's emphasis upon Jesus' knowledge. The first verb in the chapter is *eidōs*, 'When Jesus knew (*eidōs*) that the hour had come'. This verb is a 'narratological eye-catcher' (Du Rand 1990: 383) in that it alerts the reader to one of the primary rhetorical *topoi* in the narrator's repertoire, the theme of Jesus' knowledge. As Culpepper has shown, Jesus' knowledge as the incarnate *logos* has been a vital part of John's characterization of Jesus from the beginning of the Gospel (1991: 135):

Jesus knows Nathaniel before Philip has called him (1.48).
He knows all things, even what is in the hearts of others (2.24-25).
He knows that the testimony about him is true (5.32).
He knows what he is about to do (6.6).
He knows when his disciples grumble about him (6.61).
He knows those who do not believe in him and he knows who his
    betrayer will be (6.64).
He knows the one who sent him (7.29; 8.55).
He knows from whence he came and where he is going (8.14).
He knows that the Father always hears him (11.42).
He knows that the Father's command is eternal life (12.50).

Now, in 13.1-38, Jesus knows that his hour of departure is nigh (13.1, *eidōs*). Jesus knows that the Father has put all things under his power, that he has come from God and is returning to God (13.3, *eidōs*). He knows who will betray him (v. 11, *ēdei*). He knows whom he has chosen (v. 18, *oida)*.

All this contrasts with the lack of knowledge typified by Peter but shared by all the disciples. The narrator underlines this contrast between Jesus' knowledge and the disciple's ignorance in v. 22. At this point Jesus has just announced that one of the disciples is about to betray him. The narrator then remarks: 'His disciples stared at one another, at a loss to know (*aporoumenoi*, from *aporeō*, 'to be uncertain') which one of them he meant'. The narrator again intrudes in the narrative at 13.28 to make the same point: 'But no one at the meal understood (*egnō*) why Jesus said this to Judas'. Jesus himself underlines the ignorance of the disciples at several points:

'What I am doing you do not know (*oidas*) now, but later you will
understand (*gnōsē*)' (13.7).
'Do you know (*ginōskete*) what I have done to you?' (13.12)
'If you know (*oidate*) these things, blessed are you if you do them'
    (13.17).

Clearly the knowledge of Jesus and the ignorance of the disciples (especially Peter) is a vital feature of the characterization in John 13.

b. Judas. Judas begins to act out his narrative function as betrayer in Jn 13.1-38. He has appeared twice in the Gospel so far. In 6.70 Jesus declares, 'Have I not chosen you, the Twelve? Yet one of you is a devil!' The narrator then explains in an aside, 'He meant Judas, the son of Simon Iscariot, who, though one of the Twelve, was later to betray him'. The mention of Judas as a devil (*diabolos*) forms one of a number of narrative echoes between John 6 and John 13 (notice also the use of *trōgō* in 6.54, 56, 57 and 13.18).

In the second reference to Judas in 12.4-6 there is no suggestion that Judas' motives are 'diabolical'. He is portrayed in 12.4-6 as a thief (*kleptēs*) who used to embezzle the common purse. However, in the third reference to Judas (here in 13.1-38), the diabolical nature of Judas' actions, suggested in 6.70-71, is now developed.

In 13.2 the narrator informs us that 'The evening meal was being served, and the devil had already prompted (*beblēkotos eis tēn kardian*, 'put it into the heart of') Judas Iscariot, son of Simon, to betray Jesus'. Then in 13.27, as soon as Judas eats the morsel given to him by Jesus, the narrator tells us that 'Satan entered into him' (*eisēlthen eis ekeinon ho Satanas*). To put the finishing touches to this portrayal of a thoroughly Satanic betrayer, the narrator remarks that, on Judas' exit, 'it was night' (*ēn de nux*). Frank Kermode writes:

> The Greek is as terse as possible; six words cover this exit. Judas leaves the light for the darkness. It is a key moment in the plot. Judas accepts the role; he is what ancient theorists of drama used to call the person designed to bring about the catastrophe' (1987: 462; see also 1979: 92-93).

c. **The Beloved Disciple.** In 13.23 a minor character is introduced in the Gospel, 'the disciple whom Jesus loved'. It is probable, reading John's story in its own right, that the reader is supposed to see this individual as Lazarus. Lazarus has been described with the epithet 'the one whom you love' in 11.3. There the phrase was *hon phileis*. Here in 13.23 it is *hon ēgapa ho Iēsous* (*agapaō* and *phileō* are used interchangeably in John; see 21.15-19). Also, in Jn 12.2, Lazarus is described as one of those reclining (*anakeimenō*) with Jesus at dinner (*deipnou*). Now in 13.23 we see the beloved disciple reclining (*anakeimenos*) with Jesus at dinner (*deipnou*, 13.2). These narrative echo effects make it more than likely that the epithet 'the disciple whom Jesus loved' is supposed to be an honorific code name for Lazarus (Stibbe 1992: 77-82).

This disciple is portrayed in a somewhat idealized fashion in 13.23. He is described as reclining 'on the bosom of Jesus'. This suggests much more than the fact that he is Jesus' 'bosom friend' (Robinson, 1985: 119). Again there is a narrative echo with an earlier part of the Gospel. In 1.18 the narrator describes Jesus in the Prologue as *ho ōn eis ton kolpon tou patros*, 'the one who is in the bosom of the Father'. Here in 13.23 the beloved disciple is described 'on the bosom of Jesus', *en to kolpō tou Iēsou*. Though there is a difference between being 'in the Father's bosom' and 'on the bosom of Jesus', there is an analogous relationship implied here. The implicit commentary is that the beloved disciple shares the same kind of privileged relationship with Jesus as Jesus does with the Father. This is why the beloved disciple functions as an intermediary between Jesus and Peter in 13.23. The beloved disciple is the recipient of true revelation. He overhears the quiet disclosures of the Saviour. Indeed, he listens far more than he speaks in the Gospel. This is the one occasion in John when he says anything.

Implicit Commentary

As we have just seen from the evidence of 13.23, the narrator suggests much from a very few words. In 13.1-38 the reader should note the use of symbolism. Many commentators have noticed the symbolic nature of Jesus' actions in the footwashing scene. Jesus gets up from the meal and takes off his outer clothing, placing a towel around his waist. This has often been interpreted as a symbolic pre-enactment of Jesus laying down his life for the world. There are obvious similarities in that Jesus is stripped of his clothes on the cross. Indeed, in 19.23 the narrator tells us that the guards took Jesus' clothes (*himatia*, as in 13.4). More compelling still is the fact that the verb used for the laying down of Jesus' garments in 13.4 is the same verb which Jesus uses for 'laying down' his life in the good shepherd *paroimia* in 10.11, 15, 17 and 18 (*tithēmi*). It is also the verb which Jesus uses of Lazarus when he asks, 'Where have you laid [buried] him ?' (*tetheikate*, 11.34). The laying down of the outer garments in Jn 13.4 is therefore a symbol for the crucifixion.

The subsequent washing of the disciples may symbolize the salvific and purifying consequences of Jesus' death, especially since the symbol of water is used ubiquitously in the Fourth Gospel, sometimes in the context of purification (2.6; 3.23-25). What is more certain, however, is the way in which the narrator portrays Jesus putting his clothes back on in 13.12. Here the verb is *lambanō* ('take'), which was used by Jesus in 10.17 and 18 for his ability to take up his life again. The whole scene is therefore not only a moving example of the aesthetics of valediction, it is also rich in symbolism. It provides an enacted parable of the descent and ascent of jesus—a journey which involves the naked degradation of the cross.

Themes

A final comment should be made about the dominant theme of John 13. The chapter begins with allusions to the departure of Jesus and to his return to the Father (13.1, 3). This is the regulative idea in the chapter. In a neat inclusio, the text ends where it began with a return to the theme in 13.31-33. Here the verb *doxazō*, ocurring five times in two verses, is used as a metaphor for the return of Jesus to the glory of the Father.

To see how this metaphor operates, we need to look at the occurrences of *doxazō* so far in the Gospel. The narrator introduces us to the notion of Jesus' glorification in an aside in 7.39: 'By this Jesus meant the Spirit, whom those who believed in him were later to receive. Up to that time the Spirit had not been given, since Jesus had not yet been glorified'. This theme reoccurs in 8.54 and 11.4. In 12.16 the narrator provides another aside in which the *doxazō* theme resurfaces: 'At first his disciples did not understand all this. Only after Jesus was glorified did they realize that these things had been written about him and that they had done these things to him.' Jesus then refers to his imminent glorification in 12.23 before God announces from heaven that he has already glorified Jesus' name and that he is about to glorify it again.

Thus the theme of glorification is linked with the death of Jesus, a death referred to as 'the lifting up' of the Son of Man (with the sense of exaltation as well as elevation) and concomitantly as the moment of revelation (8.28). These themes are given full expression in 13.31-33. As Kurz says, 'Being glorified and "lifted up" are Johannine ironic puns that allude both to Jesus' ignominious crucifixion and to his exaltation to God through his crucifixion' (1990: 77).

John 14.1-31

Context

With the context for Jesus' farewell speech established in ch. 13, we now come to the speech itself. This speech is uttered during the evening before Jesus' departure and return to the Father (13.1). As such, the tone of Jesus' words is valedictory, the atmosphere solemn. Yet even here, the night before he dies, Jesus is eager to continue the revelation of the full extent of his love (13.1). Having himself been troubled by death in 11.33 (*etaraxen*), Jesus now exhorts his disciples not to be troubled (*tarassesthō*; the same verb occurs at 14.1, 27) by his impending death. As such the focalization changes in John 14. As far as the disciples are concerned, the focus moves from their feet (John 13) to their hearts (*kardia*, 14.1, 27).

There are parallels here with another great farewell speech, that of Moses in Deuteronomy 31–33. There too, Moses is concerned for Israel not to lose heart: 'Be strong and courageous. Do not be afraid or terrified because of them, for the LORD your God goes with you; he will never leave you nor forsake you.' Notice the intertextual echoes in John 14: 'The Spirit...will be in you' (v. 17). 'I will not leave you as orphans' (v. 18). 'Do not be afraid' (v. 27).

Form

Many of the formal characteristics of the farewell speech described by Kurz (1990) are present in John 14. There is first of all *the announcement of impending death*, understood as departure or 'going away' (*poreuō*, vv. 2, 3; *hupagō*, v. 4). There are a number of *exhortations*,

such as 'Trust in God, trust also in me' (v. 1; see also vv. 11, 21, 23, 27, 28).
There are *revelations of the future*, most notably the going away and
coming back of Jesus (vv. 28-29: 'I have told you now before it
happens, so that when it does happen you will believe'). There are
promises: 'I will do whatever you ask in my name', v. 13; 'The Father
will give you another Counsellor', v. 16. There is *didactic speech*; Jesus
teaches the disciples to obey his commands (*entolai*, v. 15, 21) and to
observe his teaching (*logos*, vv. 23, 24). There is the *question of
successors*.

The last of these is important in John 14. In vv. 16-17 and v. 26 Jesus
promises that the Father will send another *paraklētos* to the disciples.
The word *paraklētos* is a legal metaphor; it literally means 'the advocate
who comes to our defence' (the same word is used for 'advocate' in
1 John 2.1). This is a suggestive image in a Gospel which often feels like a
courtroom. The fact that Jesus promises 'another' *paraklētos* or 'advocate' shows that he is ensuring that the disciples will enjoy the presence
of a successor like himself.

In terms of the farewell genre, the whole of John 14 can therefore be
summarized as *the consolation of the inner circle*, 'I will not leave you
as orphans' (v. 18).

However, even though John makes use of the farewell genre, he also
subverts it. It is instructive at this point to compare John 14 with perhaps the most famous farewell speech in the Graeco-Roman literature,
namely the farewell of Socrates in Plato's *Phaedo*. There are some interesting (though coincidental) similarities. In both texts, the hero is on the
point of facing his own death—Jesus by crucifixion and Socrates by
drinking a cup of hemlock. Both heroes embrace this cup with
confidence and fearlessness. The tone of Jesus' words throughout John
14 is assured and bold, and we may note the Socratic tenor of Jesus'
words in 18.11: 'Shall I not drink the cup the Father has given me?' This
kind of courage is present in Plato's *Phaedo*: 'As he spoke he handed the
cup to Socrates, who received it quite cheerfully...With these words,
quite calmly and with no sign of distaste, Socrates drained the cup in
one breath' (117A).

In both stories, the hero is surrounded by a small number of disciples.
In John 13–16 the eleven disciples are present with Jesus, of which
three are named in John 14: Thomas, Philip and Judas (not Iscariot). In
Phaedo, the last day of Socrates is spent with fourteen named disciples,
of whom Cebes and Simmias are prominent. In both stories, the role of
the narrator in 'telling' the reader what was said is almost non-existent.
The style is more one of 'showing' in the form of dramatic dialogues. In
both contexts the principal rhetorical function of the hero's words is
the consolation of the inner circle, mostly through discussion of what
will happen to the hero and his disciples after his death.

The last of these similarities is important. Both Socrates and Jesus have considerable confidence about where they are going *to* after death. Jesus is sure about going to the Father. Socrates is also confident. He says, 'I have a firm hope that there is something in store for those who have died, and (as we have been told for many years) something much better for the good than the wicked' (63B). As far as Socrates is concerned, the soul is immortal and imperishable and will exist in the next world (107A).

Two important differences should, however, be noticed. The destination of Socrates' death and departure is, first of all, different from that described by Jesus. Socrates describes his destination in terms which reflect Greek culture: 'When I have drunk the poison I shall remain with you no longer, but depart to a state of heavenly happiness' (115D). Like Jesus, Socrates can say, 'I shall not stay, but depart and be gone' (115D); but unlike Jesus, Socrates is going to the realm of the invisible, reserved in the main for the souls of good and wise people. Jesus, on the other hand, is going to his Father's house (14.2), which is also the inheritance of those who in turn obey and love Jesus.

Secondly, there is an enormous difference between Socrates and Jesus in the matter of the *basis* for their beliefs in the hereafter. Socrates' confidence concerning the afterlife is arrived at via the route of philosophical logic. Throughout *Phaedo*, Socrates demonstrates his philosophical powers by deducing, through a relentless and sometimes tendentious rational argument, the necessity of proposing that the soul (and by implication *his* soul) will live again after death. It is through reason that Socrates arrives at the thesis that the soul will 'be born again' (77C). Jesus' belief in his Father's house, on the other hand, is a matter of experience (Jn 14.1-4; 17.5). He has already been there.

The differences are consequently just as revealing as the similarities. The principal way in which Jesus departs from the Platonic use of the farewell genre is in *the question of successors*. In *Phaedo*, the disciples of Socrates ask their master to give heed to the issue of a successor. Simmias is the one who asks, 'But Socrates, where shall we find a magician [an itinerant Sophist of Socrates' stature] who understands these spells now that you are leaving us?' Socrates responds by giving his disciples the task of finding a true successor: 'Greece is a large country... which must have good men in it; and there are many foreign races too. You must ransack all of them in your search for this magician' (78A). It is perhaps this lack of a successor which leaves the followers of Socrates so desolate at the end of *Phaedo*. The consolation of the inner circle in Plato's story is not the consolation of having 'another Socrates' but the comfortable belief in the afterlife of the soul. That is why the narrator (Phaedo himself) says, 'We felt just as though we were losing a father and should be orphans for the rest of our lives' (116A).

In John 14, however, the situation is very different. Jesus himself takes on the responsibility of providing a successor. His promise of 'another Counsellor' is really the promise of 'another Jesus'. Unlike Socrates, in other words, Jesus does not leave his followers comfortless. He does not leave them with the responsibility of finding another itinerant teacher. He promises the Paraclete, the Spirit of Truth, who will live within them and who will even remind them of (and interpret for them) everything he said. While Socrates' disciples therefore end up feeling fatherless and like 'orphans', Jesus' disciples are promised a continued relationship with the Father which will not leave them as orphans (v. 18).

Structure

The teaching on the Paraclete in John 14 is not only central in terms of form, it is also central in terms of narrative structure. Most commentators on this chapter confess considerable difficulties in the analysis of the structure here. R.E. Brown is not untypical; he says, 'The internal organization of chapter 14 is not easy to discern' (1966: II, 623), and that in ch. 14 'it is difficult to know where one unit ends and another begins' (1966: II, 652). Segovia notes that commentators over the years have divided the chapter into two, three, four, five, six, seven, eight and even nine major sections (1991b: 64). However, the use of inclusio and parallelism (noted throughout this present commentary) provides some clues concerning the structure of John 14 and these should be taken into account in any analysis of its literary design.

We should begin by noticing the inclusio and parallelism between 14.1-4 and 14.27-31. Both units are of roughly equal length and both have exactly the same words, 'Do not let your hearts be troubled' (*mē tarassesthō humōn hē kardia*, v. 1 // v. 27). There is also a thematic inclusio between 14.1-4 and 14.27-31. In the former, the theme of departure ('I am going away') and return ('I shall come back') are announced. In 14.28, Jesus harks back to this theme by quoting his earlier remarks at the beginning of the chapter: 'You heard me say, "I am going away and I am coming back to you"'. What this use of both inclusio and parallelism shows is that Jn 14.1-4 is supposed to function as the overture to the chapter, and 14.27-31 as its conclusion. The suggestion of closure in 14.27-31 is indicated by the note of actual leave-taking: 'Peace I leave with you' (v. 27), and 'Come now; let us leave' (v. 31).

The structure of vv. 5-26 presents a major challenge. However, there is yet another use of parallelism in the statements made by the three minor characters in John 14. Thomas's words in 14.5 *must* begin a new unit because 14.1-4 is the introduction to the chapter. His words should therefore be taken seriously as an indication of the kind of construction which signifies the start of a unit. If we look at 14.5 closely we see a comment made by the narrator ('Thomas said to him') followed by a question asked by Thomas: 'Lord (*kurie*), we don't know where you are going, so how can we know the way?'

Since this verse clearly indicates the opening of a unit, we should now look for parallels elsewhere in John 14. The second, similar construction is in 14.8. Here Jesus' words break off and a new minor character joins the dialogue. Again the verse begins with a comment made by the narrator ('Philip said to him') and proceeds to a statement made by Philip in direct speech, 'Lord (*kurie*), show us the Father and that will be enough for us'. This parallels 14.5, where Thomas also begins his statement with the word *kurie*. We may justly infer, therefore, that 14.5-7 is the second narrative unit of John 14, and that a third begins at 14.8.

The third and final example of this parallel construction is in 14.22. Here again we find a statement by the narrator ('And Judas [not Iscariot] said to him') followed by a question, again beginning with the vocative, *kurie*: 'Lord, why do you intend to show yourself to us and not to the world?' Here the actual verbal construction precisely mirrors that used in the remark by Thomas. Both are interrogatives and both are negative in form ('We don't know...so how can we know?' // 'Why not to the world?'). This should indicate to the reader that 14.5-7 (Jesus and Thomas) and 14.22-26 (Jesus and Judas) are parallel and complete sections.

It is with these comments in mind that I propose the following structure for John 14:

1-4	Introduction	'Do not let your hearts be troubled.'
5-7	Dialogue with Thomas	The disciple comes to the Father through the Son
8-21	Dialogue with Philip	a. vv. 9-14, 'The Father is in me and I am in the Father'.
		b. vv. 15-21, 'I am in the Father and you are in me, and I am in you'.
22-26	Dialogue with Judas	The Father and the Son come to the disciple
27-31	Conclusion	'Do not let your hearts be troubled.'

This analysis reveals that the central section is the longest, and focuses on the role of the Paraclete. That 14.8-21 comprises one section is supported by the use of inclusio between the opening sentences (vv. 9-10) and the concluding sentences (vv. 20-21). Both the first and the last words of this section are to do with 'showing' or revelation. In vv. 8-9, the theme is that of Jesus showing the disciple the Father. In v. 21, the theme concerns Jesus showing himself to the disciple. There is some suggestion of parallelism between Jesus' words in 14.9, 'Anyone who has seen me has seen the Father', and his words in 14.21, 'He who loves me will be loved by my Father'. There is certainly a parallel between Jesus' words, 'I am in the Father and the Father is in me' (v. 10), and 'I am in the Father and you are in me' (v. 20). In between these opening and concluding statements there is evidently some transition of thought between v. 14 ('You may ask me for anything in my name and I will do it') and v. 15 ('If you love me, you will obey what I command'). This suggests that the long central section of the chapter is composed of two sub-sections of equal length, vv. 9-14 and vv. 15-21. Both of these sub-sections are entirely composed of the words of Jesus in response to Philip. They are both taken up with the theme of 'indwelling' (see the outline above).

Characterization

In John 14, the role of the narrator is confined entirely to occasional notifications as to who is speaking (vv. 5, 6, 8, 9, 22, 23). There are no comments describing either the thoughts or the expressions of the four characters (Jesus, Thomas, Philip and Judas). Here, as so often in John, characterization is inferred entirely from direct speech.

In Jesus' case, the suggestion of divinity is again implicit. Jesus' descriptions of his Father's house as well as his confident assertions concerning the future are consonant with a divine figure. The use of the predicative *egō eimi* in 14.6, again indicative of the divine 'I Am', also contributes to this impression. The reader should note, however, the suggestion of a theology of subordination in 14.28. Having made the great affirmation of his identity with the Father in 10.30 ('The Father and I are one'), Jesus now introduces an element of hierarchical distinction between himself and God in his words, 'the Father is greater than I'. Here a dialectical understanding of the relationship between Jesus and God is depicted. While the Son and the Father are one in being (10.30), they are not entirely equal in 'greatness' (14.28).

This identification with the Father's divine being does not mean that Jesus is a remote deity. The characterization of Jesus in John 14 demonstrates that his divinity is the furthest remove from the Greek idea of God. If the Greek conception of God stresses *apatheia* (nine steps removed from humanity, as it were), the Johannine portrayal of the incarnate deity in John 14 stresses sympathy. Thus Jesus is concerned to put the hearts of his disciples at rest, to console them, and to provide an abiding sense of his presence even after his death and departure.

The portrayal of Jesus in John 14 is therefore a positive portrayal. The same cannot, of course, be said of Thomas, Philip and Judas, the three minor characters in the dialogue. Here the theme of the disciple's ignorance, prevalent throughout John 13, is carried over into John 14 and focused in the remarks of three individual disciples. The statements of Thomas, Philip and Judas are used by the author to signal either misunderstanding or unbelief. John's recurrent use of misunderstanding follows a common pattern. Alan Culpepper has developed the lists of misunderstandings provided by Leroy (1968) to highlight the ubiquity of this device in the Fourth Gospel (Culpepper 1983: 161-62):

Misunderstandings in John

Passage	Ambiguity	Partner	Theme	Explanation
2.19-21	'this temple'	the Jews	death and resurrection	by narrator
3.3-5	'born anew'	Nicodemus	how one comes to be one of the children of God	restatement in other terms
4.10-15	'living water'	the Samaritan woman	the revelation or spirit which comes from Jesus	deferred (cf. 7.38)
4.31-34	'food'	the disciples	Jesus' relation to the Father	by Jesus
6.32-35	'the bread from heaven'	the crowd	Jesus' origin, identity, and mission	by Jesus
6.51-53	'my flesh'	the Jews	Jesus' death	by Jesus
7.33-36	'I go...where I am you cannot come'	the Jews	Jesus' glorification	no explanation
8.21-22	'I go away...'	the Jews	Jesus' glorification	no explanation
8.31-35	'make you free'	the Jews	the freedom conferred by Jesus to those who receive him	implied by contrast of 'son' and 'servant'
8.51-53	'death'	the Jews	eternal life	no explanation
8.56-58	'to see my day'	the Jews	Jesus as the fulfilment of God's redemptive activity (?)	no explanation
11.11-15	'sleep'	the disciples	death and eternal life	by the narrator then by Jesus
11.23-25	'your brother will rise again'	Martha	Jesus as the source of resurrection and eternal life	by Jesus
12.32-34	'lifted up'	the crowd	Jesus' death and glorification	no explanation

Passage	Ambiguity	Partner	Theme	Explanation
13.36-38	'I am going'	Peter	Jesus' glorification	no explanation
14.4-6	'Where I am going'	Thomas	Jesus' glorification	metaphorical explanation by Jesus
14.7-9	'you... have seen him'	Philip	Jesus' revelation of the Father	by Jesus
16.16-19	'a little while...'	the disciples	Jesus' death and return to the disciples	metaphorical explanation by Jesus

From Culpepper's table we can see that the remarks of Thomas and Philip constitute examples of the misunderstanding. Thomas fails to understand either the destination or the means of Jesus' departure from the world in 14.5-6. Jesus therefore has to explain both to Thomas using the metaphor of the 'way'. Philip fails to understand in 14.8 that Jesus is the revelation of the Father. Jesus therefore has to rebuke Philip for his rather otiose comment. This leaves Judas' question in 14.22: 'Lord, why do you intend to show yourself to us and not to the world?' This is not an instance of the misunderstanding. The question has some parallels with the statement made by Jesus' brothers in 7.4: 'You ought to leave here and go to Judea, so that your disciples may see the miracles you do. No one who wants to become a public figure acts in secret. Since you are doing these things, *show yourself to the world*'. In this instance, the narrator signals to the reader that the request of the brothers of Jesus stems from unbelief (7.5). The question posed by Judas in 14.22 should therefore be regarded as a sign of unbelief rather than of misunderstanding alone.

Plot

The narrator uses suspense to good effect in John 14. In the beginning of John 14 (vv. 1-7), the note of suspense is introduced as Jesus speaks of his impending departure: 'I am going away'. In the long central section of the chapter (vv. 8-21, the middle of the plot), this sense of imminent death largely disappears from view. In the conclusion of the chapter, however (the end of the plot, vv.27-31), the suspense is intensified. This is largely because the announcements of impending death and departure (one of the formal characteristics of the farewell genre) are increased. Indeed, there is a valedictory note struck in v. 27, 'Peace I leave with you'. In v. 28 Jesus reminds the disciples of his statement about going away to the Father. In v. 30, the suspense is intensified even further in Jesus' warning that 'the prince of this world [Satan,

12.31] is coming'. In v. 31 the suspense of the chapter reaches its climactic point. The proximity of Jesus' enemies means that he must now move from the supper room to a new location: 'Come now; let us leave'.

This imperative in 14.31 has spawned a great deal of comment by scholars. Most have complained that Jesus makes to leave, but then proceeds to deliver more speeches in John 15–17. Surely chs. 15–17 must have been clumsily added at this point, so that the smooth flow from Jn 14.31 to 18.1 has been spoiled? Surely 14.31 is a classic (if not *the* classic) example of what source critics have called the Johannine *aporia* (the *non-sequitur* which interrupts the narrative flow)? John 14.31, it is often argued, was originally the conclusion of the farewell discourses.

In this commentary I am committed to discovering the sense and significance of Jn 14.31 in the final form of the narrative. As C.H. Dodd remarked,

> Unless the redactor was strangely irresponsible, he must have given some thought to the arrangement of the material, and unless he was more obtuse than we can easily believe, he must have seen the difficulty about *egeiresthe, agōmen* as clearly as we do. Presumably he thought the words had some intelligible meaning as they stand (1965: 407).

This is the position taken here. John 14.31 is significant in the plot of the farewell discourses because it keeps alive the most important theme of the Gospel, the theme of the elusive Christ. Jesus can neither be apprehended nor comprehended by his enemies. This inability to grasp Jesus is again implied in Jesus' words in Jn 14.30. Here he says that the prince of this world 'has no hold on me' (*kai en emoi ouk echei ouden*, a difficult expression to translate). The devil cannot catch Jesus. However, the fact that the prince of this world is now coming means that it is time to move. In order to evade his captors for one final time, Jesus addresses the whole group of disciples, saying 'Come now; let us leave'. This statement makes very good sense provided we have understood that John wants to portray Jesus as the elusive Messiah.

Reader Response

From the commentary above it is clear that John 14 is one of the more poignant chapters of the Gospel. The emotive character of John's story-telling derives from his exploitation of what I have termed the aesthetics of valediction. There is a subtle dialectic of leave-taking and homecoming in the story. Much of Jesus' language in John 14 indicates the imminence of his departure. This aspect of his farewell has received attention in the analysis above. However, much of the poignancy of Jesus' words derive from the fact that they are devoted to the subject of 'homecoming' in the context of leave-taking. Thus Jesus speaks of returning to the disciples in order to take them to the Father's house (*oikia*) where there are many dwelling places (*monai*). Jesus promises his disciples a 'homecoming'.

The realized eschatology in the rest of John 14 suggests that this house is not so much an eternal home in heaven as a post-resurrection, empirical reality for true disciples. In Jn 2.16 Jesus refers to the Temple as 'my Father's house'. Later in the same passage the Temple is identified as a metaphor for Jesus' body (2.21). When Jesus promises to return to take the disciples to his Father's house in 14.1-4, he is indicating that the disciples will find their true dwelling place in the body of Christ, the church, after the resurrection. This realized interpretation of the Father's house is further supported by the imagery in 14.23. Here Jesus promises that the Father and the Son will make their home (*monē*, as in 14.2) in the lives of obedient disciples. To these true ones, Jesus promises both a home and a Father. No wonder Jesus declares, 'I will not leave you as orphans' (14.18).

It is important to conclude with a few remarks on the relationship between storytelling and homecoming (Stibbe 1992: 166-67). Homecoming is one of the archetypes of literature. Ancient stories such as Homer's *Odyssey* and Euripides' *Bacchae* focus on the theme of frustrated homecomings. In both, the hero is a stranger desperately trying to come home. In Homer's story, it is the hero Odysseus, returning in disguise after the Trojan war, recognized only by his dog. In Euripides' story it is Dionysus, a god *incognito* who wishes to be recognized in his home city of Thebes.

This is a dynamic which we see at work in John's story of Jesus. The Johannine Jesus, like Odysseus and Dionysus, is a stranger who comes to his own people but is not recognized or acknowledged (Jn 1.10-11). He too is condemned to a sense of homelessness as both his immediate family misunderstand his true mission (7.1-5) and his racial family (the Jews) reject him. However, far from reap some fierce vengeance on those who have denied him his rightful homecoming, Jesus reveals the Father's love by consoling his followers with the promise of a new home. To today's reader, the symbol of the Father's house in John 14 can address one of the most fundamental needs within us, for, as J.H. Elliott has put it, 'With house and home are linked the existential issues of identity and belonging, personal and collective origin and destiny' (1982: 236).

John 15.1-11

Context

We now come to one of the most memorable passages in the farewell speech, the discourse concerning the gardener (the Father), the branches (the disciples) and the vine (Jesus). In this commentary, I am treating 15.1-11 as a distinct literary unit because v. 11 contains a rhetorical formula used by the evangelist throughout John 13–17 as an indication of closure ('I have told you this so that...'; see 14.29; 16.1, 4a, 33).

We need to notice several important features about the context for this speech. First of all, there are no spatio-temporal indicators provided by the narrator. After the leave-taking of 14.31, there are no references throughout John 15–17 to narrative settings or to the passing of hours (process time-shapes). Jesus' speech in 15.1-11 almost seems to be without a definable context (see the commentary on 12.44-50). Secondly, unlike 13.31-38 (where Peter speaks with Jesus) and ch. 14 (where Thomas, Philip and Judas are involved in the dialogue), in John 15.1–16.4a there are no questions or statements made by the disciples. The 'you' being addressed by Jesus in the present tense (e.g. 'you are already clean...', 15.3) is not specified. This makes it hard for the reader to locate the speech within a concrete setting.

However, the reader should not be led to conclude from these observations that Jn 15.1-11 has no connection with the chapters which precede it. There are two analepses in this vine discourse. Both hark back to John 13. The first concerns the theme of cleansing, which has figured earlier in the Gospel (2.6, 3.25, *katharismos*). In 15.3 Jesus describes the disciples as already clean (*katharoi*) because of the word (*dia ton logon*) which he has spoken. This reminds the reader of the foot-washing scene at the beginning of the farewell. Here the theme of the moral and spiritual cleansing of the disciples, made possible through the cross, is explored at the level of implicit commentary. In that context Jesus says, 'And you are clean (*katharoi*), though not every one of you' (13.10). Clearly some of the vine imagery is connected with John 13.

The reference to one of the disciples not being clean in 13.10 is also important for locating Jn 15.1-11 within the context of the farewell. The disciple in question is Judas Iscariot, who takes the morsel at the meal, leaves the disciples, and enters the heart of darkness to fulfil his role as betrayer. Judas is the defector *par excellence*. He is the one who does not last the distance as a disciple. He is not the kind of fruit that lasts, that stays the course (15.16). Thus, when Jesus describes the branch on the vine which is cut off (15.2), which does not remain and which is thrown away and withers (15.6), the reader is supposed to think of Judas Iscariot as the primary example of this kind of fruitlessness. He is the branch whose destiny lies in the fire (15.6), an eschatological symbol of destruction.

These two flashbacks to John 13 within the vine discourse (cleansing in the vine, removal from the vine) demonstrate that Jn 15.1-11 is very much a part of the farewell. Indeed, it functions, at the very least in the case of Judas, as a deeper commentary on the actions of characters earlier in the Gospel.

Form

John 15.1-11 seems to be another example of the *paroimia*, the symbolic word-picture, which we encountered in Jn 10.1-21. There Jesus' discourse concerning the shepherd was described as a *paroimia* in 10.5. R.E. Brown has proposed that the two *paroimiai* in 10.1-21 and 15.1-11 are examples of the *māshāl* or 'riddle' (1966: II, 668). They are vital for our understanding of the 'secret senses' elsewhere in John's story.

In the commentary on 18.1-27 I shall show how this works in the case of the shepherd *paroimia* (Jn 10.14). In the case of Jn 15.1-11, we need to ask what other passages in the Gospel are illuminated by Jesus' discourse on the vine.

The first step in establishing this is to make sure that we have understood the sense of the vine imagery itself. This imagery focuses on two major motifs, that of remaining and that of fruit-bearing. The disciples are to 'remain' in the vine (*menō*, ten times here). They cannot take it for granted that *coming* to Jesus is sufficient for salvation. They must continue in their discipleship; their commitment is about permanence. Similarly, remaining in a relationship of intimacy with Jesus (abiding in the vine) is not a static enterprise. It is not a matter of passive resting. There is a crucial, missiological task to fulfil. This task is about 'bearing fruit' (*karpos*), by which Jesus means creating other disciples. Thus, the twofold imperative for discipleship consists of remaining in Jesus and reproducing other disciples.

Understood this way we can see how the vine *paroimia* functions as the narrative code for a more detailed and profound interpretation of earlier stories in the Gospel. In Jn 4.4-42, the narrator tells the story of the transformation of a Samaritan woman. Her encounter with Jesus leads to a radical change of lifestyle—from dependent relationships with men to an effective apostolic ministry. Thus, she leaves her water jar at the well (a Johannine symbol for the relinquishing of one's former way of life) and returns to her village to encourage the inhabitants to come and see a man who told her everything about herself. The villagers start walking out to the well while Jesus himself talks to the disciples about the fruitfulness of the mission field. At this point the villagers arrive and are said to believe in Jesus. Indeed, they are so impressed with Jesus that they ask him to stay with them. Many, on the basis of Jesus' words, confess him as the Saviour of the world.

For the paradigmatic reader, rereading the Gospel story with a keen eye for interconnections, the vine discourse provides the key for a proper interpretation of the actions of the Samaritan woman. Her missionary activity is seen as an example of what Jesus desires of all disciples when he speaks in John 15 of remaining with him and of making other disciples who will remain with him. The woman's mission, in other words, is symbolic of true 'fruit-bearing'. This is why the narrator uses *dia ton logon* in 4.39 and 4.41, and the verb *menō* in 4.40 (twice). The villagers believe in Jesus on account of her words just as the disciples are made clean because of Jesus' word in 15.3 (*dia ton logon*). The villagers ask Jesus to stay with them (*menō*) because remaining with Jesus (*menō*) is a key sign of discipleship in Jn 15.1-11.

Thus the *paroimia* of the vine functions as an implicit commentary on the ministry of the Samaritan woman (and indeed on the ministry of Andrew in 1.35-42). It is a *māshāl* or riddle which helps the reader to uncover the deeper truths concerning the Johannine theology of discipleship.

John 15.12-17

Context
One of the key themes in the farewell of Jesus is the theme of love. In 13.1, the narrator says, 'Having loved his own who were in the world, Jesus now showed them the full extent of his love'. The love referred to in this context is the love of Jesus for the disciples. However, this is not the only love relationship alluded to in the farewell. A second kind of love is the love of the disciples for one another. The disciples are to imitate their master by living in relationships of self-giving love for each other. Thus, Jesus exhorts the disciples to wash each others' feet (13.14-17). He gives them a new command in 13.34: 'Love one another. As I have loved you, so you must love one another; by this all men will know that you are my disciples, if you love one another.'

This theme is carried over into ch. 14. Here a third kind of love relationship is specified, the love of the disciples for Jesus: 'If you love me, you will obey what I command' (v. 15; see also vv. 21, 23, 24, 28). In 15.12-17, this theme of love is given central attention within the context of one literary unit. Jesus begins by saying, 'My command is this: Love each other as I have loved you' (v. 12). The unit ends with a repetition of the words, 'This is my command: Love each other' (v. 17)—another example of inclusio.

John 15.12-17 is the centrepiece of the farewell both thematically and structurally. Thematically, the text is related to all previous allusions to love relationships depicted in John 13–14, particularly the love commandment in 13.34. This theme is continued in John 16 (see v. 27) and in the high priestly prayer in John 17. Indeed the farewell finishes on the theme of love (17.25-26).

Structurally, Jn 15.12-17 forms the very centre and heart of the farewell discourses. There are seven major sections to the farewell (13.1-38; 14.1-31; 15.1-11; 15.12-17; 15.18–16.4a; 16.4b-33; 17.1-26) in a chiastic arrangement. The focal point in this design is this reminder of the commandment given by Jesus to the disciples to love one another. This commandment is renewed in 15.12-17. Thus John 15.12-17 is a unit which functions as the focus of the farewell discourses, both in its structural situation and in its thematic concerns.

Form

The reader should note the introduction of a new element of the farewell genre as identified by Kurz (1990). First of all, there is what Kurz calls *the renewal of a covenant*. The covenant is established at 13.34: 'A new commandment (*entolē*) I give you: Love one another (*agapate*). As I have loved you (*ēgapēsa*) so you must love (*agapate*) one another.' This covenant is renewed in 15.12-17. Jesus says in v. 12: 'My command (*entolē*) is this: Love (*agapate*) each other as I have loved (*ēgapēsa*) you'. In v. 17, Jesus again says, 'These things I command you (*entellomai*): Love (*agapate*) each other'. The element of the *renewal of a covenant* enters the narrative at this stage. This covenantal character is indicated by the prevalence of *entolē* here and at 13.34. This word is used 11 times in John's Gospel and in Paul's writing is 'the characteristic mark of the Mosaic Law' (Brown 1966: I, 504). The frequency of this term in John 13–17 should be seen as a sign that John is consciously employing the farewell genre.

Themes

A very dense concentration of Johannine themes is to be found in 15.12-17. As I have already indicated, 'love' is the principal theme (*agapaō/ agapē*). Closely related to this is the theme of friendship (*philos*, ×3). Disciples who love each other are the friends of Jesus because their mutual love manifests their obedience to him. The theme of the commandment of Jesus is also pervasive (*entolē*, ×3; *entellomai*, ×2). This is related to the theme of love because the commandment of Jesus to the disciples is to love one another. The theme of remaining continues here (*menō*) as does the theme of knowledge (*oida*, once; *ginōskō*, once). The idea of 'asking in Jesus' name' in v. 16 has also occurred in 14.13-14 and 15.7 and will occur again in 16.23-24. Thus Jn 15.12-17 interconnects very widely with the thematic tapestry of the farewell as a whole.

John 15.18–16.4a

Context and Form

Jesus now takes a new direction in his farewell speech. Using the terminology of the farewell genre we can see that the primary rhetorical function of John 14 is *the consolation of the inner circle*, while 15.1-11 can be summed up as *exhortation* and 15.12-17 as *the renewal of the covenant* (of love). Now, in 15.18–16.4a, we move from consolation and exhortation to prophetic *warnings*. Jesus warns the disciples that they will be hated by the world just as he has been hated. 'If the world hates you', Jesus says, 'keep in mind that it hated me first' (v. 18).

In drawing attention to the hostility which he himself has faced, Jesus links this present discourse with the Gospel story in John 5–12. In these chapters Jesus was hounded by the Jews even though his miracles proved his credentials. Thus, Jesus speaks of the Jews in John 1–12 as ones who 'have seen the miracles (*erga*), and yet they have hated both me and my Father' (15.24). John 15.18–16.4a therefore harks back to the first part of the Gospel story.

If the words of Jesus in 15.18–16.4a are linked with the events of the Book of Signs, they are also linked with the farewell discourses thus far. In 15.20 Jesus reminds the disciples of the words he spoke in 13.16: 'No servant is greater than his master'. In 15.26, Jesus' words about the coming of the Counsellor echo his words in 14.26: 'But the Counsellor, the Holy Spirit, whom the Father will send in my name, will teach you all things and remind you of everything I have said to you'. Thus 15.18–16.4a is very much a part of the whole Gospel story. It is important in terms of the plot in the farewell.

It is also important in terms of the overall structure of John 13–17. In the analysis of Jn 15.12-17, we saw how this section incorporating the love commandment stands at the very centre of John 13–17. Immediately on either side of this centrepiece stand two sections with entirely contrasting themes. In the first section (15.1-11), the theme is one of remaining in community. Here Jesus exhorts his followers to abide in the vine. In the second flanking section (15.18–16.4a), the theme is one of exclusion from community. Here Jesus warns his disciples that they will be hated by the synagogue and even excommunicated (16.2, *aposunagōgos*, as in 9.22 and 12.42-43). Thus, around the great love commandment (15.12-17), the narrative explores a fundamental, binary opposition between abiding in community on the one hand, and separation from community on the other.

Furthermore, the theme of hatred in John 15.18–16.4a, indicated by the pervasive use of the verb *miseō* (vv. 18 [×2], 19, 23 [×2], 24, 25), creates another significant binary opposition in the plot of John 15, one between love and hatred. If the major theme of Jn 15.12-17 is love, the major theme of 15.18–16.4a is hatred. The reader should be alert to the careful and often artistic development of narrative themes in the structure and plot of the farewell discourses.

Structure

Something of this narrative artistry can be seen in the way in which John 15.18–16.4a has been designed. The beginning of the unit is clearly 15.18. The abrupt transition from *agapate allēlous* ('love one another') in 15.17 to *ei ho kosmos humas misei* ('if the world hates you') marks the start of a new section.

However, it is not so easy to discern where the unit ends. Some commentators argue that this part of Jesus' farewell speech concludes at 16.3 with the words, 'They will do such things because they have not known the Father or me'. This enables the reader to detect a neat inclusio in the following unit between 16.4 and 16.33. Both contain the statement, 'I have told you these things'. Others contend that the proper ending is at 16.4a: 'I have told you this, so that when the time comes you will remember that I warned you'. This argument is usually based on the observation that the formula, 'I have told you this so that...' (*tauta lelalēka humin hina*..., 16.1, 4a) marks the end of sections elsewhere. A third view is that the unit ends at 16.4b, 'I did not tell you this at first because I was with you'.

Of these three views, the second is the most convincing. Throughout the farewell discourses, the formula translated 'I have told you these things' functions as an indication of narrative closure. This is true in 14.29, 15.11, 16.1, 4a and 16.33. Therefore, I propose that the start of this fifth major section of the discourse is at 15.18 and its conclusion is at 16.4a. The reason why 16.4b is an unlikely conclusion is because there is a clear flow of thought from 'I did not tell you this at first because I was with you' (16.4b), to 'Now I am going to him who sent me' (16.5)—note the confusion in the NIV translation at this point.

As far as the internal structure of 15.18–16.4a is concerned, Francis Moloney (1987) has provided some insightful pointers. Though Moloney argues that 16.3 is the conclusion of the unit, his comments are still helpful. Moloney argues that there are three sub-sections in 15.18–16.4a. In 15.18-21, the hatred of the world is spelt out in general terms. In 16.1-4a, however, there is a specific application of these general terms to the

Johannine community's experience: expulsion from the synagogue and martyrdom (1987: 37). This leads Moloney to propose the following overall structure in the unit (1987: 43; though keep in mind that I see the conclusion at 16.4a):

1. 15.18-21	The world–disciples (18-19)	The first
	The word of Jesus (20a)	explanation
	The world–disciples (20b)	of the hatred
	Cause: Ignorance (20)	of the world
2. 15.22-25	Jesus and his word shows	Results of the
	sin (22)	hatred
	Hatred of Jesus=hatred	
	of the Father (23)	
	Jesus and his works show	
	sin (24-25)	
3. 15.26–16.3	Paraclete–disciples (26-27)	Second
	The word of Jesus (16.a)	explanation
	World–disciples (16.2)	of the hatred
	Cause: Ignorance	of the world

Thus, 15.18-21 and 15.26–16.4a function as the first and third sub-sections, while 15.22-25 functions as the centrepiece.

Time

Something of John's artistry is also visible in the use of narrative time in 15.18–16.4a. There are a number of 'external prolepses' (Culpepper 1983: 67) in this section. 'External predictive prolepses are those statements which refer to events outside the temporal framework of the narrative' (Reinhartz 1989: 4). In other words, they are predictions of the fate of the disciples after the conclusion of John's story (the resurrection in John 20–21) and during the story of the Johannine community. 15.18–16.4a contains a noticeable concentration of such prolepses (Culpepper 1983: 67):

15.18	If the world hates you...
15.20	...they will persecute you...
15.21	But all this they will do to you
16.2	They will put you out of the synagogues; indeed, the hour is coming when whoever kills you will think he is offering service to God
16.3	And they will do this because...
16.4	But I have said these things to you that when their hour comes you may remember...

As Culpepper puts it,

> The references just cited have the effect of collapsing or
> compressing time. That which was expected in the future of the
> story may have already occurred in the reader's past. In a sense,
> therefore, not only the eschatology of the Johannine community
> but also its history is 'realized' in the Gospel story (1983: 68).

Characterization

Adele Reinhartz has spelt out the implications of these predictions for
the characterization of Jesus (1989). There is christological significance
to be discerned in the presence of prolepses in the speeches of Jesus.
Many of these predictive prolepses are 'internal'. That is to say, they are
fulfilled in the course of John's story. Thus, when Jesus tells the arresting party to let the disciples go, the narrator is quick to point out that
this was to fulfil the words spoken by Jesus, 'I have not lost one of
those you gave me' (18.8-9). Other prolepses are 'external'; they are
fulfilled during the history of the Johannine community.

Reinhartz infers from Jesus' predictive statements that John is charac-
terizing Jesus first as the prophet-like-Moses (Deut. 18.15-21) and
secondly as a divine revealer. With respect to the second, Reinhartz
alludes to texts in Deutero-Isaiah where Yahweh announces things
before they happen (1989: 10): 'I am the Lord, that is my name...
Behold, the former things have come to pass, and new things I now
declare; before they spring forth I tell you of them' (Isa. 42.8-9; see 44.7-
8, 46.9-10). As Reinhartz concludes:

> There are at least two different christological points being made by
> means of this device [prolepsis]. The first is that Jesus is a true pro-
> phet whose role is to transmit accurately the words given to him by
> God. This point views Jesus and God as separate entities, the latter
> acting as the trusted agent of the former. The second focuses on the
> content of his prophecy as divine speech. In contrast to Deutero-
> Isaiah, the Fourth Gospel views this speech primarily as verifying
> the identity not of God the Father, but of Jesus the Son (1989: 10-11).

A vital contribution to the characterization of Jesus is therefore made by
John 15.18–16.4a. Here again we see direct speech as the exclusive
means of revealing important character traits.

John 16.4b-33

Context

We should remind ourselves of the overall structure of John 13–17 if we are to appreciate the place of Jn 16.4b-33 in the context of Jesus' farewell. I have proposed the following outline:

A^1	13.1-38
B^1	14.1-31
C^1	15.1-11
D	15.12-17
C^2	15.18–16.4a
B^2	16.4b-33
A^2	17.1-26

If this chiastic outline is correct, then we will expect to find a number of parallels between B^1 and B^2. This is indeed what appears. Note the following similarities (Brown 1966: II, 589-91):

	16.4b-33		*14.1-31*
5	I am going to him who sent me.	29	I am going to the Father.
5	None of you asks me, Where are you going?	5	Thomas said to him, 'Lord we do not know where you are going?' (see also 13.36).
6	Your hearts are full of sadness	1	Do not let your hearts be troubled (see also v. 27).
7-11	(Paraclete passage)	15-17	(Paraclete passage)
7	I will send him to you.	26	The Father will send him in my name.
10	I am going to the Father.	12	I am going to the Father.
11	The prince of this world has been condemned.	30	The prince of the world is coming.
13-15	(Paraclete passage)	26	(Paraclete passage)
13	He will guide you into all truth.	26	He will teach you everything.
14	It is from me that he will receive what he will declare to you.	26	He will remind you of all that I told you.

	16.4b-33		*14.1-31*
16	In a little while you will not see me any more, and then again in a little while you will see me.	19	In just a little while the world will not see me any more, but you will see me.
23	On that day...	20	On that day...
23-24	If you ask anything of the Father, he will give it to you in my name. Until now you have asked nothing in my name. Ask and you will receive.	13-14	If you ask anything of me in my name, I will do it. Whatever you ask in my name, I will do it.
25	I have said this to you...	25	I have said this to you...
27	The Father himself loves you because you have loved me.	21	Whoever loves me will be loved by my Father.
28	I am going to the Father.	12	I am going to the Father.
33	I have said this to you so that in me you may have peace.	27	Peace is my farewell to you.
33	Have courage.	27	Do not be afraid.
33	I have overcome the world.	30	The Prince of the world... has no hold on me.

The number of parallels between B[1] and B[2] shows how 16.4b-33 recapitulates many of the the themes of 14.1-31. Note also the similar tone in both sections. In the commentary on Jn 14.1-31, we saw how the focus moves from the disciples' feet in John 13 to their hearts (*kardia*) in John 14 (vv. 1, 27). In John 14, Jesus is concerned to comfort the disciples as he prepares to depart. This same rhetorical strategy of *the consolation of the inner circle* resurfaces in Jn 16.4b-33. Here again Jesus focuses upon the *kardia* of the disciples (16.6, 22), as he endeavours to console them in the grief (*lupē*, 16.6, 20-22) which they are now about to experience as he returns to the Father. The presence of such repetition and narrative echo effects accentuates the care with which the author has located Jn 16.4b-33 in the context of the farewell.

Structure

In the analysis of the structure of Jn 14.1-31, we observed how the questions of the disciples function in that context as structural markers. They are indicators that a unit is about to begin. We see a return to this strategy in Jn 16.4b-33 (which further highlights the parallelism between these two sections). As in John 14, there are three units in 16.4b-33, all indicated by the reactions of the disciples (whose presence has not been registered by either word or action in Jn 15.1-11; 15.12-17; 15.18–16.4a).

The first reaction of the disciples is ironically registered as a lack of a response. Jesus indicates the presence of the disciples as questioners in 16.5 by complaining of an absence of reaction on their part. In 16.5 he says, 'Now I am going to him who sent me, yet none of you asks me, "Where are you going?"' The second reaction of the disciples is registered by the narrator, whose voice re-emerges in 16.17 for the first time since 14.23. Here we read, 'Some of his disciples said to one another, "What does he mean...?"' The third reaction of the disciples is observed in 16.29: 'Then Jesus' disciples' said, "Now you are speaking clearly"'. These three responses function as structural markers. They mark the presence of three units centred upon 16.5, 16.17 and 16.29.

Note the progression in these responses. The first response (16.5) is really an absent response. The disciples do not speak to Jesus at all. The second is really an indirect response. They do not speak to Jesus directly but speak to one another instead. The third response is, however, a distinct intervention. Here their words (16.29-30) are a direct response to Jesus' words and are actually addressed to Jesus rather than to one another. The threefold role of the disciples therefore creates a sense of progression in the plot of Jn 16.4b-33.

I propose therefore that Jn 16.4b-33 comprises three units which focus upon the responses of the disciples. F. Segovia, in his recent literary analysis of John 13–16 (1991b), also argues that the progressive role of the disciples functions as a crucial indication of both structure and plot. Segovia proposes that Jn 16.4b-33 is composed of these three units. Each of these contains the following characteristics: 1. a declaration of Jesus; 2. a reaction by the disciples; and 3. a further declaration of Jesus in response to the disciple's reaction (1991: 222).

Thus, the first unit comprises: 1. the declaration of Jesus in 16.4b-5a ('I did not tell you this at first because I was with you. Now I am going to him who sent me'); 2. the response of the disciples in 16.5b; and 3. a further declaration of Jesus in vv. 6-15.

The second unit comprises: 1. the declaration of Jesus in v. 16 ('In a little while you will see me no more, and then after a little while you will see me'); 2. the reaction of the disciples in vv. 17-18; and 3. the response to Jesus' reaction in vv. 19-24.

The third unit consists of: 1. the declaration of Jesus in vv. 25-28; 2. the reaction of the disciples in vv. 29-30; and 3. the final response to the disciples by Jesus in vv. 31-33. The overall structure of Jn 16.4b-33 therefore looks like this (Segovia 1991: 224):

1.	4b-15	Jesus' departure and the disciples
2.	16-24	Jesus' departure and return and the disciples
3.	25-33	Jesus' revelation and the disciples

Characterization

a. The Disciples. The similarities between John 14 and John 16.4b-33 are important for our appreciation of the characterization of the disciples in Jn 16.4b-33. This section begins with a question asked by Jesus to the disciples. Here Jesus says, 'Now I am going to him who sent me, yet none of you asks me, "Where are you going?"' This is a passage over which many commentators have struggled. Many have argued that this verse is an example of clumsy editing. How can Jesus say that none of the disciples have asked where he is going when Peter has asked precisely this question in 13.36 ('Lord, where are you going?'), as has Thomas in 14.5 ('Lord, we don't know where you are going, so how can we know the way?')? Many contend that a later editor has simply inserted the discourse material of Jn 16.4b-33, forgetting to check all the details. If this redactor or editor had done the job properly, the tensions between 16.5 and 13.36//14.5 would have been seen and the text altered accordingly.

However, this kind of argument fails to take into account the dynamics of a chronological reading experience of the farewell discourses. A sequential reading reveals something of the importance of Jesus' question in 16.5 for the characterization of the disciples. The reader knows that a proper response to Jesus' 'Now I am going to him who sent me' (16.5a) is the question, 'Where are you going?' asked by Peter in 13.36 and by Thomas (less overtly) in 14.5. The silence of the disciples at this point reveals their caution. When Peter asked this question before, it led to a severe warning: 'I tell you the truth, before the cock crows, you will disown me three times!' (13.38). When Thomas asked this question in 14.5, it led to a thinly veiled rebuke: 'If you really knew me, you would know my Father as well'. The silence of the disciples in Jn 16.5 is therefore entirely explicable. The disciples have become very cautious about asking questions. In spite of the constant invitations by Jesus to ask things of both himself and the Father (14.13-14, for example), the paradox is that every time a disciple asks a question in John 13.31–14.31 it is greeted less than enthusiastically by Jesus. No wonder then that the disciples are reticent in 16.5. They have learned the hard way that this is a Messiah who does not need anyone to ask him questions (16.30).

b. Jesus. We need to remind ourselves that the primary characteristic of John's portrayal of Jesus is elusiveness. In Jn 16.4b-33, this elusiveness of Jesus reappears. It is focused in his use of language rather than in his movements. His use of the *māshāl* in 16.16 proves hard to *grasp* as far as the disciples are concerned. Jesus says, 'In a little while you will see me no more', a riddle which recalls 7.33-34, where Jesus tells the Jews, 'I am with you only for a short time...You will look for me, but

will not find me.' Like the Jews in that context, the disciples have a
hard time understanding the riddle in 16.16. This is indicated in the
reappearance of the theme of 'seeking' in 16.19. Here Jesus says, 'Are
you seeking (*zēteō*) the meaning of my words?'

However, a change of strategy is promised by Jesus in 16.25. He says,
'Though I have been speaking figuratively (*en paroimiais*), a time is
coming when I will no longer speak in riddles (*en paroimiais*) but will
tell you plainly (*parrēsia*) about my Father'. There follows in v. 28
a lucid summary of the whole plot and purpose of Jesus' life: 'I came
from the Father and entered the world; now I am leaving the world
and going back to the Father'. With this clear announcement of Jesus'
descent and ascent, a change of perception and faith occurs in the
minds of the disciples. Suddenly they understand Jesus' origins and his
destiny. They have met the major challenge of the Gospel, which is to
know where Jesus has come from, and where he is going to. With this
anagnorisis or 'recognition', the disciples proclaim that Jesus is now
speaking clearly (*parrēsia*) and not in riddles (*paroimiai*). Having been
slow to understand during the plot of the first two sub-sections (16.4b-
15, 16.16-24), they now know the answer to the key question in John's
story of Jesus: the question of Jesus' real origins. They exclaim, 'This
makes us believe that you came from God!' (v. 30).

Themes

There are a large number of familiar Johannine themes in 16.4b-33
(sending, leaving, sin, the world, judgment, knowledge, glorification,
faith, sight, asking, speaking in riddles, speaking openly), but two in
particular should be given attention. There is first of all a fine summary
of the cosmic journey of Jesus in 16.28: 'I came from the Father and
entered the world; now I am leaving the world and going back to the
Father'. The importance of 16.28 consists not only in the fact that it acts
as a catalyst for the disciples' faith development, but also that it underlines one of the major themes both in 16.4b-33 and John 13–17 as a
whole. As Culpepper has shown (1983: 37-38), 'The importance of
Jesus' eternal whence and whither in the farewell discourse is clearly
illustrated by its recurrence in the following statements:

14.12	. . . I go to the Father.
14.28	You heard me say to you, 'I go away, and I will come to you'. If you loved me, you would have rejoiced because I go to the Father.
16.5	But now I am going to him who sent me; yet none of you asks me, 'Where are you going ?'
16.10	. . . because I go the Father, and you will see me no more.
17.11	. . . and I am coming to thee . . .

17.13   But now I am coming to thee...

17.18   As thou didst send me into the world, so I have sent them into the world.

17.24   Father, I desire that they also, whom thou hast given me, may be with me where I am, to behold my glory which thou hast given me in thy love for me before the foundation of the world.

John 16.28 functions as the parade example of this theme of the eternal origin and destiny of Jesus the Messiah.

If the origin and destiny of Jesus is a crucial theme in Jn 16.4b-33, so is the theme of the advent of the *paraklētos*. We have seen this theme at a number of strategic places in the farewell discourses: 14.15-17, 14.26 and 15.26-27. We now see it again in 16.7-11 (the longest Paraclete passage) and 16.12-14.

Symbolism

The symbolism requires attention as well as the themes in Jn 16.4b-33. Worthy of note is the symbol used by Jesus in 16.21. Here Jesus uses an image taken from childbirth as a parable of his coming death and resurrection. He says to the disciples, 'A woman giving birth to a child has pain because her time has come; but when her baby is born she forgets the anguish because of her joy that a child is born into the world'.

In this statement, a poignant link is made between two spheres of meaning, between the agony of the expectant mother and the *lupē*, the grief, of the disciples after Calvary. This link between the mother's pain and that of the disciples who are about to suffer bereavement is suggested by a typically subtle use of echo effects between 16.21 and 19.25-27 (the scene at the foot of the cross).

First of all, the concept of the hour (*hōra*) links the two texts. In the symbolism of the agony of childbirth, Jesus speaks of the woman's pain because her time (*hōra*) has come. This resonates with the concept of Jesus' hour of return, which evidently involves Calvary. Indeed, the word *hōra* occurs at 19.27. Secondly, the word 'woman' (*gunē*) appears in both 16.21 and 19.25-27. Obviously it is a *gunē* who is in labour in 16.21. But in 19.26, the crucified Jesus addresses his mother with the word *gunē*: 'Woman, behold your son!'

These narrative echo effects connect the agony of the woman in labour with the agony of the disciple's bereavement. However, this grief will turn to joy, just as the woman's pain turns to elation once the baby is born. The disciples, when they recognize that Jesus has risen from the dead, will experience the *chara*, the joy, which a mother feels after the trauma of the birth experience. They will experience the joy of new life, the life given to Jesus and the life which they too will be given by the Spirit.

The equation of the mother in labour with the disciples in bereavement seems to be the first order of reference and application. However, this symbol also seems to have a second order of reference. It seems to be multivalent. For not only is there a suggestion that the woman's pain is to be linked with the impending pain of the disciples, there is also the suggestion that her pain is to be linked with the impending agony of Jesus on the cross. After all, it is Jesus' suffering which actually produces life, not the suffering of the disciples. It is through Jesus' agony that a new 'humanity' is born into the world (the word translated 'child' in the NIV is *anthrōpos* in 16.21c). Jesus' agony, in the ordeal of crucifixion, will be like the suffering of a woman in labour. It will be painful, and yet it will bring new life into the world.

Perhaps it is therefore in the childbirth imagery of Jn 16.21 that we should look for part of the significance of the blood and water which flows from the side of Christ as he hangs upon the cross in 19.34. In that context, a soldier pierces Jesus' side with a lance and the narrator reports that blood and water suddenly flow out of the wound. These symbols ('blood and water') are symbols of life in John (see Jn 4.4-15, 6.53). Indeed, blood and water are archetypal symbols for life. They achieve this status not least because blood and water are what flows from a woman in the very final stages of labour, as a human being—an *anthrōpos*—is born into the world. The blood and water which flow from the *pleura*, the 'side', of Jesus in 19.34 (which echoes the *koilia* of 7.38, which can be translated as 'womb') must therefore be linked with the childbirth symbol in 16.21. As this link is made, a profound paradox is uncovered in this symbol, for Jesus is now seen describing his death as a childbirth-experience.

John 17.1-26

Context

We now come to the final and climactic section of Jesus' farewell, the prayer of John 17. We should keep in mind the overall structure of the farewell discourses with which I have been working throughout the commentary on these passages. I have argued for a sevenfold plan in a chiastic arrangement—see the introduction to the commentary on John 13–17. In the analysis of Jn 16.4b-33, I showed how much of this text repeats the themes of 14.1-31. If this structure really exists in the text rather than in this commentator's mind, then we shall expect to find a number of parallels between the first section of the farewell (Jn 13.1-38) and the prayer in 17.1-26. This is indeed the case. Notice in particular the remarkable parallels between the opening passage in both chapters:

John 17.1-26		John 13.1-38	
1	'Father, the hour has come.'	1	Jesus knew that the hour had come...
2	'You granted him [the Son] authority over all people.'	3	Jesus knew that the Father had put all things under his power.
4	'I have brought you glory on earth by completing (*teleioō*) the work you gave me to do.'	1	He loved them to the end (*telos*).

John 17.1-26 is not only the climactic section of John 13–17, it also foreshadows the coming events of the arrest and passion of Jesus. Three factors in John 17 suggest that the death and departure of Jesus is now imminent in the plot of the Gospel. First of all, we should note the use of the adverb 'now' in this chapter. In the previous section, 16.4b-33, the word 'now' (*nun*) begins to appear with increasing regularity: 'Now I am going' (16.5), 'Now is your time of grief' (16.22). In John 17, Jesus says, 'And now, Father, glorify me' (v. 5); 'Now they know that everything you have given me comes from you' (v. 7); 'But now I am coming to you' (v. 13). This increase in the word 'now' creates a sense of suspense. It shows that the hour of Jesus is *now* here (compare 4.23, 5.25: 'An hour is coming and *now* is...').

Secondly, the theme of completion in John 17 indicates to the reader that we are nearing the end of the story. Put another way, the use of *teleioō* reminds the reader of the teleology of John's plot. In 17.4 Jesus declares, 'I have brought you glory on earth by completing (*teleioō*) the work you gave me to do'. Here the idea of the fulfilment of Jesus' mission, the completion of his quest (4.34, 5.36), is reintroduced. This creates suspense.

Thirdly, the theme of 'protection' signifies the approach of danger. In the very next section of the story (Jn 18.1-11), we shall see Jesus standing at the entrance of the olive garden protecting his disciples. We shall see him performing the function of the good shepherd, who lays down his life for the sheep (Jn 10.1-21). These actions are prefigured in John 17 in the petitions for the disciples' safety. In 17.11, Jesus prays that the Father would protect the disciples (*tēreō*). He continues, 'While I was with them, I protected them' (*tēreō*, v. 12). Now he is leaving, so he prays, 'protect them from the evil one' (*tēreō* again).

Time

The second of these statements, 'While I was with them I protected them', highlights one of the most enigmatic features of John 17: the way in which a future action in the narrative (Jn 18.1-11) is presented as a past event. This sense of paradox is also evident in 17.4: 'I have brought you glory on earth by completing the work you gave me to do'. Here again a future reality (the completion of Jesus' work, signalled to the reader by Jesus' words, 'It is finished!' in 19.30) is portrayed as a past accomplishment. We are confronted again with a frequent paradox of the farewell discourses: the remembrance of things hoped for.

As far as 17.12 is concerned, the prime example of Jesus' protective stance towards the disciples is about to be narrated in the following chapter. Yet here Jesus speaks of it in the past tense. What should be a prolepsis (flash-forward) is described as an analepsis (flashback). If the reader interprets this as a flashback, he or she is in trouble; a visible example of Jesus' protection of the disciples prior to John 17 is not forthcoming. Clearly there is something very unusual going on in the narrative time.

All this shows how important it is for us to relate the narrative time of John 17 to the realized eschatology of much of the Fourth Gospel. Throughout John, there is a powerful sense of the presence of the eschatological future. Though the last day is still anticipated as a future event, many of the characteristics of that future day (resurrection of the dead, judgment, the giving of eternal life) are dispensed to a needy humanity in and through the ministry of Jesus. The realities of God's tomorrow are present in the today of Jesus' life. In this respect, normal notions of time have collapsed. The eternal has entered history *in medias res* and, as such, Jesus can speak of future actions as past realities. Jesus can revel in temporal paradoxes because he perceives history always from the perspective of eternity.

Space
If this sense of paradox is explicit in the narrative time of John 17, it is also equally explicit in its narrative space. At the very start of John 17, the binary opposition between earth and heaven is established. Jesus turns his eyes upwards to heaven in v. 1, and then speaks of what he has achieved 'on earth' in v. 4. In the opening of this prayer, the petitioner (Jesus) seems to be praying to the Father while still on earth. However, later on, matters become more complex. In v. 11, Jesus says, 'I am in the world no longer' (present tense, not future as in the NIV translation). This implies that Jesus is already on his journey back to God, 'halfway between this world and the Father's presence' (Brown 1966: II, 747). Yet in v. 13, Jesus says, 'I am saying these things while I am still in the world'. This implies that Jesus is still on earth. So while all seemed clear in vv. 1-4, now in vv. 5-19, the reader is confronted with yet another paradox: a Jesus who not only transcends normal understandings of time, but also normal understandings of space. Jesus is both 'in the world' and 'out of this world' simultaneously.

Characterization

These insights are fundamental to our understanding of the character of Jesus in John 17. John's use of both narrative time and narrative space highlight Jesus' divinity. This is a human person who can pray as if the differences between future and past, heaven and earth are transcended. This is a Jesus whose consciousness is imbued with a supra-human understanding of time and space. Thus, the Jesus of John's story obeys very different laws of gravity. In our Newtonian perspective, 'what goes up must come down'. In the Johannine law of gravity, the opposite seems to be true: 'what comes down [Jesus] must go up!' What John gives us in John 17 is therefore a Jesus at the very edge of our human understanding. This is a Jesus 'at the limits': a Jesus who crosses (*metabainō*, 13.1) human boundaries.

Form

The prayer of Jesus is therefore a fascinating narrative phenomenon. In many ways it is a conventional, formal characteristic of the farewell genre. As Brown rightly says, 'It is not unusual for a speaker to close a farewell address with a prayer for his children or for the people he is leaving behind' (1966: II, 744). Brown points to the first canticle of Moses in Deuteronomy 32 as an example. Here (as in Jn 17), Moses turns from the people to address the heavens. But John goes much further than any other storyteller in his use of the farewell prayer. John's Jesus utters his prayer not as a human being on earth but as a divine being somewhere beyond both time and space.

Jesus' prayer in John 17 therefore transcends the formal conventions of the farewell genre. Like the prayer of Jesus in Jn 11.41-42 and 12.27-29, this is more an example of revelation than of petition. This is a prayer which is 'overheard' by an audience. The reader and the disciples overhear the prayer of Jesus in John 17 and are taken, for a moment, into the heart of Jesus' intimate relationship with the Father. As Käsemann puts it,

> This is not a supplication, but a proclamation directed to the Father in such manner that his disciples can hear it also. The speaker is not a needy petitioner but the divine revealer and therefore the prayer moves over into being an address, admonition, consolation and prophecy. Its content shows that this chapter, like the rest of the farewell discourse, is part of the instruction of the disciples (1968: 5).

J.S. Mill once made the comment that 'prose should be heard, but poetry should be overheard'. What Mill said of poetry can also be said of Jesus' prayer (which many scholars have praised for its poetic qualities). Jesus' prayer in John 17 is supposed to be 'overheard'. Throughout this chapter, the reader is permitted the greatest privilege, the gift of 'overhearing the Godhead'.

Structure

The prayer itself is carefully and artistically constructed. As so often in John's Gospel, the section comprises three equal sub-sections. Many commentators point out that this threefold structure is indicated by the three different objects of Jesus' prayer: himself (vv. 1-8), his disciples (vv. 9-19) and the world (vv. 20-26). All three sections begin with a reference to Jesus praying. Sections 2 and 3 both begin with Jesus saying 'I pray' (*erōtō*, v. 9 and v. 20), and section 1 begins with an indication by the narrator (the only narratorial intrusion in Jn 17) that Jesus is praying (v. 1). The theme of 'glorification' unites all three sections (vv. 1-5, 10, 22), as does the direct address to God as Father (vv. 5, 11, 21). Furthermore, the now expected device of inclusio is used. The beginning and end of John 17 are linked by the description of Jesus' relationship with the Father before the creation of the world (vv. 5, 24), and by the motif of the revelation of God's name (vv. 6, 26).

Within this structure, everything moves towards the climactic petition in v. 21, expressed in the *hina* clause, 'that they may be one'. Jesus' great desire (*thelō*, 'I desire', v. 24) is that the disciples may be one, even as he and the Father are one (v. 22). In a prayer which is itself a literary unity, Jesus prays for unity among believers. As such, form matches content with consummate artistry.

John 18.1-27

Context

The first part of the Book of the Passion comprises chs. 13 to 17, the farewell discourses. The second part is composed of chs. 18 and 19, the Johannine passion narrative. This part of the Gospel contains three major sections of equal length: 18.1-27, 18.28–19.16a and 19.16b-42. What the narrator gives us here is a kind of triptych of narrative Christology. In the first section (18.1-27), Jesus is portrayed as the good shepherd; in the second section (18.28–19.16a), he is portrayed as king; and in the third section (19.16b-42), he is portrayed as the Paschal Lamb. These chapters are a complete narrative unit, as can be seen from the fact that the action begins in a garden in 18.1 and ends in a garden in 19.38-42 (though not the same garden). Alongside this inclusio, we should note the way in which narrative and discourse are woven intricately together, as in the story of the raising of Lazarus (11.1-44). Here we see John's narrative style at its very best.

Structure

John 18.1-27 is composed of three sub-sections. The first sub-section begins at 18.1, a clear departure from the prayer of Jesus in 17.26. It ends with Peter striking Malchus and with Jesus' bold question in v. 11: 'Shall I not drink the cup the Father has given me?' There then follows a small bridge passage in 18.12-14, in which the narrator describes the movement of Jesus from the olive garden to the house of Annas. In the third sub-section, 18.15-27, two separate scenes are described alongside each other. John creates a dual stage-setting in which Peter is seen denying Jesus three times (vv. 15-18, 25-27) while, in the centrepiece, Jesus is telling his interrogators to ask the disciples to come forward as witnesses (vv. 19-24).

In this third unit (18.15-27) John cleverly uses the literary device of ironic juxtaposition. We last saw this strategy used in 4.4-42. In that instance the Samaritan woman was depicted bringing many people to Jesus (vv. 27-30, 39-42) while in the centrepiece (vv. 31-38) Jesus declared that the fields of mission were ripe for harvest. There John juxtaposed Jesus' declaration concerning the fruitfulness of the missiological harvest with a description of many being 'gathered in' to the kingdom. A similar device is used in Jn 18.15-27. In this case, John juxtaposes Jesus' declaration concerning the reliability of his disciples with a description of Peter's weaknesses. In the case of 18.15-27, the irony is to be found in the gap between Peter's failure as 'witness' and Jesus' recommendation that Annas question his disciples (of whom Peter is the representative).

Looking at the unit as a whole, I propose the following arrangement:

1.	1-11	The arrest of Jesus and the bravado of Peter
2.	12-14	The arresters take Jesus to Annas
3.	15-27	The interrogation of Jesus and the denials of Peter
	a. 15-18	Peter's first denial
	b. 19-24	Jesus' first interrogation
	c. 25-27	Peter's second and third denial

There is a clear sense of contrast between the first and third units. In the first, Jesus is in the foreground and Peter in the background. In the third, Peter is in the foreground and Jesus in the background. In both units the conduct of Jesus and Peter are contrasted. Both units, we should note, conclude with a reference to Malchus (vv. 10, 26).

Characterization

In complete contrast to John 13–17, where there is a very limited number of minor characters, in Jn 18.1-27 we meet a large cast of actors: first Judas, then the maniple of Roman soldiers, the officials from the chief priests and Pharisees, Malchus, the commander of the maniple, Annas, another disciple, the girl at the gate, the servants and officials, a guard,

Caiaphas, and another servant of the high priest. Of these, Judas and the other disciple are the most important. They are presented as contrasting examples of discipleship. While Judas functions as a traitorous guide to the arresters, the other disciple (almost certainly the beloved disciple) functions as a faithful guide to Peter.

The two protagonists in this dramatic narrative are Jesus and Peter. Jesus is portrayed as a person in sovereign control of events. Thus he goes to the olive grove where he and his disciples have frequently met (v. 2), knowing full well that he is going to a venue known by Judas. Once the captors do arrive, Jesus goes out to them and confidently reveals his identity (vv. 4-8). This is quite unlike the Synoptic accounts, where Judas takes the initiative. Thereafter Jesus orders the captors to let his disciples go, in fulfilment of his words earlier in the Gospel (vv. 8-9), and ends the section by asserting, with Socratic composure, that he must drink the cup which the Father has given to him. Everywhere in this first sub-section Jesus seems in control of events.

Peter, on the other hand, seems to be very much controlled by them. In the heat of the moment, he brandishes a sword and cuts off Malchus's right earlobe (v. 10), thereby evoking a sharp rebuke from Jesus. In vv. 15-16, Peter relies on the beloved disciple to get him into the courtyard of Annas' house. In v. 17, his bravado with Malchus turns into timidity before a servant girl. In vv. 25-27, he again fails to declare his allegiance to Jesus, this time on two occasions. At the end of the section, a cock crows, reminding us of Jesus' prophecy of Peter's denials in 13.36-38. Everywhere in this third sub-section there are indications of Peter being controlled by his circumstances. His conduct is the very opposite of Jesus'.

Narrative Echo Effects

The poignancy of this contrast between Jesus and Peter is carefully explored in the use of echo effects. In the first sub-section (18.1-11), the arresters declare that they want 'Jesus of Nazareth' (v. 5). Twice thereafter (vv. 5, 8) Jesus identifies himself with the words, 'I am' (*egō eimi*). In the third sub-section (18.15-27), the interrogators of Peter ask him whether he is one of Jesus' disciples. Peter answers twice in direct speech with the words 'I am not' (vv. 17, 25). Here the phrase is *ouk eimi*, the very opposite of Jesus' *egō eimi*. Again we see Peter's conduct contrasted in ironic fashion with that of Jesus.

A second use of narrative echo effects is worthy of mention. The narrator uses the verb *histēmi* ('to stand') twice in this section, first of all in v. 5, and secondly in v. 18. In v. 5, the narrator explains (in what appears at first glance to be a redundant aside) that Judas the traitor was *standing* with 'them'. The group referred to are the arresting party, which includes the *hupēretai* (guards) carrying their lanterns and torches. By standing with them, Judas shows his true colours. He stands with the world, the *kosmos* opposed to Jesus. In v. 18, the narrator tells us that Peter was standing round a fire with the servants and *hupēretai*. In an aside which sounds very similar to v. 5, the narrator says 'Peter also was standing with them, warming himself' (v. 18). Like Judas, then, Peter stands with the world which is opposed to Jesus. This further highlights the anti-Petrine satire in this passage. To be equated with the world is one thing. To be equated with Judas is quite another.

Settings

Another way in which the narrator constructs this anti-Petrine satire is through narrative settings. In vv. 1-11, the setting is a walled garden. We know that it must be an enclosure because of the references to 'going in' and 'going out'. In v. 1, we read that Jesus and the disciples 'went into' the garden. In v. 4, we read that Jesus 'went out' of the garden. This *kēpos* or garden takes on symbolic significance as the narrative progresses. However, this garden is not symbolic of Eden, as so many commentators propose. It is reminiscent and symbolic of the sheepfold in Jn 10.1-5, where there is also a constant sense of 'going in' and 'going out' (Stibbe 1992: 102):

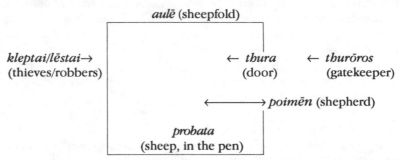

Thus, when Jesus stands at the entrance protecting his disciples in John 18, we are reminded of the *aulē*, the sheepfold, whose entrance is guarded by the good shepherd in Jn 10.1-21. When Judas approaches this walled garden in 18.3, we are reminded of the *kleptēs*, the thief, who tries to get into the sheepfold (Jn 10.1). Indeed, Judas is described as a *kleptēs* by the narrator in 12.6. When Jesus demands that his disciples should be allowed to go, the narrator points out that this was to fulfil Jesus' words, 'I have not lost one of those you gave me', a statement which points to Jesus' role as pastor. In symbolic terms, the walled garden remind us of the sheepfold, the approach of Judas remind us of the thief, the disciples huddled in the garden reminds us of the sheep in the fold, and the protective stance of Jesus reminds us of the good shepherd at the gate. In diagrammatic form, these similarities can be seen clearly (Stibbe 1992: 103):

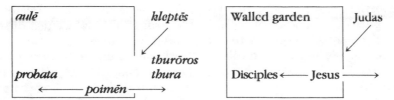

What is the purpose of this use of setting in 18.1-11? Mark Powell has written,

> Mieke Bal suggests that one dynamic frequently relevant for spatial settings of stories is the contrast between inside and outside. Inside settings sometimes carry the connotation of protection or security, but they may also suggest confinement. Likewise, outside settings may connote danger in one narrative and freedom in another. This possibility for different connotations opens the door for paradox, and many stories have seized upon the notion of equating security with confinement, or danger with freedom (1990: 71).

In 18.1-11, the disciples on the 'inside' of the garden are in a setting connoting security and protection. Jesus on the 'outside', however, is in a place of danger. This situation is ironically reversed in the next major unit of Jn 18.1-27. In 18.15-27 the narrator again creates a setting which exploits the inside/outside dualism. Here again the setting is reminiscent of the sheepfold in John 10, but this time 'being on the inside' does not mean security and safety for Peter.

Annas's courtyard is actually called an *aulē* (18.15), the word translated 'sheepfold' in John 10. The door of this *aulē* is mentioned (*thura*), just as the door (*thura*) of the sheepfold is stressed (10.2). A gatekeeper (*thurōros*) is mentioned in 18.16, just as the gatekeeper (*thurōros*) of the sheepfold is stressed (10.3). The beloved disciple is mentioned going in and out of Annas' *aulē* in 18.15-16, just as the shepherd's going out nd coming in is stressed (10.1-5). These parallels are again made clear in diagrammatic form (Stibbe 1992: 103):

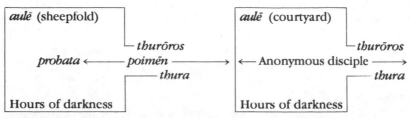

This shows how being on the 'inside' of the courtyard for Peter does not connote protection. In 18.15-27, this setting is now paradoxically the place of danger, the place of interrogation.

The reason why these two settings (the walled garden of 18.1-11 and the courtyard of 18.15-27) are important in the satire of Peter relates to the implicit commentary in these texts. Through this subtle use of settings, the narrator equates the roles of Jesus, Judas, Peter and the beloved disciple with certain roles in the shepherd discourse of John 10. Obviously, Jesus plays the part of the good shepherd, and Judas of the thief in 18.1-11. In 18.15-27, however, the beloved disciple plays the part of the shepherd who walks in and out of the fold, and the girl at the gate plays the part of the gatekeeper. This leaves Peter, who runs away in the hour of danger in 18.15-27. Here the flight is not a literal desertion, but a metaphorical flight from confession. This means that Peter can only be equated with one role in the shepherd discourse: the role of the hired hand, who runs away in the hour of danger (10.12-13).

Themes

The dominant theme of the passage relates to this critique of Peter: it is the theme of discipleship. It is said that Peter and another disciple 'followed' Jesus (v. 15). Here the verb *akoloutheō* is a dynamic verb which is used symbolically. We have already seen how the narrator uses a stative verb symbolically as an indication of where individual disciples stand (vv. 5, 18). In 18.15 the narrator uses a verb of motion in a similar way. At the surface level the verb 'follow' indicates the movement of the beloved disciple and Peter, and helps the reader to see how both of them managed to get into Annas' courtyard. At the symbolic level, however, it connotes discipleship, as the noun 'follower' reveals. The beloved disciple is one who truly 'follows' Jesus; Peter is not. His example is a far cry from that of Jesus, whose conduct under interrogation (where the issue of his disciples is prominent) functions as paradigmatic for all persecuted believers (18.19-24).

A secondary theme is that of the elusiveness of Jesus. Jesus has proved elusive throughout the Gospel with those who have functioned in the narrative as 'negative seekers'—those who have sought to arrest Jesus. This theme of seeking appears again in 18.4-8 where Jesus twice asks his captors, *tina zēteite*, 'Whom are you seeking?' These words were the first uttered by Jesus in the Gospel, to the two followers of the Baptist in 1.38. The verb *zēteō* is used 34 times in John, often of those who want to kill Jesus. In 18.4-8, the surprise in the story is the fact that the arresters now actually catch up with Jesus. They not only find him, they bind him. Maybe this is the principal reason why they fall to the ground in 18.6. This, at one level, is the standard response to a theophany. At another level we can see it as a symptom of the captor's amazement. They fall back in amazement not so much because Jesus is divine as because they have at last apprehended the elusive Christ.

Narrator and Point of View

The many subtleties of this section of the passion narrative have revealed the importance of the narrator. Like the beloved disciple, the narrator is our guide throughout the events of the arrest of Jesus and the denials of Peter. Without this dextrous, bold and subtle assistant, we would not gain entrance to an insider's perspective on these events.

After a lengthy spell of being largely 'off duty' in John 13–17, the narrator's voice emerges once again intrusively at 18.1. From here on we move from 'showing' to 'telling'. The narrator guides us in the matter of Jesus' movements, taking us with Jesus across the Kidron valley into the olive grove, and from the olive grove to the courtyard and house of the high priest Annas. Truly the narrator is our guide in matters of movement, location and character.

The narrator also provides us with details which suggest a particular mood for the whole story. In Jn 13.30, we are told that 'it was night' when Judas left the supper room. In 18.2, with the re-emergence of Judas, we enter again the heart of darkness. That is why the narrator, after reintroducing Judas, speaks of the torches and lanterns carried by the arresters. The mood established is one of darkness, of evil, of tragedy. It is also one of coldness, of death. That is why we are told of the 'winter-flowing' Kidron, and of the charcoal fire in 18.18. It is why we are told that Peter was trying to warm himself (conative participle) in 18.18 and 25. Everywhere the narrator works hard to create a mood of thick darkness and macabre deathliness.

If the narrator is our guide in relation to movement and mood, the same is true in relation to motive. The narrator guides the reader into the minds of the characters involved. Thus, it is revealed that Judas knew the place where Jesus had often met with his disciples (v. 2). This, I infer, is why he takes the arresters to the garden. Similarly, the narrator tells us that Jesus knew everything that was about to befall him (v. 4), thereby emphasizing Jesus' full intentions. This is a saviour who voluntarily allows himself to be arrested.

Other functions are fulfilled by this omniscient narrator: he or she describes settings (vv. 1, 15, 18), interprets events in the light of Jesus' teaching (v. 9), provides brief glimpses of violent action (vv. 10, 22), identifies characters in the drama (v. 10), gives sometimes minute details (the right earlobe in v. 10, the charcoal fire in v. 18), provides a Who's Who of high priests (v. 13), reminds us of events earlier in the story (v. 14), and explains certain important relationships (vv. 15, 26). Without the narrator we would indeed be lost.

John 18.28–19.16a

Context

After the informal interrogation before Annas (18.19-23), Jesus is sent to Caiaphas for further questioning. The narrator does not describe this second interrogation at all. We are simply told that Annas sent Jesus to Caiaphas (v. 24) and that the Jews subsequently led him from Caiaphas to the palace of the Roman governor, Pontius Pilate (v. 28). The reason why the Jews bring Jesus to trial before the Roman governor is spelt out in 18.31: 'We have no right to execute anyone'. This lack of capital jurisdiction means that the Jews are forced to elicit Pilate's help. They have, after all, decided that Jesus must die in 11.45-54. The narrator has reminded us of this decision in 18.14: 'Caiaphas was the one who had advised the Jews that it would be good if one man died for the people'. If this plan is to be fulfilled, then Pilate must be involved in the matter. What follows is an artfully reconstructed account of Jesus' trial before Pilate.

Settings

The narrative begins with a notation of setting. The Jews take Jesus to the praetorium of the Roman governor. They do not enter this palatial residence, however, because they do not wish to become ceremonially unclean (18.28). This refusal to enter the building sets in motion an alternation between a setting outside the praetorium and one inside. As in 18.1-27, there is a sense of 'going out' and 'going in', with Pilate now the subject of these dynamic verbs.

In v. 29, Pilate comes out to the Jews. In v. 33, he goes back inside to Jesus. In v. 38, he goes back outside to the Jews. In 19.1, Pilate goes back inside (implied movement) and has Jesus flogged. In v. 4, Pilate goes out to the Jews again; this time Jesus comes out too, dressed in a purple robe. In v. 8, Pilate goes back inside the palace again to talk, in confidence, with Jesus. In v. 13, finally, Pilate comes out with Jesus and passes judgment. The dramatic effect of this to-ing and fro-ing between the inside and outside of Pilate's residence is undeniable. It creates an alternation between private and public debate which allows confrontation between Pilate and Jesus as individuals, and between Pilate and the crowds.

Structure

R.H. Strachan wrote that, 'The trial is presented dramatically in a series of scenes, which are laid out alternately outside and inside the praetorium' (1941: 315). This creates a two-stage setting with Pilate going out to the Jews, and then back inside to Jesus. R.E. Brown rightly observes that Pilate goes 'back and forth from one to the other in seven carefully balanced episodes' (1966: II, 858). These seven scenes are structured as follows:

A¹	18.28-32	Outside: the Jews demand Jesus' death.
B¹	18.33-38a	Inside: Pilate questions Jesus about his kingship.
C¹	18.38b-40	Outside: Pilate finds Jesus innocent. Barabbas is chosen.
D	19.1-3	Inside: the soldiers humiliate Jesus.
C²	19.4-8	Outside: Pilate finds Jesus innocent. 'Behold the man!'
B²	19.9-11	Inside: Pilate talks with Jesus about authority.
A²	19.12-16a	Outside: the Jews secure the death sentence.

Notice how the alternation of scenes contributes to the characterization of Pilate. It mirrors the uncertainty within himself about Jesus. Also notice the device of inclusio. In A^1, the Jews hand Jesus over to Pilate because they cannot put Jesus to death. In A^2, Pilate hands Jesus back to the Jews, with the authority now to crucify him.

Progression

As always, there is a sense of progression in the plot of John's story. The fact that the story begins with the Jews handing Jesus over to Pilate without jurisdiction and ends with Pilate handing Jesus back to them for crucifixion proves the point. In between, there is a definite sense of increasing conflict and tension. The Jews in particular are responsible for this. They begin by describing Jesus as a 'criminal' (18.30). They then develop the charge in 19.7, after Pilate has now declared Jesus innocent on two occasions. They say that Jesus has committed the crime of blasphemy because he claimed that he was the Son of God. This suggestion does not help their cause; in fact it causes Pilate to be even more afraid. He now tries to set Jesus free (v. 12). At this point the Jews play their trump card: 'If you let this man go, you are no friend of Caesar. Anyone who claims to be a king opposes Caesar' (19.12). This is the real turning point in the trial. Hearing these words, Pilate brings Jesus out to the Jews and acquiesces. Throughout this trial, as in John 9 (the trial of the man born blind), the narrator uses the device of 'progression' to create suspense.

Characterization

a. Jesus. Though Jesus is principally portrayed as 'king' (see comments on irony below), his elusiveness is again prominent. Jesus' defence is not a coherent, logical response to Pilate's interrogations. It is in fact a fine example of what A.D. Nuttall calls 'discontinuous dialogue'. As Nuttall explains,

When Jesus is asked if he is king of the Jews, he answers neither yes or no but instead asks a question of his own. When he is asked what he has done, he answers not that question but the earlier one with the mysterious, 'My kingdom is not of this world'. Even so, he skips one logical stage; to make the logic fully explicit he would presumably have had to say something like, 'I am a king, yes, but not of the Jews nor of anything earthly'. This logical ellipse seems to trouble Pilate and he asks, seeking confirmation, 'Art thou a king, then?' and hears in answer the words, 'Thou sayest I am' (Nutall 1980: 129).

The reason why this 'discontinuous dialogue' creates suspense is because Jesus' technique of deliberate transcendence actually contributes to his own condemnation. It is even more destructive than silence.

b. Pilate. The characterization of Pilate also contributes to this sense of increasing drama and conflict. At the beginning of the trial he opens the debate with confidence: 'What charges do you bring against this man?' (18.29). However, from this moment onwards what looked like an inconvenient, legal formality is transformed into a political and judicial nightmare. Pilate finds himself confounded by the Jews, who know exactly what they want and how to get it. He finds himself confounded by Jesus, whose language is deliberately evasive. He finds himself in conflict with something divine, indeed with the plan of God (19.8). With these forces ranged against him, Pilate now begins to make some serious errors of judgment.

He first of all offers the Jews the choice of Jesus or Barabbas, seizing on the Passover amnesty as a diplomatic solution to a growing crisis. However, in presenting Jesus to them, he calls him 'the king of the Jews!' (18.39) a title which can hardly have predisposed his audience towards the one he knows is innocent (v. 38). Pilate ends up having to free Barabbas (surely the very last thing he wanted) and to keep Jesus.

Secondly, he has Jesus flogged in the middle of the trial in order, presumably, to make the Jews back down. Pilate's hope is that a Jesus who has been flayed and humiliated will be a figure of such pathos that this will be enough to purge the Jews of their hostility (a sort of mass catharsis). And so Pilate presents the stricken Jesus to the Jews with the words, 'Behold the man!' Here again, the choice of words is unfortunate. To a Jewish mind, *ho anthrōpos* (the man) might have roused even more anger, especially if it had connotations of 'the Heavenly Man'. As in 18.39, Pilate's possible solution in reality increases the bloodlust of Jesus' accusers.

In the end, Pilate's growing fear before a man who could be divine (19.8) is not enough to make him overrule Jesus' accusers. It is the possibility of being reported to Rome as an enemy of Caesar that proves the most powerful argument. Pilate brings Jesus out to the Jews, knowing now that his hand has been forced into doing something which he realizes is wrong. Manipulated in this way, Pilate brings Jesus out with the deliberately provocative words, 'Behold your king!' This leads the Jews to shout even louder for Jesus' crucifixion. In the end, Pilate hands Jesus over to be crucified. What began as a legal formality has ended in a travesty of justice.

c. **The Jews.** If Pilate evokes our sympathy (he cannot overturn the destiny of Jesus, indicated in 18.32), the Jews evoke the reader's antipathy. They are the ones who are condemned in the trial, not Jesus. They are manifestly hypocritical in 18.28, worrying about ceremonial uncleanness and at the same time showing themselves unconcerned about the act of gross injustice (indeed of deicide) which they are about to commit. They choose an insurrectionist called Barabbas rather than Jesus, when offered the choice by Pilate (18.40). They shout 'crucify' twice when they see Jesus after his flogging. They manipulate Pilate with the friend of Caesar argument. Finally, they misquote a Passover hymn in 19.15, changing the words, 'We have no king but thee' (Yahweh) to 'We have no king but Caesar!'

Irony
The author constantly uses irony in order to expose the hypocrisy of the Jews and the misunderstanding of Pilate. This literary device has been examined by Paul Duke in his seminal study, *Irony in the Fourth Gospel* (1985). In John's Gospel, irony usually involves a lack of recognition: 'He was in the world, and though the world was made through him, the world did not recognize him' (1.10).

The following ironies should be noted in John 18.28–19.16a:

18.28 The Jews refuse to enter Pilate's palace for fear of ceremonial uncleanness. The irony here derives from two facts: first, that the paradigmatic reader recognizes that 'These soon-to-be murderers are at pains to maintain their purity. They are quite eager to enlist a pagan in the disposition of their crime, but they will not dream of entering his house' (Duke 1985: 128); secondly, 'they fear that ritual impurity will prevent their eating the Passover lamb, but unwittingly they are delivering up to death him who is the Lamb of God (1.29) and thus are making possible the true Passover' (Brown: II, 866).

18.30 The Jews protest to Pilate, 'If this man were not a criminal we would not have handed him over to you'. Here the irony centres upon the use of the verb 'to hand over' (*parodidōmi*). This verb is used frequently in the passion narrative: 18.2, 5, 30, 35, 36; 19.11, 16. In John's Gospel, it means not only 'hand over', but 'betray'. Thus, in 13.21, Jesus says, 'I tell you the truth, one of you is going to betray (*paradidōmi*) me'. Here the reference is to Judas. The irony in 18.30 derives from the *double entendre* in the protestation of the Jews: 'If this man were not a criminal we would not have betrayed him to you'.

18.31 The Jews say, 'We have no right to execute anyone'. Here the Jews are confessing more than they realize. In their own minds they are declaring their lack of capital jurisdiction. In the mind of the paradigmatic reader, they are publicly confessing the illegality of what they are doing to Jesus.

18.32 At this point the narrator reveals another irony. In other words, instead of letting the paradigmatic readers spot the irony for themselves, the narrator guides them into another difference between the perception of the Jews and the perception of informed readers. The narrator points out that the Jews protest in 18.31 because they plan to have Jesus undergo the shame of Roman execution. However, this 'plot' of the Jews is in reality part of the divine 'emplotment' of Jesus. 'Their carefully plotted plan to put Jesus on a Roman cross is only in fulfillment of what Jesus himself has already chosen' (Duke 1985: 128).

18.33 Pilate confesses more than he knows. By calling Jesus 'king', Pilate is describing Jesus without realizing it. Jesus is indeed a king! This irony is repeated in 18.37. Jesus' kingship is the central theme of this section of John 18–19. As Duke says, 'Jesus is called king no less than eleven times in the Johannine Passion account' (1985: 129).

18.34 By asking a question of Pilate, Jesus turns the dialogue into a trial of Pilate. The paradigmatic reader spots from Jesus' interrogative an ironic reversal at this point: the judge becomes the judged.

18.38 Pilate asks 'What is truth?' in the presence of the one who is the incarnation of Truth (14.6).

18.40 The narrator's aside is full of irony: 'Now Barabbas was a robber'. The word here is *lēstēs*, used in Jn 10.1 and 8 to signify the robber who tries to steal from the fold. As Wayne Meeks puts it, 'The Jews reject their king and choose instead a *lēstēs*; unable to hear the voice of the Good Shepherd, they follow one of the "robbers" who comes before him' (in Duke 1985: 131). We should note here the continuation of the narrator's subtle implicit commentary begun in John 18, where Judas represents the *kleptēs* or 'thief' of Jn 10.1. We should also note the coincidental irony of the name 'Barabbas' (literally, 'son of the father'). In a Gospel where Jesus is the Son of the Father in heaven, it is ironic that the Jews reject the true 'Bar Abbas' and, instead, chose an insurrectionist by the same name.

19.1-3 The reader sees the scourging of Jesus as a punitive action. The irony here consists of the fact that Pilate has pronounced Jesus innocent in 18.38, and will do so again in 19.4 and 19.6! Clearly Pilate's sense of justice is warped (Duke 1985: 132). Furthermore, Josef Blank is one of a number of scholars who have detected the beginning of an ironic distortion of a king's epiphany in these verses (cited in Duke 1985: 132). Pilate has already proclaimed Jesus king (the proclamation). In 19.1-3 we have an ironic investiture (the crown of thorns placed on Jesus' head, a purple robe draped over his stricken body). In 19.3 ('Hail, king of the Jews!') we have an ironic reception. In 19.15 ('Behold your king!') we will have another ironic, royal proclamation, and in 19.16b-37, we will have an ironic enthronement (the crucifixion of Jesus with the *titulus*, 'King of the Jews', above his head).

19.5 The narrator says that Jesus 'came out', and not 'was led out'. Here the use of an active rather than a passive verb reveals that Jesus is in command of the situation. The sovereign control over events which we noted in the characterization of Jesus in 18.1-27 is still visible here. Notice also Pilate's 'Behold the man!' Pilate means, 'Look at this wretched human being! What danger can he pose?' To the paradigmatic reader, the statement is a revelatory, credal statement: 'Behold, the Son of Man, the ultimate human being!' Again, Pilate confesses more than he realizes.

19.9 Pilate's question, 'Where do you come from?' is the ultimate concern of John's Gospel. Pilate, without knowing it, has put his finger on the central issue of the Fourth Gospel: the origins of Jesus.

19.10 Pilate tells Jesus that he has the authority to release him. There is a twofold irony here. First of all, Pilate's reference to his authority constitutes a grandiose claim which hardly rings true in the light of his pathetic attempts to get Jesus released (Marsh 1968: 608). Secondly, as Barnabas Lindars puts it, 'Pilate's unqualified claim to be above reason and justice, like an absolute monarch, makes him ascribe to himself the almost divine prerogative which is actually true of Jesus' (1972: 568).

19.12 Here the Jews play their trump card: 'If you let this man go you are no friend of Caesar'. Having presented the Jews with a choice, Jesus or Barabbas, Pilate is now himself faced with a choice by the Jews. The roles are reversed. Pilate, who is really the one on trial, is confronted by the choice, 'Christ or Caesar' (Duke 1985: 134).

19.13 The narrator leaves it ambiguous here whether Pilate sits on the *bēma*, the 'judgment seat' (an intransitive use of *kathizō*), or whether Pilate seats Jesus on the *bēma* (a transitive use). This ambiguity creates a further sense of irony. The paradigmatic reader perceives Jesus as the true judge in the trial, even in his condemnation.

19.14 The narrator provides an important process time-shape at this juncture. The day on which this trial is occurring is the day of Preparation, the day on which the Passover lambs were slaughtered in the Temple. There is a twofold irony here. First of all, this synchronization of the death of Jesus with the sacrifice of the passover lambs creates, in the paradigmatic reader's mind, the suggestion that Jesus is the true Passover sacrifice, the Lamb of God who takes away the sin of the world (1.29). Here narrative chronology and narrative Christology are inseparable. Secondly, as Duke has shown, the Passover context is crucial for covenantal reasons. Passover is a celebration of God's faithfulness to his covenant with Israel. 'How terribly ironic that the chief priests will abandon Israel's faith at the very moment when they are to begin preparations for the celebration of God's faithfulness to them!' (Duke 1985: 135).

19.15 The Jews cry out, 'We have no king but Caesar!' Duke highlights the irony here with his customary insightfulness: 'It is a sacrilege no Jew could utter without forfeit of faith. Israel has but one King (Judg. 8.3; 1 Sam. 8.7; Isa. 26.13). In the Passover Haggadah soon to be rehearsed, the concluding hymn of the Greater Hallel, the *Nismat*, would read:

> From everlasting to everlasting thou art God;
> Beside thee we have no king, redeemer, or saviour,
> No liberator, deliverer, provider.
> None who takes pity in every time of distress or trouble.
> We have no king but thee (1985: 135).

19.16a The Roman governor hands Jesus over to the Jews. Here the word for 'hand over' is again *paradidōmi*. The narrator therefore incriminates Pilate in the farcical illegality of Jesus' condemnation. Pilate may be guilty of a lesser sin (19.11) but he is still guilty. He 'betrays' Jesus to the Jews in 19.16a, and without any formal sentence.

Plot-Type
The pervasive use of irony is the most remarkable literary feature of John 18.28–19.16a. It indicates that the genre of this trial narrative is predominantly ironic. However, I have also shown in *John as Storyteller* (1992: 139-47) that there are elements of the tragic genre in John 18–19, and these surface with particular power in the trial narrative. This is principally because the central theme of tragedy, 'the killing of the king', starts to surface in the references to Jesus as 'king' in the dialogue between Jesus and Pilate (a dialogue which has a number of similarities with the exchange between the god Dionysus and King Penthius in Euripides' tragedy of the *Bacchae*).

The dramatic arraignment of Jesus in 19.1-3 provides us with the *pathos*, the spectacle of extreme suffering, necessary in the tragic portrayal of regicide. Indeed, it has been suggested by more than one scholar that the soldiers who performed this action may well have found the idea in spectacles of humiliation performed on the stage. R.E. Brown refers to a game called 'mock king' enjoyed by Roman soldiers and learnt from Graeco-Roman plays (1966: II, 888-89). The reader should note that there is a humiliation scene in the *Bacchae* in which King Pentheus is dressed up in shameful garb.

If this humiliation of Jesus provides us with the tragic *pathos*, the constant ironies in John 18.28–19.16a provide us with the necessary *hamartia* or 'tragic flaw'. The classic *hamartia* in Greek tragedy is *agnoia*, a failure of recognition. Throughout the trial of Jesus, both the Jews and Pilate are portrayed as the victims of *agnoia*. Like King Pentheus (who cannot see that Dionysus is divine), they are simply ignorant of who it is they are condemning.

What this shows is that the narrator has told the story of the arrest, trial and execution of Jesus as an ironic tragedy. Both the religious institution and the secular state are seen, for once, writing in the archetypal, tragic action of 'the killing of the king'. The dramatic qualities of John 18.28–19.16a seem to confirm this observation.

John 19.16b-42

Context

From the dramatic and highly ironic trial scene we are swiftly taken to the scene of Jesus' execution. Here the crucifixion of Jesus takes place. The actual process of the crucifixion is unimportant to the narrator. This is described with the greatest economy, 'Here they crucified him' (v 18). What is much more significant to the narrator is the conduct of Jesus and that of the *dramatis personae* around or near the cross. These run to a large number: the soldiers, the two victims beside Jesus, Pilate, the Jews, the chief priests of the Jews, the women, the beloved disciple, Jesus' mother, Joseph of Arimathea, and Nicodemus. Each of these are used as foils for understanding the profound implications of the death of Jesus.

Structure

R.E. Brown has noted the artful, literary design of Jn 19.16b-42. He sees seven scenes in a chiastic arrangement (1966: II, 911):

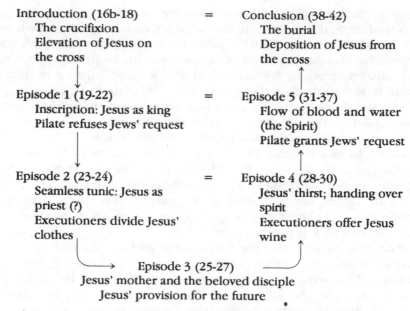

Introduction (16b-18)   =   Conclusion (38-42)
   The crucifixion   The burial
   Elevation of Jesus on   Deposition of Jesus from
   the cross   the cross

Episode 1 (19-22)   =   Episode 5 (31-37)
   Inscription: Jesus as king   Flow of blood and water
   Pilate refuses Jews' request   (the Spirit)
                                                     Pilate grants Jews' request

Episode 2 (23-24)   =   Episode 4 (28-30)
   Seamless tunic: Jesus as   Jesus' thirst; handing over
   priest (?)   spirit
   Executioners divide Jesus'   Executioners offer Jesus
   clothes   wine

                        Episode 3 (25-27)
             Jesus' mother and the beloved disciple
             Jesus' provision for the future

Two things should be noted. First of all, Brown's structure makes it clear that the adoption scenario in 19.25-27 is the focal point of this narrative section. If the beloved disciple was the founding father of the Johannine community then this would make sense. The original readers of the Gospel would take heart from this narrative vignette because it reveals how their leader was the only male disciple at Golgotha and how Jesus adopted him effectively as his successor.

Secondly, the reader should note the use of contrast in this section. The first of these involves Pilate. A request is made to him by the chief priests in 19.21 but it is not granted. A request is then made to him by Joseph of Arimathea in 19.38 and is granted (note the inclusio). The second involves the soldiers and the women in 19.23-27. It is very likely that the narrator intends a contrast between these two groups (note the *men...de* clause in 19.23-25). The four male soldiers, representatives of the unbelieving world, stand in opposition to the four female by-standers, representatives of the believing community. The third involves the soldiers. They take something from Jesus in 19.23-24 (his clothes) but give something to him in 19.28-30 (a drink). These contrasts serve to underline the plausibility of Brown's structural divisions.

Settings

Within this section the narrator again provides us with a clear description of narrative space. In 19.17, the place of execution is described as 'Golgotha', 'The Place of the Skull'. This designation suggests a somewhat macabre scenery. The narrator also makes sure that we see Jesus crucified in the middle of two others. We are then made to see the quaternion of soldiers beneath the cross and the women 'near' (19.25) the place of execution. In the final unit (vv. 38-42), the narrator moves us from Golgotha (the primary setting) to the garden where Jesus is to be buried. This secondary setting helps to create a sense of closure in John 18–19 as a whole. Though the two gardens are different, there is a certain circularity involving the garden of arrest in 18.1 and the garden of burial in 19.38-42.

Time-Shapes

If the narrator's use of narrative space helps to locate the reader within certain settings, the use of narrative time helps to locate us within a definable chronological framework. Indeed, Jn 19.16b-42 is remarkable in terms of spatio-temporal detail. As far as time is concerned, the narrator uses process, retrospective, barrier and polytemporal time-shapes in this unit. There is an obvious sense of process time in the repeated references to the day of Preparation (19.14, 31, 42). These references are important the day after this is described as a special Sabbath (19.31). This creates an element of suspense because Jesus must be dead and his body removed before the Sabbath begins at sunset on the Friday evening. To leave a dying Jew outside Jerusalem on the Sabbath would have been to infringe the most sacred of purity laws.

The use of process time-shapes creates not only a sense of suspense but also of the flow of time. The retrospective time-shape helps to remind the reader of events earlier in the Gospel story and to link the present scene with circumstances related to it. The most obvious of these time-shapes is in 19.39 where Nicodemus is reintroduced. The narrator at this point takes us to one side and reminds us that this was the man who had earlier visited Jesus by night.

The narrator not only uses process and retrospective time-shapes, but also the barrier time-shape which have often been noted earlier in this commentary. The prescribed time limit or 'barrier' by which Jesus must have fulfilled his mission is referred to as his 'hour'. We know from Jn 13.1 and 17.1 that this hour has now arrived. In 19.27 there is a reminder of this predetermined hour of Jesus when the narrator says that 'from that hour/time' the beloved disciple took the mother of Jesus to his own home. This cannot be a literal 'hour', otherwise the beloved disciple would leave the cross at 19.27, thereby making it impossible for him to witness the effusion of blood and water in 19.34. This hour must therefore be a much broader, metaphorical category. It marks the time of Jesus' return to the Father.

The narrator therefore uses temporal indicators for both literal and metaphorical purposes. The use of polytemporal time-shapes contributes to the metaphorical rather than the literal horizons of time in

Jn 19.16b-42. In 19.34-35, the narrator fuses the past of Jesus' death with the present of the reader's experience by taking leave of the story world for a moment. In 19.35, the narrator makes an overt truth-claim in what amounts to a direct address to the reader: 'The man who saw it has given testimony, and his testimony is true. He knows that he tells the truth, and he testifies that you also may believe.' Here the transition from the past tense of the narrator's storytelling to the present tense of this direct appeal creates a noticeable polytemporal effect in the narrative. Nowhere else in New Testament narrative will we find such an obvious attestation of the truth value of an incident involving the historical Jesus.

This is not the only instance of the polytemporal time-shape in Jn 19.16b-42. If 19.35 fuses the past of Jesus history with the present of the reader's experience, the Old Testament citations fuse the eternal with the temporal. The reader should note the vast increase in discernible intertextuality in John's narration of the crucifixion. There are four OT quotations here, in 19.24, 29, 37a and 37b (from Ps. 21.19; Ps. 68.22; Ps. 33.21/ Exod. 12.46; Zech. 12.10 respectively). The effect of these quotations is to indicate that the death of Jesus is in fulfilment of OT prophecy. This means that there is a polytemporal quality in the story of Jesus' death. This death is foreseen and willed by the eternal God.

Implicit Commentary

In creating this sense of a deeper significance to the cross, the narrator uses symbolism and irony. A number of details have been seen as symbolic by the commentators. One of these is the stalk of hyssop used by the soldiers to raise the drugged sponge to the lips of Jesus in 19.29. Since hyssop was used by the people of Israel to daub the blood of the Passover lambs on their lintels and doorposts, it has often been proposed that there is a Passover symbolism intended here. This is very probable. By emphasizing three times that the day of crucifixion is also the day of Preparation there can be little doubt that the narrator is synchronizing the death of Jesus with the slaughter of the Passover lambs in the Temple. This in turn creates an implicit commentary on the death of Jesus as the perfect paschal sacrifice, and shows how narrative chronology and narrative Christology are inseparable in John. The hyssop branch is a further aspect of this Passover symbolism and functions as a reminder to the paradigmatic reader that there is much more to this death than the execution of a religious subversive.

This deeper dimension of meaning is also created through the symbolic meaning of the effusion of blood and water from the side of Jesus in 19.34. Whatever explanation can be offered for this phenomenon on purely medical grounds, the fact is that the narrator clearly regards this stream of blood and water as extremely important. In the commentary on 16.21 (the childbirth *māshāl*), I indicated that the symbolism here may well have to do with the age-old paradox of life in death. Blood and water are life-giving properties in John's Gospel (see Jn 4.4-42 and 6.25-71). Blood and water are also what flows from a woman before she experiences her contractions. Origen expresses the beauty of this paradox perfectly: 'Even in death, Jesus manifested signs of life in the water and the blood and was, so to speak, a new dead man'.

Irony is used in a potent way here. Again, the narrator sets up a distinction between what characters within the narrative world can see, and what the paradigmatic reader standing above this world can see. Thus, when the soldiers crucify Jesus in the middle of two others (19.18), the paradigmatic reader sees this as an unconscious testimony to the centrality of Jesus. When Pilate places a *titulus* above Jesus' head in Aramaic, Latin and Greek, the paradigmatic reader sees this as an unconscious testimony to the universal kingship of Jesus. When the soldiers place the sponge of wine vinegar on a stalk of hyssop in 19.29, the paradigmatic reader sees this as an unconscious testimony to the sacrificial efficacy of Jesus' death. When the same men decide not to break Jesus' legs in 19.32-33, this as an unconscious testimony to the blamelessness of Jesus as the supreme Lamb of God (Jn 1.29, 35).

Characterization

Jesus is therefore, as always, in the centre of the narrative. The feature of his characterization which is most obviously evoked here is his divine sovereignty. Unlike the synoptic accounts (where Simon of Cyrene is brought in), Jesus carries his own cross in 19.17. He has no need of helpers because he is an all-sufficient king. In vv. 25-27, the evocative and moving centrepiece of this section, Jesus thinks not of his own pain but of the needs of his mother. This is the selfless heroism of a divine figure. In 19.28, Jesus performs various actions in the knowledge that they mark the fulfilment of Scripture. This supernatural *gnōsis*, 'knowledge', further sets him apart from ordinary mortals. In 19.30, after a long scene in which Jesus has appeared largely passive, Jesus appears to choose the moment to die. He is the subject of an active verb in 19.30: 'With that, he bowed his head and gave up his spirit'.

All these details reinforce the sense that in 19.16b-30 we have been the witnesses of what is in reality an act of regicide. The piece ends, it should be noted, with Nicodemus providing a prodigious amount of myrrh and aloes with which to anoint Jesus' body (19.39-40). This extravagant quantity of aromatic embalming fluids could only befit one who is in reality a king. Indeed, what Nicodemus provides is a burial fit for the king of kings.

Narrator

In arriving at this kind of interpretation, we rely very much on the narrator in Jn 19.16b-42 who helps us to understand the symbolic value of historical details, the intertextual significance of incidents (through OT references), the meaning of words (note the aside in 19.17), the motives behind Jesus' words (19.28), and the rationale for various actions (19.31, 38). The quality which comes across most strongly in this section is the *precision of detail* provided by the narrator: the three languages of the *titulus* (19.20); the exact nature of Jesus' clothing (19.23); the names of the women bystanders (19.25); the process by which Jesus was given a drink (19.29); the details concerning dates (19.31); the issue of blood and water (19.31); the nature and quantity of Nicodemus's spices (19.39); the Jewish burial customs (19.40); the location of the new tomb (19.41).

It is possible to argue, as does Frank Kermode in the *Genesis of Secrecy* (1979: 101-14), that such details are 'reality effects' designed to create a history-like quality in a blatantly fictional narrative. However, the narrator's aside in 19.35 suggests a more conservative solution. The narrator makes it clear that he or she is dependent on the eyewitness testimony of the one who saw the crucifixion. The witness in question has to be the beloved disciple who featured in 19.25-27. This means that the beloved disciple is not the author of the story but its eyewitness source. From this source came the historical details so faithfully preserved and artfully redescribed by the narrator.

John 20.1-31

Context

The last sentence of John 19 places the reader at the new tomb in the garden where Jesus is buried. The first sentence of John 20 brings us to the same tomb. In John 19 the tomb is occupied. In John 20, we shall see that the same tomb is now empty. This chapter will focus upon a number of responses to the resurrection: the responses of Peter and the beloved disciple (vv. 1-10); Mary Magdalene (vv. 11-18); the disciples (vv. 19-23); and Thomas (vv. 24-29). In the immediate context, John 20 takes us from the tomb as a place of despair to the tomb as a place of discovery.

The place of John 20 in the whole Gospel is more complex. If John 21 was added to the first edition of the Gospel, as many scholars suppose, then John 20 would have formed the original conclusion to John's Gospel. In many ways it makes sense on literary grounds to argue for John 20 as the original conclusion because it forms such an obvious inclusio with John 1 (the introduction to the Gospel). Notice first of all the way in which Jesus is introduced in both chapters. In Jn 1.19-28, Jesus is described by the Baptist as 'one who stands among you' (1.26). The Baptist is speaking here to his Jewish interrogators. We see something similar in Jn 20.19 and 20.26 when the risen Jesus comes and stands among the disciples: 'Jesus came and stood among them'. In both 1.26 and 20.19 and 26 the narrator uses the verb *histēmi* (stand) and the word *mesos* (middle). There seems to be an intentional parallelism between the mysterious way in which Jesus appears in John 1 and the way in which he appears in John 20.

Secondly, there is an inclusio between the theme of the Holy Spirit in John 1 and in John 20. In Jn 1.29-34 the Baptist describes the *katabasis* or descent of the Holy Spirit (1.34) upon Jesus. In Jn 20.22, Jesus breathes upon the disciples and they receive the Holy Spirit. The Gospel begins and ends with the giving of the Holy Spirit—in the first case to Jesus, in the second case to the disciples.

Thirdly, there is a return to the passing of days in John 20. In John 1 we had frequent references to the passing of days at 1.29, 35 and 43. Now, in John 20, we have very clear references to days at 20.1, 19 and 26. In John 1 (if 2.1 is included), we have a period amounting to about one week in story time. In John 20 we have exactly the same period of time (see 20.26, 'one week later'). The Gospel therefore begins and ends with two of the most important weeks in history.

Fourthly, there is a reference to 'turning round' in John 1 and in John 20. In Jn 1.38, Jesus turns round to see the two disciples following him. In Jn 20.14 and 20.16 Mary Magdalene turns round to see the risen Jesus (the first time she fails to recognize him). In both cases the verb for 'turn' is *strephō*.

Finally, and most obviously, the first words spoken by Jesus in the Gospel are, 'What are you seeking?' (1.38). These words are repeated by Jesus in his question to Mary Magdalene in John 20, 'What are you seeking?' (20.15). The verb in both cases is *zēteō*.

It would appear that John 20 was the original conclusion to the Gospel. Various features support this thesis. There is the parallelism between John 1 and John 20 already mentioned. This creates a sense of closure through the device of 'circularity'. There is also the very obvious sense of closure suggested by 20.30-31. Here the narrator announces the conclusion of the Gospel by making a bold declaration of its purpose: 'these things have been written that you may believe that Jesus is the Christ, the Son of God, and that by believing you may have life in his name'. Finally, there are the parallels between the way in which the author concludes John 1–12 (the Book of Signs) and John 13–20 (the Book of the Passion).

This last point is important. The major story in the conclusion to the Book of Signs is the raising of Lazarus. In Jn 11.1-44, the story of Lazarus is based around his tomb. We saw in the commentary how the narrator, through a highly subtle use of focalization, gradually brings Jesus closer and closer to the tomb (*mnēmeion*) of Lazarus. In John 11, however, Jesus does not actually enter the tomb. In Jn 20.1-18, the narrative setting is again the environs of a tomb, this time the tomb into which Jesus himself has entered as a dead man and from which he has emerged as the risen Lord. The constant emphasis upon the tomb of Jesus in John 20 reminds the reader of John 11 which formed part of the conclusion to the Book of Signs. The reference to the head-cloth (*soudarion*) of Lazarus in 11.44 and the *soudarion* of Jesus in 20.7 seems further to support this impression of parallelism in the conclusions to the Book of Signs and the Book of the Passion.

Structure

John 20 is composed of a short scene-setting prologue (vv. 1-2), two sub-sections (vv. 3-10, 11-18, 19-23, 24-29) and an epilogue (vv. 30-31). The two sub-sections are divided into two pairs (vv. 3-10, 11-18 and vv. 19-23, 24-29). The first pair of units describes events at the tomb of Jesus. The second pair depicts events in the house where the disciples are hiding for fear of the Jews. Once again the narrator uses the inside/outside dualism with great creativity.

The overall structure of John 20 appears to be as follows:

A^1	1-2	The prologue
B^1	3-10	The two disciples race to the tomb
B^2	11-18	Mary Magdalene looks into the tomb
C^1	19-23	The disciples meet the risen Jesus
C^2	24-29	Thomas meets the risen Jesus
A^2	30-31	The epilogue

Section B^1 (20.3-10) is divided into five parts. John 20.3 sets the scene: 'So Peter and the beloved disciple started for the tomb'. In 20.4-5, the beloved disciple outruns Peter and arrives at the tomb first. It is stressed that he sees the burial clothes of Jesus but does not enter. In 20.6-7, Peter arrives at the tomb and enters. He sees the burial clothes. Then in 20.8, the beloved disciple also enters the tomb, sees the interior and believes. The narrator adds an aside in v. 9 to the effect that these two disciples did not yet understand from Scripture the necessity of the resurrection. Finally, in v. 10, the disciples return to their homes.

Overall, the first episode of John 20 looks like this:

a^1	3	The two disciples run to the tomb
b^1	4-5	The beloved disciple arrives first, sees but does not enter
c	6-7	Peter arrives second, enters first and sees
b^2	8-9	The beloved disciple, having arrived first, enters second and sees
a^2	10	The two disciples leave the tomb

It should be noted at this stage that it is the details of the interior of the tomb which form the centrepiece of this first episode: 'Peter saw the strips of linen lying there, as well as the burial cloth that had been round Jesus' head' (20.6-7).

Section B² is beautifully constructed. There are essentially two stages in the narrative of Mary Magdalene's encounter with the risen Lord. Both are designed in exactly the same way. In the first stage of the encounter, the two angels in the tomb ask Mary a question ('Woman, why are you crying?' v. 13), she responds with a statement about her despair ('They have taken my Lord away and I don't know where they have put him', v. 13) before turning to see Jesus whom she mistakes for the gardener (v. 14). This first stage is constructed in a tripartite sequence: 1. question to Mary about the reason for her tears; 2. response from Mary about Jesus' body; 3. Mary turns to see Jesus.

In the second stage of the encounter, the same tripartitie sequence is repeated. Mary is first of all asked a question about the cause of her weeping. This time it is Jesus who asks, 'Woman, why are you weeping?' (v. 15). Again Mary responds with the exclamation that she is desperate to know the whereabouts of Jesus' body: 'Sir, if you have carried him away, tell me where you have put him, and I will get him' (v. 15). Jesus calls out her name 'Mary', and she turns to him and cries out, 'Rabboni!' ('My Master!' v. 16). Here the same sequence of question–response–turning is repeated, only this time Mary recognizes Jesus.

The structure of this third unit of John 20 is therefore as follows:

a¹	11-12	Mary sees two angels in the tomb
b¹	13-14	Question-Response-Turning
b²	15-16	Question-Response-Turning
a²	17-18	Mary is told to announce the news

There is an obvious parallelism between B¹ and B². Notice also the suggestion of inclusio between A¹ and A². This is indicated through the use of puns. In vv. 11-12 Mary meets two angels (*angelloi*). In vv. 17-18 Mary goes off to announce (*angellō*) the good news of Jesus' return to the Father. The echoes between *angellos* and *angellō* are unmistakable in the Greek text.

Section C¹ is structured in a fashion similar to the immediately preceding episode (vv. 11-18). Again, two tripartite sequences are juxtaposed. In the first, vv. 19-20, Jesus comes and shares his peace with the disciples. He then shows his hands and his side to them, before the narrator describes the disciples' joy. In the second, vv. 21-23, Jesus shares his peace, breathes the Holy Spirit upon them, and then authorizes the disciples to forgive or retain people's sins.

In section C², from vv. 24-29, the action begins with Thomas having not seen the Lord and with his statement about believing only when he sees Jesus (vv. 24-25). In the next part of the narrative (vv. 26-27),

Jesus appears again, shares his peace for the third time (notice the literary device of the threefold number pattern here), and tells Thomas to place his finger in Jesus' hands and his hand into Jesus' side. In v. 28, Thomas confesses Jesus as 'my Lord and my God!'. The narrative unit then ends where it began: with a statement about seeing and believing, this time with Jesus' blessing, 'Blessed are those who have not seen and yet have believed' (v. 29).

The chapter ends with an epiloguc (Λ^2) in which the narrator makes an open declaration concerning the rhetorical purpose of the book (*biblion*) as a whole (vv. 30-31). The material has been selected and expressed in such a way that the reader may continue to believe that Jesus is the Christ, the Son of God, and experience life in the name of Jesus as a result of that faith.

Themes

The theme which unifies John 20 as a whole involves 'seeing' and 'believing'. In 20.1, Mary goes to the tomb and *sees* that the stone has been rolled away. In 20.5, the beloved disciple bends over the entrance of the tomb and *sees* the strips of linen. In 20.6, Peter *sees* the same items. In 20.8, the beloved disciple *sees* and believes. In 20.11 a similar process is repeated as Mary bends over to *look* into the tomb. She *sees* two angels. They address her and she turns to *see* Jesus. In v. 20, Jesus *shows* the disciples his hands and side. The disciples are described as 'overjoyed' when they *see* the Lord. In v. 25, the disciples tell Thomas, 'We have *seen* the Lord!' In the same verse Thomas says to them that he will not believe unless he *sees* for himself. In v. 27, Jesus appears to Thomas and tells him to *see* his hands and side. In v. 29, Jesus explores the relationship between 'seeing' and 'believing' in what amounts to the climactic summary statement of this theme.

Throughout John 20 the narrator explores the relationship between faith and sight. The concern here is with the faith-responses of each of the characters on the basis of what they see. This begins in vv. 1-2. Here Mary sees the empty tomb but does not yet believe (vv. 1-2). This sets the scene for the whole chapter.

Peter sees the empty tomb in vv. 3-10 but it is not stated whether he believes or not. The beloved disciple, on the other hand, sees the empty tomb and believes (v. 8). His faith-response seems to have something to do with the burial clothes, and in particular the *soudarion* or 'head-cloth' which has been set on one side.

In vv. 11-18 we return to Mary's faith response. We left her in vv. 1-2 running to Peter and the beloved disciple and declaring her ignorance concerning the whereabouts of Jesus' body. Now in vv. 11-18 we see a gradual progression in resurrection faith. At first she sees the risen Jesus but mistakes him for the gardener. She calls him 'Sir' (*kurie*, v. 15). Then, in v. 16, Mary at last recognizes Jesus and cries out, 'Rabboni!' This moment of recognition is in fulfilment of 10.3-4. The use of 'Rabboni!' ('My master!') instead of 'Rabbi' (Master) shows that this is what has been called 'owned' faith rather than 'affiliative' faith. In other words, Mary's resurrection faith is a personal one, not one which depends on others.

In vv. 19-23, the disciples are seen to be overjoyed when they see the Lord. This joy is the result of a correct faith-response. In vv. 24-29 Thomas progresses from unbelief to faith on the basis of seeing Jesus. He too uses the personal pronoun in his confession, '*My* Lord and *my* God!' (v. 28). Like Mary Magdalene, Thomas has made the journey to 'owned' faith. His is not the 'affiliative' faith embraced by the disciples as a group. It is his own faith in Jesus as Yahweh, 'Lord and God'.

Finally, in the epilogue, the narrator turns to the reader. Having explored the faith responses of Mary Magdalene, Peter, the beloved disciple, the disciples and Thomas, the narrator addresses the reader and tells us that he or she has written the Gospel in order that we might believe. Thus John 20 concludes with a sense of 'Dear Reader'. It ends with a question mark, rather than a full stop: 'And do you, the reader, believe?'

In reading John 20, we should therefore be particularly alert to the verbs of 'seeing' and 'believing' which give thematic unity to the chapter as a whole.

Plot

In exploring the faith-responses of the characters in John 20 the narrator makes use of a plot device which we have seen throughout the Gospel. In just about every episode of John the key question has always been, 'Will characters *recognize* who Jesus really is?' The device of *anagnorisis* is fundamental to the emplotment of John's Gospel and indeed, in the present context, to John 20. Here the story examines various moments of recognition: the recognition of the resurrection of Jesus by the beloved disciple (v. 8); the poignant recognition of the risen Jesus by Mary Magdalene in v. 16; the recognition of Jesus by the disciples as a group in v. 20; and the climactic recognition of Thomas in v. 28, 'My Lord and my God!' In every case except that of Peter (whose response is not described), the characters eventually make the correct and fundamental response that Jesus has risen from the dead. As such, the disciples in John 20 see who Jesus really is, just as they do in John 1.

Characterization

However, recognition does not come easily to the characters in John 20. One of the factors which makes it difficult for them to make the journey to resurrection faith is the elusiveness of the risen Jesus. The chapter begins with one of the classic problems of detective fiction, the missing body (20.1-2). This sense of unexpected absence right at the start of the story reminds the reader of Jesus' tendency to thwart peoples' attempts to find him. John 20 then proceeds to another staple ingredient of detective fiction. Jesus is absent when the two disciples arrive at the tomb, but he has left his clothes in a neat pattern. This neatness is a perplexing clue, one which leads a disciple to believe (the beloved disciple).

The elusiveness of the risen Jesus continues in the episode involving Mary Magdalene. She turns round the first time to see Jesus standing near her but does not recognize him. She mistakes him for the gardener! Furthermore, the theme of seeking, always associated with the portrait of the elusive Christ, reappears in the words of Jesus in v. 15: 'Who is that you are looking for?' (*zēteō*). Mary eventually does recognize Jesus, but he then warns her not to hold on to him (v. 17), a statement which again seems to reinforce the picture of a Jesus who will not be grasped in any final sense.

The primary characteristic of the portrayal of Jesus in John 20 therefore has to do, once again, with elusiveness. The Jesus of John 20 is a Jesus whose resurrection body is not immediately recognizable as the same as his pre-resurrection body (20.14). Furthermore, this is a Jesus who can overhear the exact words of characters even when he is not physically present (see 20.25, 27) and who can slip through locked doors (20.26). This is a Jesus who tells Mary not to hold on to him in 20.17 (because he has not yet ascended), and yet who encourages Thomas to touch him in 20.24-29 (when he still has not ascended). Clearly this is an elusive Messiah, a Messiah who is not easy to grasp in any conventional sense.

The other characters who appear in John 20 are all given the challenge of recognizing that Jesus is risen even though that discovery is not made easy for them. Of the characters who are given this challenge in John 20, only Peter seems to remain unchanged. The narrator is strangely reticent about his faith-response. Peter is neither described as believing or not believing. This 'gap' will prove to be important when we come to examine John 21.

The faith response of the beloved disciple, on the other hand, is very much a believing one. He sees the neatly folded grave clothes of Jesus and comes to faith (v. 8). What is it that stirs faith in this disciple? This is the primary 'gap' in the entire chapter. If we subscribe to the view that the beloved disciple was Lazarus, then this 'gap' can be filled by the reader. The beloved disciple sees the *soudarion*, the 'head-cloth' neatly folded on one side and recognizes the same burial garment which he himself had worn in 11.44. The *soudarion* therefore functions as a sign which triggers faith in Lazarus. What happened to him in

Jn 11.1-44 he now believes has happened to Jesus.

Mary Magdalene is the next *dramatis persona*. She is portrayed in a stylized fashion. Her tears at the tomb (20.11) remind us of Jesus weeping at the tomb of Lazarus in 11.35. This echo effect suggests a Christ-like quality to Mary's characterization.

More stylized still are the narrator's description of her movements. In 20.11-18 she turns and sees Jesus, she understands in her heart that he is the risen Lord and experiences healing from her grief. This seems to be a positive counterpart to the narrator's description of unbelief in 12.40. Quoting Isaiah, the narrator says:

> He has blinded their eyes
> and deadened their hearts,
> so they can neither see with their eyes
> nor understand with their hearts,
> nor turn—and I would heal them.

This text provides a commentary on the symbolic importance of Mary Magdalene's movements in 20.11-18. The reader should note the emphasis on seeing, recognition and turning in 12.40 (*strephō*, as in 20.14, 16).

Most stylized of all is Mary's desire to hold on to Jesus in the garden. There are intertextual echoes here with Song of Songs 3.1-3:

> All night long on my bed
> I looked for the one my heart loves;
> I looked for him but did not find him.
> I will get up now and go about the city,
> through its streets and squares;
> I will search for the one my heart loves
> So I looked for him but did not find him.
> The watchmen found me
> as they made their rounds in the city.
> 'Have you seen the one my heart loves?'
> Scarcely had I passed them
> when I found the one my heart loves.
> I held him and would not let him go...

The picture of Mary Magdalene searching for Jesus (notice *zēteō* in 20.15) in the dark hours before dawn (20.1), of her finding Jesus and then wanting to hold onto him and not let go (20.17), is similar to the emotive quest of the woman in Song of Songs. This reintroduction in John 20 of motifs associated with comedy (resurrection) and romance (the lover's quest) shows that the narrator is returning to the prevailing mood of John 2–4, which I described as 'comic romance'.

If the narrator's characterization of Mary is stylized, so is the portrayal of the disciples in the episode which follows (20.19-23). Their faith-response is depicted in language reminiscent of Jesus' promise in

16.22: 'Now is your time of grief, but I will see you again and you will rejoice, and no one will take away your joy'. These words are evoked in the mind of the paradigmatic reader when the narrator says in Jn 20.20, 'The disciples were overjoyed (*echarēsan*) when they saw (*idontes*) the Lord'. Again, an earlier part of the Gospel provides an important commentary on the faith-response of characters in John's resurrection narrative.

The final character in John 20 is Thomas. We have already met him on two occasions in the Gospel. In 11.16 the narrator introduces him as 'Thomas (called Didymus)'. Here he calls the other disciples to go back to Judea with Jesus so that they all may die with him. Here Thomas sounds like a rash pretender to martyrdom. In 14.5 Thomas is introduced again. This time he says to Jesus, 'Lord, we don't know where you are going, so how can we know the way?' If false bravado is the weakness visible in Thomas in John 11, misunderstanding is the weakness visible in John 14. In John 20, false bravado and misunderstanding have progressed to 'unbelief'. 'Unless I see the nail marks in his hands and put my finger where the nails were, and put my hand into his side, I will not believe it'.

John 21.1-25

Context

We saw in the commentary on John 20 that there is a major 'gap' in the information provided. The omission in question is the faith-response of Peter. How did he react to the empty tomb? How did he respond to the risen Lord? Given that he had committed such a shameful act of denial in the courtyard of Annas's house, such an encounter must have caused something of an ambivalent response: joy at the reunion, trepidation at the prospect of confession. But even saying this much is filling in the gap with speculation rather than with knowledge inferred from the text. There is an artful reticence about the characterization of Peter in John 20 which creates a sense of expectation in the reader. When will we be told how Peter felt?

The primary narrative function of John 21 is therefore to describe the inevitable meeting between Peter and the risen Jesus. The chapter begins with some of the narrator's favourite link-words, *meta tauta* ('after these things'). The 'things' referred to are the events of John 20. The continuity between John 21 and John 20 is not only suggested by '*meta tauta*' but also by the reappearance of Simon Peter and Thomas (called Didymus) in v. 2 and the beloved disciple in v. 7. These three men were among the most prominent characters in John 20.

Furthermore, the comment in v. 14 that this appearance on the shore was the third resurrection appearance *to the disciples* (as a group) establishes even closer continuity. The first appearance to the disciples was in 20.19-23, the second in 20.26-29. The events in John 21 will constitute the third and final one of these resurrection appearances to the disciples.

Whoever was the author of John 21, there has been a conscious attempt to make the chapter fit into the immediate context of the Gospel narrative. The same can be said of the overall context. There are a number of examples of inclusio in John 21, again involving John 1. The mention of Nathaniel in 21.2 (see Jn 1.43-51) creates the sense of circularity in the reader's mind. There is a clear and deliberate sense of the end returning to the beginning here. This impression of ring composition is further strengthened by the inclusio involving Peter. John 1.40-42 is devoted to the call of Peter. There Jesus addresses him as 'Simon, son of John'. In Jn 21.15, Jesus again meets Peter and addresses him as 'Simon, son of John'. Most obvious of all is the inclusio involving the imperative *akolouthei moi*, 'Follow me!' (21.19). This harks back to the same command to Philip in 1.43.

So the author of John 21 (wherever he or she was) has composed a narrative which possesses the same literary style as the rest of the Gospel. Thus there are many features in John 21 which are typical of John's literary style (see Pfitzner 1986: 68):

1. The use of distinctive names, such as Simon Peter (son of John), Thomas (called Didymus), Nathaniel of Cana

2. The prominence of the beloved disciple

3. The failure of various characters to recognize Jesus and to understand what he means

4. The hesitancy of the disciples to ask a question

5. The analepsis with Jn 6.11 in 21.13, where Jesus takes the bread and the fish

6. The tripartite number pattern (third resurrection appearance, three questions to Peter)

7. The use of synonyms for 'love', 'sheep' and 'know'

8. The use of the sheep and shepherd imagery, which recalls the *paroimia* of John 10

9. The literary device of the double *amēn* formula in 21.18

10. The use of asides by the narrator (see the commentary below)

11. The analepsis with 13.25 in 21.20, with the description of the beloved disciple as the one who had lain on Jesus' chest

12.   The obvious analepsis between 21.19 ('Follow me') and Jesus' warning to Peter in 13.36 ('You cannot follow me now')

13.   The motif of misunderstanding (21.23)

14.   The examples of inclusio between John 21 and John 1 mentioned above

15.   The reference to the *anthrakia* or 'charcoal fire' in 21.9, which shows that the narrator is consciously linking the restoration of Peter with his denials (which took place by an *anthrakia* in 18.15-27)

16.   The story time, which shows a marked interest in night-time and the early hours of the morning

Form

The author uses three literary forms in John 21. There is the epilogue in v. 25. There are the two dialogue scenes in 21.15-19 and 21.20-24 (a literary form used frequently throughout the Gospel). Most obvious of all is the miracle story in 21.1-14. This shows some marked similarities with the sea stories in Jn 6.1-21 and indicates that the author is drawing upon the same source for Jn 21.1-14 which proved to be the basis for the storytelling in Jn 6.1-21.

At various points in this commentary I have distinguished between four forms of miracle story in the Fourth Gospel, each one deriving from a different source. There are first of all the Cana signs in Jn 2.1-11 and 4.46-54. There are secondly the Jerusalem pool miracles (called 'works') in Jn 5.1-15 and 9.1-41. There is thirdly the somewhat idiosyncratic Bethany miracle involving Lazarus in 11.1-44. There are finally the three miracles based in the same geographical and narrative setting: the feeding of the five thousand by the sea of Galilee (called Tiberias) in 6.1-15, the miraculous crossing of the same sea in 6.16-21, and the miraculous catch of fish in the sea of Galilee (called Tiberias) in 21.1-14.

There are noticeable similarities between the feeding of the five thousand in Jn 6.1-15 and the catch of fish in 21.1-14. The narrative settings are identical (the sea of Tiberias). The reference to bread and fish as the meal in both stories (6.9 and 21.13) forms another similarity. The manual actions of Jesus also reinforce this sense of parallelism: 'Jesus then took the loaves, gave thanks, and distributed to those who were seated as much as they wanted. He did the same with the fish' (6.11) // 'Jesus came, took the bread and gave it to them, and did the same with the fish' (21.13). These echo effects show that the author of Jn 21.1-14 has drawn on the same source as was used for the sea stories in 6.1-21.

Narrator and Point of View

As always, the author tells the story through the persona of an omniscient narrator. The narrator in John 21 names settings carefully

(vv. 1, 4, 8, 9), names certain characters specifically (vv. 2, 4, 7, 8, 10-17, 19, 20-22), leaves some characters unnamed (vv. 2, 7), identifies speakers (vv. 3, 5-7, 10, 12, 15-17, 19, 21, 22), describes action with brevity (vv. 3, 4, 7-9, 11, 13, 15, 20, 25), tells the time (vv. 3, 4), only occasionally explains thought processes (vv. 4, 12, 17, 19), interprets actions for the reader (vv. 6, 8), and provides asides (vv. 7, 12, 14, 17, 19, 20, 23-25).

Of special interest are two particular features of the narrator in John 21. First of all, the narrator shows an unusual interest in precise details or 'reality effects'. We are told that the net was so full that the disciples were unable to bring it into the boat (v. 6), that Simon Peter wrapped his outer garment around him (v. 7), that the other disciples were about 100 yards from the shore (v. 8), that there was a charcoal fire burning on the beach (v. 9), that there were 153 fish in the catch (v. 11), and so on. This specificity is unusual in terms of the Gospel as a whole. However, I made a note of the same provision of reality effects in the commentary on Jn 6.1-15, which I have argued comes from the same source as 21.1-14. The reality effects provided by the narrator in Jn 21.1-14 are therefore signs of a marked predilection for detailed historical reminiscences in John's sea-story source.

Secondly, the narrator in John 21 (as elsewhere in the Gospel) conceals as much as he or she reveals. At the same time as being impressed with the quantity of information given by the narrator, the reader is also frustrated by what is not provided. Indeed, there are a number of 'gaps' in ch. 21. For example, who are the two unnamed disciples in v. 2 (whose anonymity is in marked contrast to everyone else in that verse)? Why are the disciples who met Jesus in John 20 now fishing at the start of John 21? Why are we now in Galilee after spending so much time in Jerusalem? Why do the disciples not recognize Jesus in v. 4? Why does Peter put on his clothes before jumping into the water in v. 7? Why does the narrator tell us that there were exactly 153 fish? Why does Jesus ask Peter the same question three times? Why is Peter so aggrieved at the third time of asking? Why is the beloved disciple exempt from martyrdom in v. 22? Why does the narrator feel the need to end the book a second time in v. 25?

Characterization

Many of the questions which I have just asked are only answered as we go through the text, asking the question, 'What do the details of this verse suggest about the portrayal of Peter?' Peter, after all, is the character whose presence links every episode of John 21. Indeed, even though Jesus' presence is again unmistakable, for the first and only time in this Gospel the spotlight seems to fall not on Jesus but on another character, Simon Peter. In the following analysis we shall go through each verse, using a narrative approach informed by psychological insights.

Verse 1 The narrative setting of the chapter is established right at the outset. From the primary setting of the Book of the Passion (Jerusalem and surrounding areas, in chs. 13–20) we move to the sea of Tiberias or Galilee. This setting, associated with Peter and the sons of Zebedee in the Synoptic tradition, sets up some kind of expectation of meeting these fishermen.

Verse 2 The first words of this verse start to fulfil this expectation. They are, 'There were together Simon Peter...' The reference to the 'sons of Zebedee' also contributes to the sense of fulfilment.

Verse 3 Peter's declaration, 'I'm going out to fish', now comes, at one level, as no surprise. It is precisely what the narrative setting and the mention of Peter and the sons of Zebedee have led us to expect. At another level, however, it comes as an inexplicable turn of events. In John 20, after all, Jesus has given the disciples their commission. He has breathed the Holy Spirit upon them and told them to go and forgive or retain people's sins. Yet now, in 21.3, Peter is encouraging a group of disciples to go out fishing with him. At a psychological level, the only explanation is that Peter is in a state of what is called 'denial'. Having failed Jesus so obviously in 18.15-27, he now seeks to suppress and even obliterate the shame in his life by reverting to 'life before Christ', to fishing. He seeks to deny the three denials. This attempt to fill his 'hole in the soul' with work fails dismally. The narrator laconically remarks that 'they caught nothing'. Peter's gesture is a futile one.

Verse 4 In v. 3 the narrator indicates that it was night-time when the fishing expedition began. Now we learn that it is 'early in the morning'. This is the time when Jesus chooses to appear (v. 4), standing (*estē* from *histēmi*) on the shore. The significance of this note of process time should not be missed. The time between night and the early hours of the morning was precisely the time when Peter denied Jesus in 18.15-27 (see 18.28, 'early in the morning'). Jesus chooses to appear at this time because it is the time associated with Peter's shame. At this stage, however, the disciples on the boat do not recognize that the man standing on the shore is Jesus. Possibly this is intended to be seen as an indication of the distance between boat and land. It is more likely, however, that we are supposed to interpret this as a failure of recognition (the theme of *anagnorisis* once again). From now on the plot of the narrative will be taken up with whether Peter is prepared to face up to and recognize reality.

Verses 5-6 If Peter is secretly and fearfully expecting Jesus to come to him with a word of condemnation and to give him a punitive penance, nothing could be further from the truth. Jesus addresses the disciples as 'Children!' (*paidia*, a term of affectionate endearment) and then proceeds to show them where there is a superabundance of fish (note again Jesus' use of supernatural *gnōsis*). Far from condemnation and penance, Jesus returns to Peter with a word of affection.

Verse 7 The narrator now introduces another character, the beloved disciple. The main narrative rationale for this is because this same disciple has been paired with Peter throughout the Gospel, not least in the context of Peter's denials (18.15-27). Again it is the beloved disciple who is portrayed in a more favourable light. It is he who, yet again, has to help Peter (see 13.23-25; 18.15-27; 20.3-10). It is he, not Peter, who recognizes Jesus: 'It is the Lord!' This prompts Peter to put on his outer garment and throw himself into the sea, so as to swim to his master.

This is entirely explicable on psychological grounds. The fact that Peter puts his clothes on before jumping into the water reveals the profound shame in his life. If Peter had no shame, then, like Jesus in Jn 13.3-5, he would be able to stand naked before others. However, unlike Adam and Eve before the fall, Peter is unable to be naked and unashamed (Gen. 2.25). The shame of the denials has caused a deep loss of innocence in Peter as a disciple. He therefore throws himself upon the mercy of Jesus in v. 7. Here he not only throws himself *towards* Jesus but *into* the water. This act should remind the reader of 13.9, where Peter invites Jesus to wash not only his feet but his whole body. This request of Peter in 13.9 should warn us against attributing the shame in Peter's life solely to the denials in John 18. There is clearly a root of toxic shame in Peter's life even before his rejection of Jesus in the courtyard of Annas.

Verses 8-9 Peter swims to the shore and the other disciples follow in the boat, towing the net behind them (as opposed to dragging it on board). On the shore, Jesus has lit an *anthrakia*, a 'charcoal fire' (v. 9), with fish and bread cooking on it. The importance of the charcoal fire is of course related to the scene of Peter's denials. Jesus is recreating the setting in which Peter denied him (see 18.18). This fire will function as a trigger mechanism, stimulating Peter into remembering his denials as opposed to denying them.

Amy and Thomas Harris write:

> Sights, sounds, and smells affect us differently because of our uniqueness. For example, if you see a red car today, your 'red-car circuits' hum with all the previous impressions you have had of red cars. If your first teenage romance was with someone who drove a

red convertible, the sight of a red car today might flood you with
happy feelings. If, however, you had a head-on collision in a red
car and ended up in a body cast for eight months, the sight of a red
car today would probably produce markedly different feelings from
those of the person with the romance (A. Harris and T. Harris, 1985:
21-22).

These insights provide a useful commentary on Jn 21.9. Jesus' appearance at the time of Peter's denials (early in the morning), and his recre-
ation of the setting of those denials (the charcoal fire) are presented as a
careful and loving attempt to help Peter to face reality. For Peter, the
truth is this: 'no pain, no gain'. Therefore, Jesus triggers his 'shame-
circuits' in order to help him towards the wholeness he will need in
order to be a true shepherd of the sheep.

Verses 10-11 When Peter and the disciples arrive at the shore, Jesus
asks them to bring him some fish. Peter is the one who responds, eager
to please the one whom he has offended. Again this is a mark of Peter's
unhealed state. He has not yet understood that grace is given, not
earned.

Verse 12 The invitation to breakfast is a delightful touch. It shows that
Jesus is concerned with the whole person, not just with shameful memories. The reticence of the disciples at this point is worth noting too. It
fulfils the prolepsis of Jesus in 16.23: 'In that day [the day of Jesus'
return to the disciples] you will no longer ask me anything'.

Verse 13 The meal which Jesus now provides has powerful
eucharistic overtones. There are strong similarities between this meal
and the eucharistic meal in Jn 6.1-15, as I have shown. This sacramental
quality to the breakfast is significant because the eucharist itself is an act
of remembrance ('Do this in remembrance of me'). We see Jesus using a
remembrance-oriented meal to heal Peter's memories.

Verse 14 The story of the miraculous catch and the subsequent meal is
rounded off with the narrator's description of this appearance as the
third one involving the risen Jesus and the disciples. This provides a sense
of closure. There is an inclusio with 21.1 which starts: 'Jesus appeared
[*phaneroō*, as in 21.14] again to his disciples [*mathētai*, as in 21.14]'.
However, the notation of closure creates a sense of anticipation in the
reader (similar to that experienced at the end of Jn 20). Peter has met
the risen Jesus, but he is still unhealed. Will there be a subsequent
episode in which the denier of Jesus is restored to wholeness?

Verse 15 The immediate answer is 'yes'. A new dialogue scene now
opens. The meal has ended (v. 15a). The narrative does not record

what conversation took place during the breakfast, but the absence of questions in v. 13 would imply that it is a silent meal. This, of course, would have given Peter no opportunity to avoid the issue of facing the pain evoked by the setting. In v. 15b, the silence is now broken by Jesus, who addresses Peter as 'Simon, son of John'. This is a conscious reminder by Jesus of Peter's call to discipleship in 1.40-42, where Jesus addressed Peter in the same way. The question, 'Do you love me more than these?' is intended to put Peter on the spot concerning his life priorities. What does Peter care most about: the fishing, the disciples whom he has taken fishing, or Jesus? Peter confidently answers, 'Yes, Lord. You know that I love you.' Jesus then replies, 'Feed my lambs'.

The call to feed lambs (and then sheep, twice) is important. The reader should recall the implicit commentary in 18.1-27, where Jesus was depicted at the symbolic level as the model shepherd, Judas as the thief who attacks the fold, the beloved disciple as another model shepherd, and Peter—by implication—as the hired hand who runs away in the hour of danger. By evoking pastoral imagery at this point, Jesus is seen helping Peter confront the fact that he behaved like a hired hand, and calling him back to his vocation as a model shepherd.

Verses 16-17 Jesus poses the question concerning Peter's commitment three times. The verbs *agapaō* and *phileō* are used interchangeably in this interrogation. The narrator tells us that Peter, after the third time, was hurt. What is it that hurts Peter? It is not *what* Jesus asks, but *how often*. As countless commentators and preachers have discerned, the threefold interrogation of Peter by Jesus is a re-enactment of the threefold interrogation of Peter in the courtyard of Peter's denials. This strategy of re-enactment used by Jesus at last forces Peter to confront his shame. The breakthrough is signalled by the transition from Peter's twofold, 'You know that I love you...' (21.15, 16), to his remark, 'You know all things' (21.17). Peter confesses that Jesus has seen through his defence mechanisms. The shame can now be dealt with and healed.

It is important at this point to understand the relationship between remembering and feeling if we are to appreciate how it is that Peter is healed. Amy and Tom Harris write,

> The brain functions as a high-fidelity recorder of the events of our lives...These recording are in sequence and continuous...The *feelings* which were associated with past experiences are also recorded and are *inextricably locked* to those experiences...[This means that] recorded experiences and *feelings associated with them* are available for replay today in as vivid a form as when they happened...We not only remember how we felt, but we feel the same way. We not only remember the past, we relive it. We are there! (1985: 19).

The narrator tells us in Jn 21.17 that Peter was 'hurt' (NIV) when Jesus asked him the same question a third time. Notice that the author does not describe Peter remembering Jesus' warnings about the denial in 18.15-27 (at the time of the denials). The remembering and grieving of Peter must wait, in John's Gospel, until this seaside encounter with the risen Lord.

Peter's grief is emphasized at this point by the narrator. This word *elupēthē* is the verb form of the noun *lupē*, meaning 'grief' (see Jn 16.6, 20-22). The use of this word shows that Peter is not only remembering the denials, but also reliving them. He is experiencing again the feelings of shame which he felt at the actual time of denying Jesus. The reason why this experience is a healing event for Peter is because this grief must be felt and vocalized if it is to be dealt with.

Verses 18-19 With the past confronted (the denials), the present defined ('feed my sheep'), Jesus now turns to Peter's future. Jesus uses an enigmatic *māshāl* or riddle to warn Peter that he will one day, when he is old, have his hands stretched out, and someone else will dress him and take him where he will not want to go. The narrator then explains that the riddle was intended to indicate the kind of death by which Peter would glorify God. Any preoccupation with past failure is now discouraged. Peter has a present commission ('Follow me!') and a future destiny (martyrdom) which will not allow him to re-excavate and dwell upon that which his master has healed.

Verses 20-23 The narrator indicates in v. 20 that this dialogue between Jesus and Peter was a personal one, confined to them during a walk together. Now Peter turns round and sees the beloved disciple following behind. Having heard about his own destiny, Peter enquires what will become of the beloved disciple. Jesus tells Peter not to worry about the beloved disciple. What matters is to be obedient to his own calling. There then follows an apology provided by the narrator. Because of Jesus' words, 'If I want him to remain alive until I return', a rumour had spread among 'the brothers' (a term for the Johannine community, not the original disciples) that the beloved disciple would not die. The narrator corrects this rumour by pointing out that Jesus had used a conditional statement, 'If I want him to remain', not a descriptive statement, 'He will remain'.

This incident again points to the legitimacy of identifying the beloved disciple with Lazarus rather than with John son of Zebedee. It makes no sense at all for a rumour to spread concerning the immortality of a Galilaean fisherman. But it is eminently reasonable to suppose that such a rumour could spread concerning Lazarus. He, after all, had already tasted death once but had been raised. It would be easy to imagine some of 'the brothers' in the Johannine community mistaking that temporary resuscitation for a permanent resurrection. The beloved disciple in John 21 should therefore be identified with Lazarus, the founder of the community and the authority behind the Gospel.

But does this mean that Lazarus, the beloved disciple, actually wrote the Gospel? The narrator seems to insist that this is so in v. 24: 'This is the disciple who testifies to these things and who wrote them down. We know that his testimony is true.' However, the reference to what the beloved disciple has written down should be seen as a reference to the written source behind John 21 and not to the final form of John 21 as we have it. The narrator in 21.24 is pointing to the authority, authenticity and credibility of the written source material from which he or she has drawn, not to the nature of the chapter in its final form. Thus, the narrator informs us that the incidents in John 21 derive from the written reminiscences of the beloved disciple, Lazarus.

Epilogue

Verse 25 In the final verse of the Gospel, the narrator somewhat wistfully moves on from a reference to sources to a statement concerning the infinite potential for telling stories provided by these sources. Something of a Johannine hermeneutic can be discerned here. In the writing of this *biblion*, the author of the Fourth Gospel has had to be selective. Though there has been a huge repertoire of narrative possibilities at the author's disposal, a ruthless process of selection and imaginative redescription has necessarily been employed. For this reason there is a note of lament in the narrator's voice in v. 25: 'If only there was world enough and time to do this magnificent subject some justice'. Perhaps there is some explanation here for the narrator's seeming inability (or even refusal) to end the Gospel at the logical place (20.31). To end the Gospel means to put a full-stop on a narrative that, by rights, should be infinite. The narrator does, however, end the story; a pragmatic view-point prevails. A collection of books entitled the *Vita Jesu* would have produced a library which the world could simply not contain. And so the narrator is content with this little book about Jesus—a book which offers a brief and yet enticing narrative of Jesus the Messiah.

Bibliography

Alter, R.
    1981   *The Art of Biblical Narrative* (New York: Basic Books).

Barrett, C.K.
    1978   *The Gospel according to St. John: An Introduction with Commentary and Notes on the Greek Text* (London: SPCK).

Beasley-Murray, G.
    1987   *John* (Word Biblical Commentary, 36; Waco, TX: Word).

Brown, R.E.
    1966   *The Gospel according to John* (2 vols.; London: Geoffrey Chapman).

Carson, D.
    1991   *The Gospel according to John* (Leicester: Inter-Varsity Press).

Crossan, J.D.
    1980   'A Structuralist Analysis of John 6', in R. Spencer (ed.), *Orientation by Disorientation* (Pittsburgh: Pickwick Press): 235-52.

Culpepper, A.
    1983   *Anatomy of the Fourth Gospel: A Study in Literary Design* (Philadelphia: Fortress Press).

Dodd, C.H.
    1965   *The Interpretation of the Fourth Gospel* (Cambridge: Cambridge University Press).

Duke, P.
    1985   *Irony in the Fourth Gospel* (Atlanta: John Knox).

Du Rand, J.A.
    1990   'Narratological Perspectives on John 13.1-38', *Hervormde Teleogiese Studies* (Pretoria) 46.3: 367-89.

Elliott, J.H.
    1982   *A Home for the Homeless: A Sociological Exegesis of I Peter, its Situation and Strategy* (London: SCM Press).

Ellis, P.
    1984   *The Genius of John: A Composition-Critical Commentary on the Fourth Gospel* (Collegeville, MN: Liturgical Press).

Forster, E.M.
    1962   *Aspects of the Novel* (New York: Penguin Books).

Frye, N.
    1971   *Anatomy of Criticism* (Princeton: Princeton University Press).

Genette, G.
    1980   *Narrative Discourse: An Essay in Method* (trans. J.E. Lewin; Ithaca, NY: Cornell University Press).

Grayston, K.
    1990   *The Gospel of John* (Epworth Commentaries; London: Epworth).

Greimas, A.J.
    1966   *Semantique Structurale* (Paris: Larousse).
    1970   *Du Sens* (Paris: Editions du Seuil).

Haenchen, E.
    1984   *A Commentary on the Gospel of John* (trans. R.W. Funk; 2 vols.; Philadelphia: Fortress Press).

Harris, A., and T. Harris
    1986   *Staying OK* (London: Pan).

Higdon, D.
    1977   *Time and English Fiction* (New Jersey: Rowman & Littlefield).
Käsemann, E.
    1968   *The Testament of Jesus According to John 17* (trans. G. Krodel;
                Philadelphia: Fortress Press).
Kelber, W.
    1991   'The Birth of a Beginning: John 1.1-18', *Semeia* 53: 120-44.
Kermode, F.
    1979   *The Genesis of Secrecy* (Cambridge, MA: Harvard University Press).
    1987   'John', in F. Kermode and R. Alter (eds.), *The Literary Guide to the
                Bible* (London: Collins).
Kurz, W.
    1990   *Farewell Addresses in the New Testament* (Collegeville, MN:
                Liturgical Press).
Kysar, R.
    1984   *John's Story of Jesus* (Philadelphia: Fortress Press).
Leroy, H.
    1968   *Rätsel und Missvertsändnis: Ein Beitrag zur Formgeschichte des
                Johannesevangeliums* (Bonner biblische Beiträge, 30; Bonn: Peter
                Hanstein).
Lincoln, A.
    1993   'Trials, Plots and the Narrative of the Fourth Gospel' (Unpublished
                paper delivered at the British New Testament Conference, St
                Andrews University, 1993).
Lindars, B.
    1972   *St John's Gospel* (London: Faber & Faber).
    1990   *John* (New Testament Guides; Sheffield: JSOT Press).
Malbon, E.S.
    1990   'Ending at the Beginning', *Semeia* 52: 175-84.
Marsh, J.
    1968   *Saint John* (Harmondsworth: Penguin Books).
Moloney, F.J.
    1986   'The Structure and Message of John 13.1-38', *Australian Biblical
                Review* 34: 1-16.
    1987   'The Structure and Message of John 15.1-16.3', *Australian Biblical
                Review* 35: 35-49.
    1991   'A Sacramental Reading of John 13.1-38', *Catholic Biblical Quarterly*
                53: 237-56.
Nuttall, A.D.
    1980   *Overheard by God: Fiction and Prayer in Herbert, Milton, Dante and
                St John* (London: Methuen).
O'Day, G.
    1991   '"I Have Overcome the World" (John 16.33): Narrative Time in John
                13–17', *Semeia* 53: 153-66.
Pfitzner, V.C.
    1986   'They Knew it was the Lord. The Place and Function of John
                21.1-14 in the Gospel of John', *Lutheran Theological Journal* 20.2-3:
                64-75.
Powell, M.A.
    1990   *What is Narrative Criticism?* (Guides to Biblical Scholarship, NT series;
                Minneapolios: Fortress Press).
Reinhartz, A.
    1989   'Jesus as Prophet: Predictive Prolepses in the Fourth Gospel', *Journal
                for the Study of the New Testament* 36: 3-16.

Resseguie, J.
    1982   'John 9: A Literary-Critical Analysis', in K. Gros Louis (ed.), *Literary Interpretations of Biblical Narratives*, II (Nashville: Abingdon).
Robinson, J.A.T.
    1985   *The Priority of John* (London: SCM Press).
Ryken, L.
    1979   *Triumphs of the Imagination: Literature in Christian Perspective* (Downers Grove, IL: Inter-Varsity Press).
Schnackenburg, R.II.
    1968–1982   *The Gospel According to St John* (3 vols.; New York: Herder & Herder).
Segovia, F.
    1991a   'The Journey(s) of the Word of God: A Reading of the Plot of the Fourth Gospel', *Semeia* 53: 23-54.
    1991b   *The Farewell of the Word: The Johannine Call to Abide* (Minneapolis: Fortress Press).
Simoens, Y.
    1981   *La gloire d'aimer: Structures stylistiques et interprétatives dans le discours de la cène (Jn 13–17)* (Analecta Biblica, 90; Rome: Biblical Institute Press).
Sloyan, G.
    1988   *John* (Atlanta: John Knox).
Staley, J.
    1986   'The Structure of John's Prologue', *Catholic Biblical Quarterly* 48: 241-64.
Stanton, G.
    1989   *The Gospels and Jesus* (Oxford: Oxford University Press).
Stibbe, M.
    1991   'The Elusive Christ: A New Reading of the Fourth Gospel', *Journal for the Study of the New Testament* 44: 20-39.
    1992   *John as Storyteller: Narrative Criticism and the Fourth Gospel* (SNTS Monograph series, 73; Cambridge: Cambridge University Press).
    1993a   'Return to Sender: A Structuralist Analysis of John's Plot', *Biblical Interpretation* 1-2 (forthcoming).
    1993b   *The Gospel of John as Literature: An Anthology of Twentieth Century Perspectives* (New Testament Tools and Studies; Leiden: E.J. Brill).
Strachan, R.H.
    1941   *The Fourth Gospel* (London: SCM Press).
Tasker, R.G.V.
    1976   *The Gospel according to St John: An Introduction and Commentary* (Leicester: Inter-Varsity Press).
Wahlde, U. von
    1984   'Literary Structure and Theological Argument in Three Discourses with the Jews in the Fourth Gospel', *Journal of Biblical Literature* 103: 575-84.
Whybray, R.N.
    1983   *The Second Isaiah* (Old Testament Guides; Sheffield: JSOT Press).

Index of References

Old Testament

New Testament

Apocrypha and Pseudepigrapha

Index of Authors